On the Periphery
of Europe, 1762–1825

On the Periphery of Europe
of Europe
1762–1825

THE SELF-INVENTION OF THE RUSSIAN ELITE

ANDREAS SCHÖNLE AND ANDREI ZORIN

NIU PRESS / DeKalb, IL

27 26 25 24 23 22 21 20 19 18   1 2 3 4 5
978-0-87580-785-0 (paper)
978-1-60909-241-2 (e-book)
Book and cover design by Yuni Dorr

The research for this volume and its publication were supported by a grant from
The Leverhulme Trust (RPG-357).

Library of Congress Cataloging-in-Publication Data
is available online at http://catalog.loc.gov

In Memory of **Michelle Lamarche Marrese**

Contents

Acknowledgments

This volume owes its existence to a research grant entitled "The Creation of a Europeanized Elite in Russia: Public Role and Subjective Self" awarded by the Leverhulme Trust (RPG-357). This grant supported the preparation of two books, of which this is the second. Among other things, the grant enabled the appointment of a research assistant for two years, supported the archival research undertaken by our consultants in Russia, and allowed the principal investigators some precious time off teaching. We are deeply grateful to the Leverhulme Trust for its support, as well as for its flexibility during the three-year tenure of our grant. We also thank the Ludwig Fond at New College, University of Oxford, as well as the School of Languages, Linguistics, and Film at Queen Mary University of London, which supported the translation of some contributions for our first volume from Russian into English.

The research team we assembled consisted of Alexei Evstratov as our research assistant, Stanislav Andriainen, Elena Korchmina, and Mikhail Velizhev as our archival consultants, and several scholars we invited to participate in our debates and to contribute to our collective volume: Igor Fedyukin, Alexander Iosad, Michelle Lamarche Marrese, and John Randolph. This proved to be a wonderful group, and we wish to express our gratitude to our friends and colleagues for the lively discussions they nurtured through their participation. Our collective work led to the publication of *The Europeanized Elite in Russia, 1762–1825: Public Role and Subjective Self* (Northern Illinois University Press, 2016).

To our profound distress, Michelle Marrese tragically died just as this volume came out and before she could see it. Her contribution for us will likely be her last publication. Over the last few years, she had been collecting archival sources for a book manuscript on eighteenth-century noblewomen. This would have been, no doubt, yet another hugely influential monograph, just like her work on women's property rights in imperial Russia. She cared deeply for this book, and it is a huge loss for scholars of eighteenth-century Russia (and beyond) that her indefatigable work in archives will not come to fruition. We dedicate our volume to her, to pay tribute to her inspiring contributions to our field and in gratitude for her friendship.

At different stages of the grant, we benefited greatly from the input of our Advisory Board, which consisted of Wladimir Berelowitch, Simon Dixon, Catriona Kelly, Dominic Lieven, and Derek Offord. Their commitment to our project has been much beyond the call of duty and gave rise to heady and lively discussions, which helped us avoid many pitfalls. Roger Bartlett, Andrew Kahn, and Paul Keenan also participated in some of our internal research meetings and contributed extensive feedback on our work, for which we thank them profusely. We remain, of course, solely responsible for the content of this volume.

We presented individual research papers or intermediary reports of our research at various conferences and in various seminars, notably at the University of Oxford, Queen Mary University of London, the German Historical Institute in Moscow, the annual conference of the Association for Slavic, East European, and Eurasian Studies in Boston, the annual meeting of the Study Group on Eighteenth-Century Russia in Hoddesdon, and the East European History Seminar at Humboldt University in Berlin. The questions and comments we received from panel chairs, discussants, and participants sharpened our thinking greatly. Particular recognition is due to Gary Marker and Richard Wortman, whose constructive skepticism was crucial. We thank the organizers and participants of these events for the opportunity to present our thoughts and for the feedback we received. We also thank our peer reviewers, Jelena Pogosian and Peter Sterns, for their pertinent suggestions and comments.

The project relied on extensive archival work, and for their assistance in locating materials we wish to thank the staff at the State Archive of Ancient Acts, the State Archive of the Russian Federation, the Manuscript Collection of the Russian State Library, the Division of Written Sources of the State Historical Museum, the Russian State Archive of Literature and Art, the Russian State Archive of the Navy, and the Russian State Military Historical Archive, all in Moscow; the Manuscript Division of the Institute of Russian Literature (Pushkin House), the Manuscript Division of the Russian National Library, the Russian State Archive of History, and the Archive of the Museum of Artillery, Engineering, and Communication Corps in St. Petersburg; the

State Archive of Novgorod Oblast' in Novgorod; and, finally, the National Archives in Kew. Essential library work was undertaken at the British Library in London, the Bodleian Library in Oxford, the Russian National Library in St. Petersburg, as well as the Russian State Library and the State Public Historical Library in Moscow, and we are indebted to these institutions for access to their extensive collections.

Last but not least, we are grateful to Amy Farranto and the other staff at Northern Illinois University Press for their enthusiastic response to our project and their support throughout, as well as to Christine Worobec, the series editor, for her helpful suggestions in the final stages.

Note to the Reader

This volume aims to present an original synthesis intended for a broadly educated reader not necessarily conversant with the many twists and turns of Russian history, while incorporating archival research and the conclusions drawn from an intense collective research project that took place between 2012–2015. We have therefore tried to provide background knowledge, to define critical terms, and to lighten up our bibliographic apparatus. Where called for, we provide parenthetical acknowledgments of sources and references for further reading, but to the extent possible, we have given preference to English-language publications, in keeping with the aims of this book, and refrained from using endnotes. Scholars of Russian history will hopefully find provocative ideas in this volume, despite having to return to some well-trodden fields, especially in the introduction.

As described in greater length in our acknowledgment section, our research is based in part on the findings of a research group we convened with the financial support of the Leverhulme Trust. This project led to the publication by Northern Illinois University Press of *The Europeanized Elite in Russia, 1762–1825: Public Role and Subjective Self*, edited by ourselves and Alexei Evstratov, a volume organized as a series of case studies. The present monograph incorporates additional research and proposes an original synthesis of our findings.

Dates are given according to the "old" Julian calendar, since this is what our protagonists used. For the transliteration of Russian names and terms, we adopted the Library of Congress transliteration system, with a minor simplification consisting of reducing the frequent ending -kii (as in Dostoevskii) to -ky (Dostoevsky), except in bibliographic references. We also adopted the accepted English spelling of well-known figures. Translations from foreign-language sources are ours unless otherwise noted.

On the Periphery
of Europe, 1762-1825

INTRODUCTION

A new book discussing the Europeanization of Russia requires some explanation. Not only is the existing literature quite substantial, but one can hardly mention any work dedicated to Russian political, social, or cultural history in the eighteenth and early nineteenth centuries that does not in some way deal with this issue. The scholarly attention to this problem has clear reasons—the changes initiated by Emperor Peter the Great (Peter I) in Russia in the early eighteenth century were arguably the most far-reaching attempt at enforced Westernization until the Meiji restoration in Japan in 1868 and the Ataturk reforms in Turkey in the 1920s—and their repercussions continue to resonate in Russian history to the present day. They are also important for understanding the logic of political, institutional, and cultural transformations in peripheral empires—a topic that acquired new relevance in the period of globalization.

In Russia, the ideological debate about the eighteenth-century Europeanization was launched in the 1830s by Petr Chaadaev, and the direction it took afterward was already anticipated by his notorious "First Philosophical Letter" and the "Apology of a Madman": it featured obsessive comparisons with Europe, assertions of Russian exceptionalism, and painstaking deliberations about the moment in history when the country took a wrong turn. In the wake of this cause célèbre, the elites that emerged in the process of Europeanization embarked on a reassessment of their own history and their place in the world. The historiography of the question is until now very much defined by the controversy between proponents of the idea of the Russian *Sonderweg* (that is, exceptionalism), whether positive or negative, and scholars and thinkers tending to "normalize" Russian history and to see in it just one national version of "European modernization."

The goal of this book is to refocus this debate. We are not so much interested in the eternal question whether there is something special about the Russian case and whether Russia was really Europeanized, but to analyze the world of the actual actors of this process—the Russian educated elite. Thus, the "visible" parts of this transformation—the introduction of a regular army and professional civil service; the rise of secular print and the periodical press; the development of schools, universities, and the Academy of Science; as well as the emergence and proliferation of new manners and dress codes—will be discussed here primarily from the perspective of the people who experienced these changes, shaped them, and changed themselves in the process. This volume deals not with the history of institutions or the history of ideas, but with the history of practices, emotions, and perceptions. Hence our interest in case studies, that is, in specific examples that give us a glimpse into the actual world of Russians rapidly Europeanizing themselves in order to find, define, or consolidate their identities as Russians. We believe that this approach allows us to see the controversial and dramatic history of the emergence of a great and powerful empire on the fringes of Europe and within the sphere of attraction of European culture in a more nuanced, detailed, and complex way than a traditional set of historiosophical generalities. This change of optics will then also allow us, in our conclusion, to map out what is at stake in this process of self-Europeanization and how the Russian case can help shed light on other countries that at different stages of history have embarked on similar trajectories. Our research will show that the elite did not have its own "home," as the various roles it inhabited produced a lack of coherent attachment, resulting in unstable hybridity in its subjective world.

This introduction aims first to describe our methodology, explaining how we defined the object of our inquiry and how we proceeded to trace the elite's complex subjective response to the state project of Europeanization. In order to demonstrate how fundamentally this issue shapes Russian history, this introduction will then briefly analyze the major historical narratives nineteenth-century historians and thinkers have proposed to assess Russia's Europeanization. We will also outline the trajectory of Europeanization in the twentieth century and to this date, to illustrate the continuing relevance of this debate and reveal some recurring patterns. Furthermore, in chapter 1, we will provide an overview of the key parameters of Russia's Europeanization in political, social, economic, legal, and cultural terms. This historiographic background will thus sketch out the charged and polarized field within which our study of practices, attitudes, and emotions inserts itself. Our intervention is intended less to take a stance in this grand political debate than to map out how macrohistorical factors shape subjectivities and produce patterns of behavior among individuals and to delineate how these individuals eventually seek to emancipate themselves from this sort of historical determinism and imagine new forms of living.

Who are the elite? In keeping with the emphasis on subjective identity, we have deliberately refrained from defining in social terms what we mean by "elite." And to avoid any confusion with the nomenclature of the period, we have chosen this term despite the fact that it did not exist in Russian at the time, which does not mean that the sense of distinction was absent. What mattered to us was less the social standing of a man or woman than their subjective self-evaluation—that is, whether they considered themselves as part of the "cream" of the country and acted accordingly. Neither one's position on the table of ranks nor the number of serfs owned could have worked as an adequate proxy to determine one's elitist identity. Nevertheless, by virtue of the service ethos of the times, it goes without saying that we have in mind a subsection of the nobility: those subject to an interiorized requirement to act on behalf of the public good and rise above their sole private interest.

The Russian nobility was in itself a highly stratified estate, ranging from select families that owned extensive tracts of land and thousands of serfs to provincial gentry with only a few serfs and very little exposure to the European way of life. In 1766–1767, 52 percent of the estates featured 20 (male) serfs or fewer, 34.7 percent owned between 21 and 100 serfs, 13.3 percent had up to 1,000 serfs, and only 0.6 percent more than 1,000 serfs. This latter group represented 240 families (Ivanova 2001, 182). Nobles with a pronounced sense of elitism were more likely to be found among the latter two categories, and especially in the wealthiest group, although we did not want to exclude individuals who made a speedy career progression—for example, officers who

rose quickly in the ranks on account of their talents and assumed commanding positions in the military, yet did not own substantial estates. Furthermore,
there were nobles who traced their families back to pre-Petrine boyars and
derived particular pride from this, even if their economic circumstances and
social rank were not always commensurate with what they saw as their social
standing. It goes without saying that in eighteenth-century Russia, when four
women wore the crown and ruled for a combined sixty-seven years, and where
women could legally hold title to immovable property, one did not need to be
a man to belong to the elite.

Implicit in the notion of service, which was morally linked to the privileges
enjoyed by the nobility, was a degree of public-spiritedness, which, however, can
be understood in a fairly trivial way. For the provincial gentry residing on their
estates, this public commitment might mean as little (or as much) as managing
their estates in such a way as to be able to collect the poll tax and surrender
the required number of recruits during the periodic conscriptions. For other
members of the lower gentry, service in the army or civil administration was
first and foremost a way to survive economically and escape destitution. But
higher up socially, the public good signified participation in the state project of
Europeanization on its various levels: promoting the greatness of the Russian
empire in the international arena militarily or diplomatically, contributing to
running the empire administratively, fostering the spread of European deco-
rum and elegance in society, furthering the advance of knowledge and education, establishing new institutions, experimenting with new technologies, etc.
In this way, through this service ethos, the identities of the elite were directly
implicated in the processes of Europeanization that were traversing the country.

As he embarked upon his broad-ranging reforms of Russian society, Peter
I conceived of Europeanization primarily as a technique to enlist the elite as
informal (and sometimes formal) state agents in the furtherance of his aims.
Thus he placed the emphasis on inculcating the ethos of service, providing
incentive and reward mechanisms that clearly tied the elite to its social role,
and sought to prepare it for discharging its new duties competently. These
aspirations underscored the importance of education and cultural reform as
means to changing the mindset and developing the skills of the elite. To this
effect Peter deployed legal and coercive techniques—rule by decree and the
occasional use of state violence. By the time of his death in 1725, without
security of person or property and subject to a lifelong obligation to serve, the
elite was profoundly dependent on the government.

As we describe in greater detail in chapter 1, in the decades following Peter's death, the elite started, with some success, to mobilize as a social group and lobby for legal and economic reforms that would strengthen its position vis-à-vis the government on one side and its serfs on the other. This process culminated in Peter III's promulgation of the Manifesto on the Freedom of the Nobility in 1762. The manifesto formally freed the elite from the obligation to serve, but substituted an internalized moral compunction for the coercive means Peter had used. The elite was thus given a modicum of independence, but on the condition that it developed an emotional bond with the ruler and internalized the duty to serve on behalf of ruler and country. The manifesto was hence more about moral duty than freedom.

The year 1762 marks thus the beginning of the period when the elite found itself in a subjectively ambivalent position. The European ideas about the dignity of the person, which it had started to imbibe, had raised its aspirations and given it some tacit independence, albeit no legal security, and then only to the extent that it willingly embraced the aims of the state and applied itself to their furtherance. Europeanization became a double-edged sword. While it encouraged internalized self-discipline and self-invention, it also tethered the elite to a state project, which was to compete with European countries in terms of civilizational progress. In order to become better Russians, members of the elite were expected to reinvent themselves as Europeans, yet without losing their patriotic loyalty to Russia.

Over the following decades, the elite sought more and more to assert its independence psychologically, morally, culturally, and symbolically, in a continuous dialogue and negotiation with the state in all spheres of its existence. It gained greater legal protections in 1785 when Catherine II promulgated the Charter of the Nobility. But the internalized bond between the elite and the monarch started to fray in the wake of the French Revolution, when the government took fright and began to implement repressive measures. In the wake of Russia's victory over Napoleon in 1815, expectations were ripe that Tsar Alexander I would embark on domestic reforms. When this failed to materialize, a psychological conflict or contradiction opened up between the ideological commitment of a segment of the elite toward political and social reforms on the one side and identification with the monarch on the other. For officers of the guard who had seen the liberties and amenities of life in Paris, to be a good patriot now increasingly implied turning against the ruler, who was perceived as an obstacle to reforms. This rift prepared the ground for the Decembrist uprising of 1825, when members of the guards tried to take advantage of a brief interregnum to demand constitutional reforms and install their preferred ruler. For the elite, the crushing of this uprising meant the end of the period of internalized identification with the monarch. Thus the years of 1762 and 1825 represent the thresholds of our inquiry, as they mark the limits of the period when subjective emotional identification, with all its tensions and ambivalence, was the main mechanism that tied the elite to the court.

What did Europeanization mean for the elite? As we will discuss in the following chapters, Europeanization meant first of all exposure to many facets of the way of life of European countries. From material culture to reading practices to the arts, the elite keenly observed, absorbed, consumed, and purchased whatever it could find on its journeys through Europe or obtain from intermediaries who imported goods to Russia. Europeanization also meant developing forms of sociability inspired by European models—from clubs to balls to theaters—leading notably to the incorporation of elite women into polite society. Furthermore, Europeanization encouraged the development of social networks across state boundaries, fostering the interaction with foreign elites by various means. It also became an educational project, requiring foreign tutors and often study at one of the main European universities. Through the widening influence of Freemasonry, along with pietist and mystical literature, it gained a spiritual dimension. And in practical term, it inspired costly attempts to redesign Petersburg mansions and country estates. Thus Europeanization gave rise to a whole series of practices that were socially significant as they signaled one's belonging to the circles of the elite. In the following chapters we have tried to render justice to the pervasive and multifaceted repercussions of Europeanization for the elite by analyzing, in as extensive a fashion possible, the multiple and variegated forms it assumed in its lives.

With these practices also came distinct emotions. Through its readings, the elite learned to identify sentimentally with the author behind the text and to shape and evaluate its existence in analogy with literary narratives. Through its consumption of the visual arts and its involvement with interior and estate design, it discovered the pleasures of vicarious travel to foreign places. At court, it learned to control and feign emotions, and to adapt its behavior to the setting and circumstances, including letting emotions loose to express its devotion to the monarch. In balls, assemblies, and salons, the elite started to enjoy socializing with members of the other sex. Some men discovered libertinism, interpreting the enlightenment as a license for sexual experimentation. More typically, men and women began to feel romantic attachment for one another, sometimes in defiance of marital bonds. At the highest echelons of society, romantic dalliances were pursued in full view of polite society.

Men acquired the habits of protecting their honor scrupulously, taking the risks inherent in dueling on the chin. Women learned not only to dance, but also to manage their or their husbands' estates and to represent the interests of their families at court. Through Masonic practices, the elite internalized methods to reach higher degrees of spiritual perfection. It also fleshed out what patriotic devotion to the country might mean beyond dutiful subjection to the monarch, perhaps identifying with the military regiment over and above anything else, or imagining a moral affinity with its serfs, for whose welfare it was responsible. But it also suffered from the instability of court life and developed a longing for islands of stability such as the country estate, seeking to invent lasting markers of identity independent of its position at court. Most importantly, through exposure to this manifold emotional palette, the elite acquired the techniques of self-fashioning, reflecting on its positions, inventing or reinventing itself as it saw fit, performing its identities in public, and articulating thereby its vision of its social roles.

In our previous edited volume, *The Europeanized Elite in Russia, 1762–1825: Public Role and Subjective Self*, we specifically defined this period in the life of the elite as the time when subjectivity was experienced as deeply internal and intimate, yet at the same time in need of being constantly performed, tested, and refined in the public eye. In order to feel themselves "European," nobles needed to demonstrate a mastery of their roles at court, in the company of peers, on the country estate, and not the least in the theater, which members of the elite were required to attend. The theatrical character of the Europeanization of the elite did not contradict the existential seriousness of this endeavor or its pragmatic importance. Performance could not be separated from the interiorization of new values and practices; in fact, it constituted an integral and arguably most important part in the transformations of the inner world of the nobility.

These fluid relations between subjective selves and public roles could be reconstructed only through case studies. In our book, we provided a detailed and nuanced analysis of specific cases in various spheres of life. We discussed how members of the elite dealt with their social roles and tried to negotiate and reconcile different practical and existential challenges facing them, when interiorized loyalty to the state, deeply imbibed European ideas, fashions, and emotional patterns, as well as personal aspirations and fears pulled them in various directions. We were interested mostly in a "thick description" of exceptional personalities, biographies, and conflictual situations, where the interplay of contradictory cultural and social "pulls and pushes" is particularly revealing. These case studies demonstrated the conflicts between different trends and normative systems that make it necessary for specific individuals and sometimes groups to navigate and negotiate between them.

In the current volume, we retain our interest in cases studies, but cast our gaze more widely and place them in a broader institutional and social context. By considering a more extensive array of cases, we can better demonstrate the range of options available to the elite and thus highlight the choices individual members made in fashioning their existences. As Clifford Geertz put it, in showing the pertinence of case studies, "Contextualization is the name of the game" (Geertz 2000, xi). For us, this contextualization means primarily embedding our case studies within a continuous negotiation between public roles and subjective emotions and, in particular, within a dialogue between the elite and the ruler (or the state). By necessity, as the number of these cases grew, our descriptions became less detailed, although they also gained greater representativeness as symptoms of the rapid macrohistorical political, social, intellectual, and cultural changes Russia was undergoing at the time. Furthermore, we outline the historical evolution, over six decades, in the manner in which this negotiation unfolds, tracing its increasing complexities and fluidities. One can say that while the first book described the meaning of Europeanization to individual members of the elite, here we deal with this social group as an aggregate whole and in a more stringent historical perspective.

Our focus is on the ways educated Russian nobles perceived their private lives, including their individual practices and emotional reactions, as manifestations of the political aspirations of the state to become a legitimate member of European civilization, hoping to contribute to this process both on individual and national levels. The private and the public were thus thoroughly entangled. From a retrospective point of view, one can probably say that the Russian elite failed to accomplish its historical mission, but in the process it managed to create what is now known as the Golden Age of Russian culture, not only in terms of artistic production, but also in the complexities of its inner world and polite manners.

This volume demonstrates that the emotional and intellectual life of the Russian elite was characterized by a specific type of hybridity, produced by the various competing systems of allegiance and emotional patterns it interiorized. As influences, borrowings, and identifications added to one another, they created intricate, unstable, even volatile combinations, but combinations that at least had potential for some syncretic fusing, rather than leading to an irreconcilable rift. Hence the elite's sometime extraordinary ability to navigate contradictory "pulls" and to experience the bricolage of cultures as a "natural" condition. It is only toward the end of our period, as identifications hardened into fixed ideologies, that the harnessing of different behavioral and emotional patterns became more difficult and unbridgeable contradictions opened up, which spelled an end to the period of conscious and unconscious compromises that enabled the extraordinarily intensive self-fashioning, self-reflection, and self-refining performed by the elite.

The Nineteenth-Century Historiography of Russian Europeanization

What were the main historical narratives advanced in the nineteenth century to assess the results of Russia's Europeanization? The publication of the "First Philosophical Letter" by Petr Chaadaev in 1836 can be seen as the first salvo in a historiographic battle over Russia's identity that continues to this day. It showed that this period could already be seen as belonging to the historical past. Chaadaev blamed the evils of Russian history on the fatal choice of religion. According to him, Eastern Christianity separated Russia both from the West and the East and left it in a civilizational void:

> We do not belong to any of the great families of the human race; we are neither of the West nor of the East, and we have not the traditions of either. Placed, as it were, outside of time, we have not been touched by the universal education of the human race. (Raeff 1966, 162)

In addition, Russia's culture also suffered from its imitative character. Chaadaev believed that the Petrine reforms were superfluous and could not remedy the historical reasons of Russia's backwardness, in the same way as triumphant Alexander's European campaign led only to the botched Decembrist rebellion. Repeated attempts at Europeanization notwithstanding, Russia was unable to learn from the West, because it was divided from it by a religious schism and nearly thousand years of existence outside of historical development:

> On one occasion, a great man sought to civilize us; and in order to give us the foretaste of enlightenment, he flung us a mantle of civilization; we picked up the mantle, but we did not touch the civilization itself. Another time, another great prince...led us victorious from one end of Europe to the other; returning home from the triumphant march across the most civilized countries of the world, we brought back only ideas and aspirations which resulted in an immense calamity setting us back half a century. (Raeff 1966, 167)

Thus, for Chaadaev, the period of Russia's Europeanization was an experiment that had failed resoundingly.

Both the authorities and the public took Chaadaev's argument extremely seriously, extravagant and outrageous as it may seem. Scholars still argue how this document, originally written in 1829 in French as a personal letter to a lady, could have slipped through the rigid censorship of tsarist Russia. The magazine that published Chaadaev's letter was shut down, its editor exiled, and Chaadaev was officially declared insane and forever banned from publishing. Nevertheless, the publication triggered an outburst of national self-examination. This was in part because Chaadaev was the first to openly challenge the doctrine of Orthodoxy, Autocracy, and Nationality. Forged by the minister of education, Sergei Uvarov, this doctrine represented at that time the official ideology of the Russian empire. It defined Russian national identity as consisting of the belief in the dogmas of the ruling church and the existing political order—the institutions that, according to the ideologues of the Orthodoxy-Autocracy-Nationality triad, had saved Russia from the degradation already experienced by the West. Chaadaev's letter had struck at the heart of the founding myth of national identity and political legitimacy in the Russia of Nicholas I.

The responses to Chaadaev's letter helped define the main debate that dominates Russian political thought until the present day—the opposition between the so-called Westernizers and the Slavophiles. The former followed the tradition established by Catherine's *Instruction*, regarding Russia as a fundamentally European country and Peter's reforms as an unfinished project. The educated elite's assimilation of Western manners and cultural norms was to be followed by the adoption of Western political institutions, most importantly, parliamentary democracy, equality before the law, a robust legal system, and a free press. Only by completing the process of Westernization would Russia compete with its European neighbors not only militarily, but also economically, politically, and culturally.

In contrast, the Slavophiles believed in Russia's *Sonderweg* based on its pre-Petrine historical legacy and defined by its unique spirituality and communal religiosity (the so-called *sobornost'*). According to the Slavophiles, Russia had to reject the misplaced Westernization imposed upon the country by the tyrannical will of the reforming emperor and return to its genuine peasant and Orthodox roots. Konstantin Aksakov, one of the Slavophiles' leading ideologues, wrote that Peter "brought Russia much outward glory, but within her essential integrity he implanted corruption" and demanded that the government "embrace Russian principles, which have been rejected since Peter's day" (Raeff 1966, 245). The most burning question dealt with the relations between the lower classes and the educated Europeanized society: while the Westernizers wanted to enlighten the majority of the population so that it would be able to close the civilizational gap with Europe, the Slavophiles believed that the elite should go back to the traditional values still preserved among the peasants.

The general spectrum of ideological positions with regard to Russia's historic mission in the world and its relations with the West can be systematized on the basis of the answers given by the adherents of each ideology to two basic questions that are still shaping the political debate in Russia today:

1. whether Russia is comparable with the West or has its own unique way of development;
2. whether Russia's traditions and customs are superior to Western ones or inferior to them.

	RUSSIA IS COMPARABLE TO THE WEST	RUSSIA HAS ITS UNIQUE WAY OF DEVELOPMENT AND MISSION IN THE WORLD
RUSSIA IS SUPERIOR TO THE WEST	Official Ideology (Orthodoxy-Autocracy-Nationality)	Slavophiles
RUSSIA IS INFERIOR TO THE WEST	Westernizers	Chaadaev

One of the powerful attempts to reconcile the idea of the *Sonderweg* with national messianism was made by Dostoevsky in an essay that may be regarded as his testament: the famous speech he gave at the festive unveiling of a monument to Pushkin in Moscow in June 1880, half a year before his death. By that time, Pushkin's standing as the national poet was already established and, following the traditions of romantic nationalism, Dostoevsky had to derive his conclusions about the mission of the nation from the works of its greatest author. Presenting Pushkin, the single most cosmopolitan and European among Russian poets, as a symbol of "Russian individuality" was a challenging task, but Dostoevsky found an elegant and powerful solution. He defined Pushkin's and therefore Russia's uniqueness as their exceptional ability to understand other nations better than those nations are able to understand themselves:

> In fact, in European belles-lettres there were geniuses of immense creative magnitude, Shakespeare, Cervantes, Schiller. But please point to even one of these geniuses who possessed such a universal susceptibility as Pushkin. And this faculty, the major faculty of our nationality, Pushkin shares with our people, and by virtue of this he is preeminently a national poet. (Raeff 1966, 297–298)

By "susceptibility," also sometimes translated as "responsiveness," Dostoevsky meant Pushkin's ability to absorb and internalize a myriad foreign influences and to forge something original out of them. This analysis also had a clear political dimension—the nation that can understand every other nation is a natural leader in the international order. Thus Dostoevsky managed to preserve the deeply Slavophile feeling of Russian uniqueness, while relegitimizing Petrine Europeanization and the St. Petersburg period of Russian history, in that he conceived of modern Russia as a country uniquely placed to integrate all external, foreign influences and thus lead the way to the future. By the same token, he did not deny Russia's backwardness, nor did he anticipate Russia becoming prosperous and developed in the foreseeable future. "Let our land be poor," he exclaimed, but it was "this destitute land" that was destined "to reconcile all European controversies, to show the solution of European anguish in our all-humanitarian and all-unifying Russian soul" (Raeff 1966, 300). The glorification of Pushkin's universal genius became a thinly veiled legitimization of Russian imperial politics.

The notion that Russia's poverty somehow provided spiritual conditions enabling Russia to leap ahead of European countries and take on a leading role loomed large. Alexander Herzen, paradoxically glorified by Isaiah Berlin as one of the greatest European liberals (Berlin 2008), started his career in Russia as a passionate Westernizer. But having moved to the West, he became deeply disappointed in it and began to cherish the idea that the traditions of the peasant commune make Russia the ideal place for a future socialist society. He believed that Russia lagged behind Europe in terms of civilizational development, but it was exactly this backwardness that gave it hope for a glorious future. In the late nineteenth–early twentieth century, this way of thinking defined the teachings of the so-called "populists," but even such an avowed opponent of the populists as Lenin also insisted that the socialist revolution would triumph not in the most developed capitalist countries, but in the least developed one. As a dogmatic Marxist, Lenin could not fail to see that this idea contradicted the spirit and the letter of the economic determinism he claimed to profess, but the magic of the transformational leap forward that would put his country ahead of its European peers was more attractive to him than the logic of orthodox Marxism. In short, from the middle of the nineteenth century to the Revolution of 1917, in response to the eighteenth-century paradigm of Europeanization, Russian thinkers of various stripes sought ways to affirm Russia's uniqueness and exceptionality and thus to legitimate its specific historical development.

Patterns of Europeanization in the Twentieth and Twenty-First Centuries

In the twentieth century, Europeanization, or Westernization, continued to be a sensitive political issue and once again became a state imperative. The Bolshevik revolution was initially seen by its leaders as a way to ignite workers' uprisings in more advanced European countries, especially in Germany, but after the collapse of the plans for an international socialist revolution, the Soviet Union began to see itself as the only beacon for all progressive humanity, illuminating the way to the utopian communist future. The young Soviet republic was ready to recognize its backwardness, but convinced as it was of holding the only true and scientific ideology, it nevertheless saw itself as a global leader planning to "catch up" with the United States industrially and "overcome" it (*dognat' i peregnat'*). This Petrine vision remained dominant throughout Soviet history, although the pattern of its implementation changed dramatically after World War Two. While in the 1920s and 1930s the mission of catching up was assigned to the lower classes, after 1945 Communist

authorities, following the pattern established by Peter the Great in early eighteenth century, began investing in the creation of a stratum of scientists and
engineers able to compete with the United States, especially in building nuclear
weapons and exploring the cosmos. Once again, Europeanization became a
top-down state project to be implemented by an educated elite.

Toward the end of the Soviet Union, this growing educated and professional class, very much in the vein of the post-Petrine nobility, aspired to com-
plement the country's enormous military might and political stature with the
introduction of modern Western institutions, first of all multiparty democracy, a free press, and a market economy. Once again, this desire expressed
itself initially in a skillful negotiation between loyalty to the Communist ideology and Soviet state and infatuation with the contemporary West, represented
this time especially by the United States. But eventually, it led to an outright
confrontation between this new modernized group and the state that created
it. The elite group of intellectuals in the late Soviet period strongly identified
themselves with the nobles of the late eighteenth and especially early nineteenth centuries. Parallels between Soviet dissidents and the Decembrists
became commonplace ever since the first political protests in the late 1960s.
Like their predecessors, the dissidents constituted a tiny minority of the Soviet
intelligentsia, but their uncompromising Western orientation strongly influenced the mindset not only of a majority of their peers, but also of the younger
generations of Communist leaders. The desire to "join the civilized world"
and to "live in a normal country" became the catchwords of a movement that
eventually led to the collapse of the Communist system in 1989–1991. Both
"the civilized world" and "the normal country" were, of course, euphemisms
for Western democracies.

The triumph of the Westernizers happened to be short lived. Russia's failure
to join "the civilized world" as it was perceived in late 1980s–early1990s or,
depending on the political views of the observer, the failure of the "civilized
world" to integrate Russia within itself, led to a revival of national exceptionalism, the intensity of which seems to be unprecedented in Russian history.
Currently, the majority of Russians, led by the authorities and official propaganda, see the history of relations between Russia and the West as a story of
mutual animosity, incompatible interests, and incessant attempts by Western
powers to undermine and subjugate Russia.

The most significant change in this perception since the time of romantic nationalism lies in the definition of "the West"—while in the 1830s this

notion was used more or less as a synonym for "Europe," now it means mostly the United States, who replaced France as an embodiment of Western values and attitudes. The other development is the emergence of Eurasianism—the ideological movement that regards Russia neither as a part of Europe, nor as a separate civilization, but includes it into the larger community of Eastern or third-world nations opposing the West. However, this ideological trend, which emerged in the 1920s and is now supported by many right-wing ideologues, has never resonated in the popular imagination, which is still fascinated positively or negatively with Europe and North America. The current isolationist trend is reinforced by active anti-Russian propaganda campaigns in the European Union and the United States, which continue to dominate the Russian symbolic map of the world. Despite seeing the West as intrinsically hostile to Russia, Russians are still obsessed with the Western perceptions of themselves. Newly resurgent Russia once again aspires to compete with the West, and, as usual, this competition breaks out first and foremost in the military sphere.

This task implies yet again the formation of a new elite, which will enable the country to gain a technological edge over its imaginary rivals, and this elite will inevitably have to be Western educated and Western oriented. Whether twenty-first-century Russia has the time, resources, and intellectual capital for such a task, and how this new elite, if it ever comes into existence, will navigate the ensuing conflict of values and loyalties, remains to be seen. Yet the experience of the Europeanized Russian men and women of the eighteenth–early nineteenth century is not irrelevant in understanding the potential logic of this process.

To summarize, unlike its European peers, the Russian noble service estate was created in order to forge military and bureaucratic machines that would allow the state to cope with a challenge posed by the development of the Western world. It took the rulers of the country several decades to realize that the task of educating such an elite could not succeed if its members did not internalize the ethos and values of the state. The monarchy launched this process of interiorization by publishing the Manifesto on the Freedom of the Nobility and, further on, by summoning the Legislative Commission. This initiative had unintended consequences, chief among them the eventual differentiation and even individualization of the members of the elite, who were granted a significant number of new existential choices and faced the necessity to reconcile conflicting values, ideas, practices, and emotions. This process not only led to the appearance of the great Russian literature and culture of the nineteenth century, but also defined some of the fundamental problems of Russian history, which continue to haunt it to this day.

Synopsis

We shall begin in chapter 1 with an outline of Russia's Europeanization up to 1825, emphasizing the main forms and techniques of Europeanization successive rulers have used in political, social, economic, legal, and cultural terms. Our analysis of the subjective world of the elite begins in chapter 2, "Exposure to Europe," where we describe some of the more obvious ways in which the elite came into direct contact with Europe and started to interiorize European values, ideas, practices, and emotions. In their journeys through Europe, through the development of a Europeanized material culture, by dint of participating in Westernized social practices, and through their reading habits, the elite forged direct links with Europe, which shaped their self-perception, behavior, and emotions. This process paradoxically strengthened the elite's pride in its Russianness, precisely because it participated in networks of interaction and exchange with European elites and shared in the linguistic and cultural capital of their European counterparts. In this way, Europeanization generated forms of social intercourse that helped the elite consolidate its corporate identity as distinct from court society and also from the people.

In chapter 3, "Commerce with Power: The Elite at Court," we analyze in greater detail the fluid interrelations between the court and elite society, examining on the basis of memoirs the elite's position in court society in its daily life, the sway of conventions, and the emotions the elite experienced as it fought to protect its position in the public eye. In this analysis, the court emerges as a site of raw emotionality, but also as a setting that required fine discriminations in behavior roles, as courtiers were forced to practice continuous code-switching in a way that could be felt as demeaning. The psychological burden placed on the elite by the unpredictability of court life complicated their efforts to develop a unified sense of self and, by the end of the eighteenth century, fostered the attempt to carve out spaces of interiority protected from the intrusion of courtly politics.

Chapter 4, "The Quest for True Spirituality," deals with the status of religion and the Orthodox Church within the upper echelons of society. The

Europeanizing reforms in many ways distanced the members of the elite from Orthodox religious traditions, which became less and less accessible to them as they turned to francophony and vernacular Russian, at a time when church services, along with religious publications, still used Church Slavonic. However, most nobles preserved a deep attachment to Orthodox practices and rituals, which constituted for them a significant part of their Russianness and served as a connection with the majority of the population as well as a repository of family heritage. As a rule, this sentimental attitude did not extend to the clergy, which was regarded as ignorant and socially closer to lower social estates. As a result, members of the elite looking for spiritual consolation mostly turned to different types of Western spirituality, including Pietism, esoteric mysticism, and quietism.

Given the spiritual failings of the church, the efforts to forge a completely new elite had necessarily to center on education. This focus is discussed in chapter 5, "Writing on the Tabula Rasa: Educational Theories and Practices." The perception of a young person as a tabula rasa and of education as a silver bullet that would shape the subjects of the monarch in the desired direction was typical for the entire eighteenth century. While early efforts in creating the contemporary system of education focused on the learning of skills necessary for officers and military engineers, the subsequent focus on the interiorization of service implied making the moral education of the elite the center of official policy. This utopian perception of the power of education is reflected in the statutes of the first state schools, which required the complete isolation of young nobles from their families and the corrupt environment. While noble families initially resisted the attempts to separate them from their children, they gradually realized the necessity of formal education and started to compete for places in such institutions. Despite the rapid growth of state-sponsored educational institutions, their number was still hugely inadequate to accommodate a sufficient number of pupils, and nobles were willing to pay substantial sums—sometimes well above their means—for private schools and home tuition. Education through home tutors also enabled the elite to provide the necessary education to its children while at the same time avoiding state interference in family affairs.

The displacement of Orthodox religion from its central position in the spiritual and intellectual life of the elite left a deep spiritual void that was only gradually filled by literature, which acquired utmost importance among

educated society. This process is analyzed in chapter 6, "The Rise of Literature
and the Emergence of a Secular Cult." At the beginning of the eighteenth
century, the literary profession belonged to non-noble salaried clerks mostly
engaged in commissioned translations and panegyric poetry for special
occasions. A century later it became the main moral, political, and intellectual voice of the nation, endowing poets with an acute sense of mission. The
decisive shift in the role of literature started in the 1760s with the massive
influx of noble writers, who started to perceive literary pursuits as worthy of
their dignity. Literature also increasingly started to serve educated society as
a repository of emotional and behavioral patterns, providing an alternative to
the norms propagated by the court. It thus became instrumental in shaping
the identities of the growing reading public.

In chapter 7, "The Europeanized Self Colonizing the Provinces," we look at
the ways in which the elite was deployed to the provinces of the Russian empire
in an attempt to administer and "civilize" its vast territories. While the government's administrative reforms relied on the elite to participate disinterestedly
in local affairs on behalf of the state, the elite mostly attempted to replicate
their urban lifestyle in the aestheticized enclaves of their country estates, eras-
ing regional particularities in the process. As a result, the provinces became a
mirror that complicated the development of national identity, as they featured
a fragmented landscape in which signs of Europeanization contrasted with
vast exhibits of civilizational backwardness, thus forcing the elite through various intellectual and moral contortions to sustain its European identity.

In our conclusion, we focus on the way the elite developed a number of
subject positions, forms of identification, and networks of sociability at once.
We emphasize the imaginary quality of its bonds with place, people, and
power. Due to the inherent instability of its lifestyle, the elite experienced a
form of uprootedness we call deterritorialization. This is visible in its relations
to the court, which elicited a confused mixture of feelings, from awe and vanity to acute dependency and fear, thus preventing outright identification. As a
result, the elite did not have its own "home," a durable system of attachments.
Instead, torn between the various roles it enacted and the ideas it absorbed,
it inhabited an emotional world marked by tensions and hybridity, which,
however, worked differently than the hybridity caused by colonial occupation. Superficially similar to early modern forms of globalization, this process
of self-Europeanization did not lead to social and national consolidation, as

elsewhere in Europe, but to social fragmentation. While showing a typological resemblance with processes of Europeanization in other countries on the periphery of Europe (for example, in Japan and Turkey), the Europeanization of Russia was uniquely intense, complex, and pervasive, as it aimed not only to emulate Europeans in behavior, but to forge an elite that was intrinsically European, while remaining at the same time Russian.

1

HISTORICAL OUTLINE OF RUSSIA'S EUROPEANIZATION TO 1825

The standard narrative of Russia's Europeanization is fairly straight-forward. Peter the Great had traveled on his "Grand Embassy" to Holland and England, where he studied not only shipbuilding tech-nologies and other crafts, but also matters of political philosophy and, with Gilbert Burnet, of theology. In addition to its diplomatic aims, the journey also offered the opportunity to learn new technologies and to recruit craftsmen and other specialists into the Russian service. Even though his primary aims were military and economic, upon his return to Russia, Peter ushered in a series of cultural and symbolic reforms, which signaled his intention to secularize cultural practices in Russia and eventually to transform its polity. Military, administrative, institutional, political, and religious reforms ensued, and even though the task of transforming Russian society was left unfinished at Peter's death in 1725, these changes profoundly affected Russian society throughout the eighteenth century and beyond. More than anything else, in matters as varied as behavioral and sartorial norms, print culture, architecture, landscape design, and scientific practice, it is a *cultural* revolution that Peter had launched (Cracraft 2003). In all these domains, the reforms were profoundly inspired by western models, as is vividly and impressively illustrated by the creation of St Petersburg, the geographically and stylistically westernmost city in Russia. Political, administrative, military and religious reforms were more incremental, although often likewise inspired by western ideas.

So is the standard narrative about the Petrine reforms. No doubt influenced by the towering figure of Peter the Great and the mythologies it inspired, scholarship of eighteenth-century Russia has generally posited that the imitation of Europe provides one of the macrohistorical keys to unlock and explain Russia's historical development in this period. Yet matters became more complex when it came to determining what exactly Russian rulers were imitating. In a famous, if controversial article, Mark Raeff began to question the customary argument. The Russian eighteenth century is a "heuristically convenient" historical period, but precisely because it is defined by "the conscious efforts to imitate the principal features of another polity," it is crucial to acknowledge that Russia was in fact emulating features from different centuries. For example, the political culture that most strongly influenced Peter was cameralism, a set of ideas developed in German lands in the seventeenth century, "the baroque and classical century" (Raeff 1982, 612–3). Likewise, the craftsmen Peter recruited were not at the cutting edge of science and technology, but introduced mid-seventeenth-century techniques, and even the scholars drafted to establish the Academy of Sciences espoused views that were fast becoming obsolete. Furthermore, due to weaknesses of the state, the implantation of a new political culture only reached the upper levels of the elite, while traditional culture endured on lower rungs of society and in the provinces. The age of Peter the Great thus turned into a confrontation between two "seventeenth centuries," that of "European political culture" and that of the "traditional Muscovite order" (Raeff 1982, 615). There is considerable simplification in this neat picture, not the least because on the one hand the traditional Muscovite order, under Kievian influence, had already undergone considerable changes in the second half of the seventeenth century and, on the other, there was no such thing as a unified European political culture at the time, only a set of substantially different political practices even among so called absolutist regimes.

Others have further refined the imitation paradigm. Several scholars have pointed out that theological and political debates during Peter's time were strongly inflected by catholic and protestant theologians and political philosophers. Indeed, Maria Pliukhanova has demonstrated that the so-called Old Muscovite opposition to Petrine modernization was mostly driven by people fascinated not so much by national tradition as by contemporary Polish baroque culture. Moreover, ever since Slavophile thinker Iurii Samarin defended his Masters dissertation in 1844, it has been known that the main confrontation of the period unfolded between the protestant-leaning Feofan Prokopovich, Peter's main "ideologue" and spokesman, and the catholic-educated Stefan Iavorsky, who gradually evolved from being one of the main ideologues of Petrine reforms to active resistance to them. Likewise, Kirill Rogov has demonstrated that Peter himself was not immune to the traditions of baroque symbolism (Pliukhanova 2004, Rogov 2006, Samarin 1880).

Recently, Paul Bushkovitch has argued that Prokopovich was less interested in promoting western absolutist theory, which, according to him, did not exist anyway, than in legitimating the transfer of specific legal and administrative practices (Bushkovitch 2012). In short, the point is that the more granular our understanding of "Western influence," the more contested, multivalent and diffuse it becomes, and the more it seems that opponents in the project of cultural and political reform were equally under the sway of Western influences, only different ones. Consequently, as the sources of influence multiply and become more widespread, the explanatory value of the imitation paradigm begins to disintegrate, since it can no longer account for the overall development of Russia in the eighteenth century. Nevertheless, all scholars agree that the period of Peter the Great marked Russia's dramatic opening towards Western values, ideas, norms, and practices, only that this transfer was considerably more chaotic than had been presumed heretofore.

Let us look more closely at the parameters of Russia's Europeanization. Western influence upon Russia, of course, goes back a long way. It is architects from Italy who were invited to build the Moscow Kremlin in the fifteenth century, and contacts with Europe intensified in the seventeenth century, notably under the rule of Aleksei Mikhailovich, the father of Peter the Great. Yet it is under Peter, who ruled independently between 1694 and his unexpected death in 1725, that Russia embarked on a sustained and explicit program of Europeanization, which brought about a profound cultural transformation, often in defiance of the church. The long-standing historiographic polemic whether Peter ushered in a revolution or only extended what his father and his elder brother had initiated need not preoccupy us too much here. What matters to us is the perception of Peter's reforms by contemporaries and subsequent generations, and it is obvious that Peter's reforms had radically transformed their lives. Peter's status as the creator of the new Russia, for better or worse, remained unquestioned until well into the nineteenth century.

In his reforms, Peter pursued first and foremost practical aims. The initial military defeats he sustained in Azov in 1695 and Narva in 1700 drove home the pressing need to raise a modern regular army and find sustainable ways of supplying it. At the same time, his first steps towards Europeanization predate the stinging defeat at Narva and also grow out of domestic considerations, in particular Peter's distaste for the traditional ways associated with the Miloslavsky party against which he had had to assert his own power (Anisimov 1995, 135).

Europeanization started with attempts to educate the elite and change their way of life. In November 1696, Peter issued an edict in which he peremptorily dispatched a few dozen scions of the elite abroad to study. He promptly followed suit himself, announcing the so-called "Grand Embassy" on December 6, 1696. This diplomatic mission, consisting of about 250 people, set out to Holland and England during 1697–98, with Peter traveling incognito among the dignitaries, the first time a Russian tsar had ventured beyond his dominion. While its diplomatic aims were only partially successful, the embassy allowed Peter to observe Western practices, learn about new technologies, notably in ship-building, and discuss politics and theology with high-placed figures, for example Gilbert Burnett. The journey to Europe threw into relief the developmental contrast between Russia and Europe's industrializing countries and afforded access to novel intellectual developments, notably the optimistic melioristic philosophy of the early Enlightenment (Anisimov 1993, 24–26).

Upon his return to Moscow, Peter promptly convened his boyars and cut their cherished beards, a way for him to stamp his authority and mark the beginning of new times (the Russian church had risen in defense of the beard). In 1699, Peter wielded his scissors again to cut the traditional Russian dress of his courtiers, while an edict mandating the German dress for all noblemen was issued a year later. It was clear from their inception that his reforms would have a coercive dimension. The attention to sartorial norms reflected cameralist theory, namely the notion that only a comprehensively organized social system was capable of functioning properly, so that in a well-ordered society even details of external deportment were subject to regulation (Raeff 1984, 24–31; Kamenskii 2001, 99–101).

Creating a secular culture was one of Peter's ambitions, and it extended to various spheres of life. Calendar reform, introduced by edict on 19 December 1699, mandated the count of years from the birth of Christ, rather than the notional creation of the world, and the New Year on 1 January, rather than 1 September. The edict also carefully defined spheres of life to which it applied, prominently leaving the church off the hook, and thereby beginning the work of creating a secular culture distinct from religious traditions (PSZ 1830, vol. 3, no 1735, p. 680). Henceforth Russia would follow two different calendars at once, a civil and a religious one. British teachers were invited to Moscow to teach mathematics and engineering, and a school was established for this purpose in 1700. In the same year, a typography was created in Amsterdam to print secular books translated into Russian for shipment to Russia. This was the first step of a process to create a secular literary culture, which we describe in our chapter on literature. A "Manifesto on the Import of Foreigners to Russia" promulgated in 1702 laid out an ambitious aim of social betterment and economic development and offered foreigners willing to work in Russia several guarantees, notably confessional freedom. The church was placed under greater control. As we explain in greater detail in our chapter on religion, Peter refused to appoint a new patriarch upon the death of Adrian in 1700 and introduced measures to diminish the role of monasteries, in particular as centers of learning. The first newspaper was launched in 1702 and a comedy theatre was erected on Red Square, a site traditionally perceived as sacred. Peter also promoted attitudes such as intellectual curiosity and scientific experimentation even when there was no immediate utilitarian benefit in sight (Iosad 2016). And he ordered elite women to be released from seclusion in their chambers and to participate in the emergent society. All these initiatives contributed to compartmentalizing the church and hence diminishing its sway over the everyday life and mindset of the elite.

One of Peter's most visible and consequential decisions was the foundation in 1703 of a new capital, St. Petersburg, situated amidst marshlands, in the most inhospitable of terrains and exposed to regular flooding. By shifting the capital to newly conquered land on the empire's periphery, Peter gave a spectacular example of creation ex nihilo. In a manifestation of his melioristic ambitions, Peter called it his "paradise." The cost of creating this realized utopia, in terms of human life and material resources, was forbidding, yet Peter didn't recoil from any sacrifice. His motivations were several. Demoting Moscow as the center of traditional culture was one of them, though the first government bodies moved to St. Petersburg only in 1712. Commercial and strategic considerations about reorienting Russian foreign policy and commercial interests in a North-Western direction, in particular achieving military control over the Baltic sea and thereby facilitating trade with northern Europe, were key. And designing from scratch a city embodying Peter's vision of the state, both administratively and aesthetically, was likewise important to him. The new city, built mostly by European architects in a Western architectural idiom and with a regular layout of streets, was meant to become a showcase of the new rational well-ordered Russia. It emerged by force of edicts mandating everything from the design of facades and the use of building materials to the dress of its inhabitants. It was to become the site of a brilliant court, but also of a bureaucracy, staffed mostly by nobles, which attempted vainly to gain control over the vast expanses of the Russian empire.

The emphasis on education and manners continued unabated. By a decree of 1714 nobles who had not completed their primary education were forbidden to marry, a measure that had no chance of being implemented, but showed the priorities of the ruler. And those without education could not receive promotion in the army or civil service. It is estimated that about 1000 young men were sent abroad to study during Peter's reign (Kamenskii 2001, 124). In the late 1710s, following a trip to France, Peter issued a decree on assemblies, which mandated holding public gatherings in the houses of his grandees, open to all well-dressed individuals without distinctions of rank, where men and women could interact freely, creating the semblance of an open public sphere. An etiquette book composed of various foreign sources, the *Honorable Mirror of Youth*, was first published in 1717 and saw several subsequent publications. It contained both moral admonition and advice on etiquette, including for young ladies, and urged young nobles to converse among themselves in foreign languages, both for practice and to avoid eavesdropping by servants (Wortman 1995, 54; Hughes 1998, 288–90).

Peter's reforms had profound social consequences. While the ideological underpinnings of Peter's reforms had European origins, their scope was beyond anything the rulers he aspired to imitate could possibly imagine. A number of early modern European monarchs enjoyed "absolute" power, yet they were nevertheless constrained by traditional customs, legal norms, the established practices of everyday life, and, not least of all, the moral authority of the church. Peter implanted his reforms as if he was personally responsible for everything from the external appearance of his subjects, to their mindset, family life, daily routine, and religious beliefs. As a result, he introduced a social divide between the Europeanized nobility and the rest of the population, a divide which would grow only wider over the course of the eighteenth century and whose consequences are still felt in Russia today.

Peter tightened the nobility's obligation to serve and lengthened the duration of service, making it continuous and lifelong. He changed the economic basis of the nobility: remuneration for service replaced grants of estates, which made nobles more dependent on the bureaucracy and ultimately the ruler's good will. The decree on single inheritance (1714) was in part meant to force those deprived of an inheritance to enlist in state service. Many nobles stopped residing on their family lands. The meritocratic principles at the heart of Peter's educational policies were eventually formalized in the Table of Rank (1722). The Table developed a nomenclature of titles modeled on Western examples (Ageeva 2006, 69–71), but instead of distinction by birth, it instituted the principles of length of service and merit as the basis for promotion. The Table made education a requirement and granted noble title to commoners reaching a certain rank, thus recasting the nobility as an open class. Nobles started service in the lowers ranks, alongside commoners, though they generally benefitted from speedier advancement. These reforms profoundly redefined what it meant to be a noble in Russia, placing much greater emphasis on service to the state than in other European countries. Nevertheless, historians generally agree that Peter's attempts to instill a commitment to state service did more to foster corruption than to instill a work ethic (Kamenskii 2001, 120–122; Hughes 1998, 290–91).

Peter's administrative and political reforms also took their inspiration from Western models. The introduction in 1717 of Colleges (that is specialized organs of government) and of the so called "General Regulation" (1720)—a massive administrative code—was patterned after Swedish equivalents and aimed to formalize the work of a caste of expert civil servants organized and rewarded according to a uniform administrative order. In 1721, to crown the transformation of his position as absolute monarch, Peter assumed the title of emperor. In referring rhetorically to the trappings of imperial Rome, for example by awarding himself the title of Father of the Fatherland, Peter also conjured up legitimating analogies with Roman antiquity. The contradiction between the machinery of an administrative apparatus and the tsar's reliance on personal charisma, combined with his frequent readiness to sidestep administrative procedure, endured throughout the eighteenth century and culminated in Catherine the Great's notorious favoritism (Wirtschafter 2008, 57–58).

By the time of Peter's death in 1725, the upper nobility found itself in a contradictory position. On the one hand, it had been firmly tethered to a state project, often by coercive means, which robbed it of its independence despite some privileges such as owning serfs and freedom from the soul tax, a yearly fee levied on all males except nobles, officials and the clergy, which was aimed to finance the military. The nobility was a cog in an administrative machine meant to extend over the vast Russian empire. The obligation to serve indefinitely imposed considerable financial and psychological burdens. Families were often separated, as husbands enlisted in military or civil service were dislocated. On the other hand, the ideas and values imported from Europe began to suggest the dignity and self-worth of the individual, yet nobles did not hold title to their estates and nor could they be assured of the security of their persons in the absence of any form of due process (Raeff 1991, 296). This contradiction opened up a disjunction between the nobility's social role and its sense of self.

The nobility's insecurity was compounded by political instability. In his Law on Dynastic Succession of 1722, Peter had empowered the ruler to designate his (her) successor, a way to secure his legacy. Ironically, Peter died in 1725 without nominating anyone. As a result, the law he introduced exposed dynastic succession to a battle between various parties at court, creating considerable instability in the immediate years after his death and fostering several political coups over the eighteenth century until Paul I reestablished succession by primogeniture in 1797. Thus, instead of a well-ordered bureaucratic machine, Russia's court and government became a battleground between factions, turning patronage and clientelism into the main *modus operandi* of political life. The notion of charismatic, personalistic power Peter had left behind exacerbated this tendency (Wirtschafter 2008, 118–133).

Deprived of the security of person and property and compelled to serve for an indefinite number of years, the nobility attempted to lobby for improvements, coming together as a political force for the first time. In 1730 it obtained the abrogation of Peter's single inheritance law and in 1736 the length of service was shortened to 25 years and some dispensations were allowed for one son to remain on the familial estate to manage agricultural work. The standing of the nobility was also enhanced in that years spent in education allowed men to enter service at officer rank or equivalent on the Table of Ranks.

Europeanization continued unabated after Peter's death. The emphasis on education remained, notably with the founding of the Cadet Corps School and the expansion of the Academy of Sciences. The learning of foreign languages soared, French becoming the language of choice by mid-century. To provide entertainment for her brilliant court, Elizabeth instituted the Russian Imperial Theater (1756), giving pride of place to French theatre in it, and invited numerous French, German and Italian musicians, who turned St. Petersburg into a notable musical center. She was less interested in literature, although she underwrote the publication of various books, including a translation of Fénelon's *Adventures of Telemachus* (Marker 1985, 55). In its extravagant balls and masquerades, the Russian court began to outshine its European counterparts. Elizabeth also embarked on ambitious architectural projects, notably the construction by Bartolomeo Francesco Rastrelli of the Winter Palace (now Hermitage) in St. Petersburg and a summer palace at Tsarskoe Selo. In 1755 she founded Moscow University, which provided an education destined initially more to the lower nobility and commoners than to the elite, as the latter preferred home education by tutors.

The notorious profligacy of Elizabeth's court—her 15,000 dresses come to mind—raises the question of who bore the cost of Europeanization. Much of Peter's policies had aimed to strengthen the finances and the manpower of the state at everybody's expense, but in particular of the serfs. The demands of the regular mass conscription and the introduction of the soul tax led to more stringent enserfment of the peasant population, notably by curtailing its freedom of movement (Kamenskii 2001, 132–36), and also to the constitution of the separate group of so-called state serfs. After Peter's death, the nobility gained greater control over its serfs, a process that culminated in 1760 with an edict that entitled nobles to banish serfs to Siberia and hold such exiles as credit towards the next draft. Nobles had in effect received sovereign jurisdiction over their serfs.

The elite sought to fund its Europeanization by extracting more rent from its serfs, but was constrained by the ever-present risk of serf flight or sometimes outright rebellion. In 1767, responding to a letter by the poet and playwright Alexander Sumarokov in which he defended the social harmony existing between nobles and peasants, Catherine reminded him that cases of landlords murdered by their serfs were well known (Solov'iev 1895, 27: 310).

The latent civil war simmering on noble estates broke out during the rebellion of 1773–1775 led by the Cossack chieftain Emelian Pugachev. When the rebellious Cossacks advanced into Russia's agricultural regions, the peasants started mass killings of landlords and their wives and children, hoping to eradicate the nobility. And while most of the nobles continued to support serfdom and the coercive apparatus of the state as the main source and protection of their personal security, economic wellbeing, and social status, they also could not fail to feel the presence of the fire smouldering beneath the foundations of the existing system. A small, but growing minority of educated nobles were also becoming aware that the practice of serf ownership was inherently unjust and contradicted the European ideas that they were eagerly absorbing.

Over the decades after Peter's death, in real terms the tax burden shouldered by the serfs decreased, while the rent they paid to their owners increased. In other words, the nobility appropriated an increasingly large share of the nation's agricultural product (Kahan 1966, 50–52). Alcohol distillery was another convenient source of income for the nobility, since it could use serfs as free labor. In 1754, the nobility obtained a monopoly over alcohol production, yet relatively few nobles distilled spirits, as only the richest estates produced a decent grain surplus (Kahan 1966, 59). Despite consolidating its economic position at the expense of the serfs and the state, when it came to building estate houses and gardens or purchasing a suitably decorous mansion in St. Petersburg, the elite contracted substantial debts, which towards the end of the eighteenth century began to be perceived as a serious moral problem (Korchmina 2016).

During his short reign (1761–62), Peter III conceded to the nobility its most coveted privilege, freedom from state service. The Manifesto on the Freedom of the Nobility, promulgated on 18 February 1762, acknowledged that the mandates imposed by Peter the Great—education and state service— had initially run "against the will" of the nobility and thus required "coercion" (*prinuzhdenie)* (Faizova 1999 and Marasinova 2008, 226–236). However, over time, Peter's beneficial dispositions had "implanted noble thoughts in the heart of all true patriots of Russia, boundless love and faithfulness to Us, great fervor (*userdie*), and outstanding zeal (*rvenie*) in service to Us." Therefore, the Manifesto went on, "We no longer find any need in the compulsion to serve" (PSZ 1830, vol. 15, no. 11444, p. 912). In inflecting its rhetoric with such psychological and moral terms as love, heart, fervor and zeal, the Manifesto highlighted the importance of the psychological interiorization of the disposition to serve. Hence the crucial importance of education as through it the nobility (an open estate, after all) would assimilate the inner compulsion to render service to the monarch. Contrary to Western European conceptions of nobility, honor was not seen as inborn (de Madariaga 1981, 6). In short, the Manifesto was more about internalized duty, than freedom.

After ascending to the throne, Catherine underscored the general "benevolence" of the monarch toward the nobility although she put off an explicit confirmation of the Manifesto. It wasn't until 1785 in the Charter to the Nobility that the nobility's privileges were formally codified in law. Yet even the Charter did not entirely resolve the nobility's insecurity. It was a unilateral grant by the monarch, which could be revoked (Paul I completely ignored it). And ownership of land was predicated on noble status, which could easily be stripped (Wirtschafter 2008, 89). Nevertheless, the new policy emphasis on interiorization had far-reaching legal, political, and moral implications for the nobility. It opened a period when the nobility was expected to *feel* a personal identification with the monarch as well as with the interests of the state. And this emotional bond would foster individual initiative while also tie the nobility to its political mission to contribute to the governance of the country. In so doing, the Manifesto complicated the subjective world of the nobility as it was now put in a position to experience at once its independence and its subservience to a state project embodied in the ruler. The Manifesto thus marked a threshold in the historical trajectory of the nobility, dividing the period when the new elite appeared as a product of deliberate social engineering by the autocracy from the later epoch of the gradual interiorization of European values and behavioral patterns

Catherine continued the path of Europeanization. Herself a German princess, she was well connected with European aristocracy and reached out to the intellectual luminaries of her times, in particular to the leaders of the French Enlightenment. Her initial reform projects, for example the vision of the state advanced in the *Nakaz*, her Instruction to a Legislative Commission of 1767, rested on a partial and discriminating use of Montesquieu and Beccaria (Wirtschafter 2008, 137–139). The *Nakaz* mounted a strong defense of autocracy and curiously adopted in justification some wording lifted from Montesquieu's intensely negative depiction of despotism, turning it upside down. It boldly affirmed in article 6 that "Russia is a European state" and explained that Peter's success in inculcating European ways stemmed from the fact that the manners prevailing before his time were in fact unsuitable to Russia and its climate. Hence, by "introducing the Manners and Customs of Europe among the European People in his Dominions," Peter was in fact restoring Russia to its true nature (Reddaway 1971, 216). By way of this rhetorical sleight of hand, which she largely copied from Montesquieu, Catherine fundamentally transformed the meaning of Europeanization (Montesquieu 1973, 1: 336). No longer was it about assimilating more attractive, advanced or efficient foreign ways. Instead, it became a matter of becoming oneself again, after a protracted and unfortunate historical digression. Indeed, many of Catherine's law projects argued in terms of Russia's core historical identity, rather than in terms of foreign models. In article 57 of the *Nakaz*, she stated that legislation must be based on "the people's thinking" (*narodnoe umstvovanie*— *l'esprit de la Nation* in the French version), as "we do nothing so well as what we do freely and uncontrouled, and following the natural Bent of our own Inclinations" (Reddaway 1971, 221). In giving primacy to the will and character of the people, Catherine sounded surprisingly Rousseauistic, despite her profound distrust of the *Social Contract*. In short, Catherine de-emphasized the rhetoric of imitation and instead advanced the notion that Russia belonged to Europe by its very nature, a nature that laws, mores, and practices were to espouse more closely.

Instead of fostering the *imitation* of things foreign, Catherine favored what we call the pursuit of enhanced connectivity with European countries. Far from seeking the wholesale transfer of a foreign cultural model, say to import the secular Enlightenment at the expense of traditional Orthodox practice, her intention was to stimulate the traffic of people, goods, ideas, images, values, technologies, and practices across state boundaries in both directions, as a way not only to harness Russia more firmly to its alleged European historical destiny, but also to exert influence abroad. Thus, in 1764, the Commission on Commerce issued an edict that encouraged sending the children of merchants abroad so that they would learn the basics of their trade, arguing that it considered travel "as a most useful and necessary matter" (PSZ 1830, vol. 16, no. 12150, p. 739). Similarly, in 1768, Catherine established a "Society for the Translation of Foreign Books into Russian," which convened promising young writers and commissioned translations of books, sometimes directly ordered by the empress, including works by Voltaire, Montesquieu, Mably, Swift, and Blackstone. Endowed with a considerable budget of 5,000 rubles per year from Catherine's personal funds, the society published more than 173 books and commissioned many more translations, some of which were subsequently issued by Nikolai Novikov. Founded in 1765 and patronized by Catherine, the Free Economic Society similarly aimed to foster experimentation in agricultural matters and to bring Western agronomical science to the attention of the Russian public, the praiseworthy results of what it called "our economic century."

Crucially, the material and cultural goods imported as a result of this traffic were generally not intended to replace indigenous ones, but simply to enrich incrementally, as it were, existing norms and particularities. So, to focus on the life of the elite, in sartorial matters, the penetration of Western fashions was, of course, desirable to give the court more brilliance, but not at the expense of the Russian dress or in a slavish fashion. Travel to Europe was most welcome, provided one remained loyal to the Empress, said nice things about her abroad, and eventually returned to Russia. It was certainly a good thing to be conversant with enlightenment philosophy, but not to the extent of becoming materialist or atheist. A vigorous literary culture was a most desirable appendage to the court, and satirical journals or plays could be used to correct pernicious habits or manners, but they should stop short of showing disrespect to the empress and her entourage, or of disparaging the Russian state. Instituting a law-based, regular political culture was deemed necessary, but without in any way impeding patronage and favoritism. As an independent estate, the nobility could enjoy legal freedom from service to the monarch, but should nevertheless feel morally obliged to serve. The list could go on. As we will see in subsequent chapters, this additive pattern of cultural import vastly complicated the psychological make-up and cultural universe of the elite.

As part of this strategy of enhanced connectivity, Catherine clearly aspired to influence the polity in various European countries, both through her personal involvement and by way of Russia's geopolitical might. Militarily and diplomatically, she engaged in a very active foreign policy, pursuing complicated alliances with other European countries and declaring war against foes with little hesitation (she fought seven external wars over the course of her reign and substantially expanded the empire towards the west and the south). These wars were inspired by strategic, geopolitical considerations, yet many also involved a civilizational project. For example, her war against the Ottoman Empire in 1768–1774 was informed by the "Greek project," the aim to take possession of Constantinople and thereby to establish a continuous line of genealogy between the Russian empire and Greek antiquity.

She also knew how to exercise soft power to achieve her aims. Catherine engaged in correspondence with Enlightenment luminaries to bolster Russia's prestige as a country that is tolerant and friendly to the arts and sciences, hoping that the *philosophes* would help her influence educated public opinion in France and elsewhere. Catherine's friendship with Friedrich Melchior von Grimm, who contributed articles to the *Encyclopédie* and was at the center of Parisian salons, led to a remarkably unguarded correspondence for over 20 years, a frankness perhaps encouraged by Grimm's moderate political views and his support of Catherine's wars (Dixon 2009, 224). Grimm served as a conduit for news on artistic life and social gossip, but he also acted as Catherine's agent and unofficial spokesman abroad, negotiating commissions with artists and securing the acquisition of Voltaire and Diderot's libraries. As he sought patronage or money for artists, Grimm deftly played on Catherine's ambitions to outshine Paris and Versailles. After the success of one of Giovanni Paisiello's operas in Paris, he noted the following conversation:

> Why is he not in Paris? I answered: because he is in Russia.—And why would he not come to Paris? I answered: because he wouldn't be paid as well as in Russia, not even counting the boxes with incrusted diamonds that the empress sends him and the clothes she sends to his wife when she is pleased with one of his operas.—Well, is there an Italian opera in St. Petersburg?—Yes, among other things." (Grimm 1886, 24–25)

Grimm's letters are peppered with such flattering demonstrations of his skill at public relations, a tactic he cleverly deployed to secure more support for the artists he took under his wings. Meanwhile the empress could not be happier with his apparent efforts at burnishing Russia's reputation in Paris.

Catherine wanted to be seen as a patron for the arts and letters and offered sanctuary to various public figures. Even Rousseau, despite her sometimes visceral hostility to him, received an invitation in 1766 from Grigorii Orlov, her favorite, to settle on one of his estates near St. Petersburg. When Diderot visited St. Petersburg in the winter of 1773–74, Catherine patiently indulged his radical political ideas expounded to her in private conferences, while the shabbily dressed writer cut a ridiculous figure in society (de Madariaga 1998, 225–234). Falconet designed the famous Bronze Horseman, spending 12 years in Russia but leaving in 1778 in acrimony, before the monument was completed. Portrait painters such as Johann Lampi, Richard Brompton, and

Alexander Roslin created a visual record of court figures. Marie-Anne Collot, who arrived together with Falconet, became the elite's favored portrait sculptor and was elected as a member of the Imperial Academy of Arts. On the run from the French revolution, Mme Vigée Lebrun, whom Catherine disliked, nevertheless found refuge in Russia in 1795, staying for six years, which gave her ample time to create a series of portraits of the Russian elite. Catherine twice invited Hubert Robert, the "painter of ruins," and was incensed that he declined repeatedly. She had wanted him to paint the idyllic views of her gardens at Tsarskoe Selo.

Foreign architects were, of course, central to Catherine's Europeanization project. Jean-Baptiste Vallin de la Mothe, Charles Cameron, Giacomo Quarenghi, and Antonio Rinaldi were instrumental in establishing the neo-classical style in Russia, an idiom largely devoid of vernacular inflections. They worked along, and partly influenced, a group of talented Russian architects operating in the same idiom. Together, these artists transformed the visual aspect of the new capital as well as of many country estates. Neo-classicism became the obligatory standard for the development of provincial towns and thus a kind of official architectural language.

Musicians were also in high demand. In 1791, count Andrei Razumovsky, Russia's plenipotentiary in Vienna, asked Grigorii Potemkin to invite Mozart to Russia, informing him that the composer was unhappy in Vienna and would be disposed to undertake the journey to St. Petersburg. The deaths of both Mozart and Potemkin shortly thereafter put an end to this plan, but Mozart had benefitted from the support and hospitality of Russian grandees from his first meeting in 1763 with D.A. Golitsyn in Paris, at the age of seven (Porfir'eva 1998–9, 2: 224–242). Paisiello was court Kapellmeister between 1776 and 1784, a time during which he experienced a remarkable creative outburst. He was replaced by Giuseppe Sarti, who stayed until 1802 and exerted a huge influence on the development of Russian music. Domenico Cimarosa and Vincense Martin y Soler also worked in Russia for many years, as did many invited singers and instrumentalists.

Meanwhile Catherine also intervened energetically in the European art market. Acting through Diderot, Grimm, and others, she acquired entire collections, notably Sir Robert Walpole's Houghton collection and part of the Duc de Choiseul's. It is estimated that she bought about 4000 paintings in the first twenty years of her reign (Dixon 2009, 194). These purchases gained much international resonance and prompted anguished concerns about

national despoliation in Britain and France. But it is by commissioning works
that Catherine exerted her greatest impact on European artistic life. Among
kingly patrons, the extent of her interest in contemporary art was unprecedented. Francesco Casanova, Jean-Baptiste-Siméon Chardin, Charles-Louis
Clérisseau, Marie-Anne Collot (25 commissions), Jean-Antoine Houdon,
Angelica Kauffman, Anton Raphael Mengs, and Hubert Robert were among
those who benefited from orders from her. Receiving a commission from the
empress conferred considerable public prestige to artists. Catherine was one
of the first on the continent to collect English art and she commissioned two
pieces from Sir Joshua Reynolds. The decorative arts were also in her line
of sight, as she needed to furnish the various palaces that were built on her
behalf. Wedgewood's Green Frog Service—a 50-set service which included
1222 views of British landscapes, gardens, and antiquities—is among her most
famous commissions. It is impossible to evaluate the full economic impact of
these purchases on the European art market, but it is clear that it considerably
helped sustain artistic production in Western European countries. In the late
1770s, "the profound impact of Catherine's interventions on the Roman art
market could be felt in nearly every corner of the city's artistic production"
(Frank 2006, 185).

The impact of Catherine's art purchases was magnified by the fact that
many a grandee followed suit and built up their own collections, sometimes
with refined discernment. Through his prominent commissions, count
Aleksandr Stroganov was instrumental in advancing Hubert Robert's career
in Paris in the 1770s (Deriabina 2000, 146–7). Stroganov continued to support Robert throughout his life. In 1803, he prevailed upon Alexander I to
commission six works, for which "he paid in quite a different manner than
they pay here," as Robert stated in a letter to a friend (Ibid., 146–151). By
way of their purchases, Russian collectors gained access to famous European
artists and gained knowledge, reputation, and influence across Europe, not to
speak of human contacts, which only served to enhance their cultural capital
at home.

Economically speaking, this demand for luxury goods, cultural artifacts,
and technologically advanced manufacturing also spurred domestic production. The existence of the Russian market encouraged foreign craftsmen to set
up shop in Russia. In a regulation promulgated in 1766 to foster commerce
and domestic industry, the government lowered duties on common goods
and applied higher tariffs on some imported luxury goods (PSZ 1830, vol.

17, no, 12735, p. 951; Munro 2008, 192). However, in line with physiocratic and Smithian economic theory, the new tariff of 1782 lowered duties across the board, so that in terms of international commerce, Russia became one of the most liberal countries in Europe, becoming less protectionist than even Britain. In order to foster the arts and sciences, it cancelled all tariffs on books, paintings, engravings, statues, metallic instruments, vases, urns, as well as on musical notes and instruments, i.e. on the products of the liberal arts the elite aspired to acquire. (In subsequent decades, the government changed tariffs on a regular basis, reflecting the vagaries of the battle between liberals and protectionists in the higher circles of government). Regardless of the prevailing tariff, prices on foreign luxury goods were significantly higher in Russia than in Western Europe, surely the result of misbalance between supply and demand.

In short, many of the reforms Catherine undertook contributed to bolstering Russia's European identity, while she was also keen to affirm its distinctiveness if not superiority. This feeling was strongly enhanced by the events of the French revolution, when the French court and aristocracy, which had served for many centuries as an object of imitation to all European elites, suddenly collapsed in the popular upheaval and the calamities of the civil war. A great number of French émigrés arrived in Russia in search of asylum, which allowed Russian nobles to perceive their country as a guardian of the European order and the main pillar of the system of European monarchies.

The Napoleonic wars, which broke out during the reign of Alexander I, complicated the cultural and patriotic allegiance of the elite. The confrontation with France and initial disaster at the battle of Austerlitz in 1805 made apparent the growing contradiction between the reverence for French culture traditional among the noble elite and its patriotic aspirations. The invasion of Napoleon in Russia in 1812 and the European campaign of 1813–1814, which ended with the triumphal entry of the Russian army in Paris in 1814, dramatically changed Russian national consciousness and especially the self-assessment of the elite. Even before the wars, the army and especially the guard had enjoyed significant institutional independence and served as a substitute for the nearly non-existent public sphere (Velizhev 2016b; Andriainen 2016). The anti-Napoleonic campaigns gave a huge boost of self-esteem and sense of entitlement to the officers, who saw Russia's military power and pan-European political clout as incompatible with the existence of such outdated institutions and practices as serfdom and the total lack of political representation even for the elite. Contradictions started to emerge between the elite's patriotic identification with Russia and its moral condemnation of specific institutions.

The emerging rift in the relations between the throne and the educated nobility was deepened by Alexander I's post-war foreign policy, which was based on a vision of future Europe as a transnational mystic union of Christian monarchs of different denominations. This project found its manifestation in the so-called Holy Alliance concluded between the rulers of Russia, Prussia, and Austria under strong pressure from the Russian emperor. Among the signatories of the treaty, Alexander seemed to be the only one who really believed in it and tried to act in its spirit. He inaugurated the protestant-inflected Biblical society, whose mission it was to translate the Bible, which previously existed only in Church Slavonic, into the vernacular languages of Russia's multi-ethnic empire, including Russian. Alexander announced constitutional reforms and the abolition of serfdom in Poland and the Baltic provinces, but not in mainland Russia, and he adamantly refused to support the Greek rebellion against the Ottoman Empire in 1821. All these decisions provoked opposition both among the traditionalists, who viewed the emperor's ecumenical plans with deep suspicion and mistrust, and the young radicals fascinated by the nationalist ideology quickly spreading through Europe after the Napoleonic wars. The younger generation of nobles increasingly viewed Alexander's policies as a betrayal of the Russian national interest.

While the conservatives were just grumbling about the official course, the radicals gradually began to organize themselves. Initially their discontent took the traditional form of triangulation between loyalty to the throne and the fatherland, fervent patriotism, and the unwavering belief in the necessity of Europeanization. Rooted in the tradition of Freemason lodges, the first political associations were organized in order to help the monarch implement necessary reforms. However, later, when the disappointment with official policy became stronger, the core of these loose associations, consisting mostly of officers of the guard, started forming clandestine conspiratorial groups, which prepared the military coup d'état attempted on December 14, 1825 and known in Russian history as the Decembrist uprising.

The officers of the guard regiments located in St. Petersburg were accustomed to the role of king makers, playing a decisive role in seven out of nine successions to the throne between the death of Peter the Great in 1725 and the accession of emperor Alexander I in 1801. However, their intervention in the succession crisis of 1825 following the sudden death of Alexander ended in utter disaster. The routing of the rebellious regiments by the canons of the loyal troops ended not only the political role of the military elite, but also the entire period of the cultural dominance of the Europeanized nobility.

The rebellion had a powerful impact on the national psyche. Of course, the participants in the conspiracy, numbering in the dozens, were a tiny minority among the Russian nobility in general, although the descendants of the most aristocratic families were dramatically overrepresented in their ranks. Nevertheless, despite the authorities' initial attempt to downplay its significance, for the elite, the failure of the conspiracy clearly meant that the post-Petrine period, with its relatively smooth, if not always easy coexistence of different sets of loyalties, was drawing to a close.

2

. . . .

EXPOSURE TO EUROPE

Travel, Material Culture, Sociability, and Reading

The state project of Europeanization permeated just about all spheres of noble life, from the food the elite ate to the books they read and the way they socialized. While it transformed the behavior of the elite in public, it also influenced the elite's mental horizon, subjective self, and private life. Even areas under the jurisdiction of the church were affected by Europeanization. Peter the Great, for example, intervened in matters of marital policy, traditionally in the purview of church authorities, promulgating an edict in 1724 forbidding coerced marriages. And Europeanization was hardly limited to men, as it fundamentally recast gender roles: along with a raft of edicts that brought elite women out of the *terem*, invited them to noble assemblies, and imposed various behavioral and sartorial conventions, Peter's policies significantly improved the position of women at court, an attempt in part to give elite sociability a veneer of European politeness (Hughes 1998, 186–202).

To illustrate the breadth of Europeanization and to give some concrete idea of the lifestyle of the elite, in this chapter we will describe some of the more obvious ways in which members of the elite came into direct contact with European culture and incorporated its conventions, values, practices, and fashions into their mundane existence. By way of an analysis of the elite's travels, their material culture, their social practices, and their reading habits, in this chapter we will depict the pervasiveness of European models. But we will also demonstrate that one cannot simply think of the adoption of European models as a process of straightforward imitation; in their migration to Russia, these cultural norms underwent various transformations and assumed specific functions that differed from those they had discharged in their original environments. As a result, the import of these models elicited variegated responses from social actors in Russia, thus fostering the coalescence of distinct social groupings. Notably, toward the end of the century, this transfer of social practices increasingly led to a polarization between the court and some quarters of noble society, while also consolidating the elite's sense of its distinctiveness from lower provincial nobles and commoners.

Travel

Travel to Europe was, of course, one of the most obvious ways to become a European and the crowning stage of a Europeanized education—a way not only to perfect one's learning, but also to measure oneself against European aristocracies. Catherine and Alexander I generally encouraged travel to Europe, albeit within limits and with some degree of control, while Paul temporarily clamped down on the practice. Scions of the upper nobility were often dispatched on educational journeys, which included extended periods of study at one of the fashionable universities (Leiden, Leipzig, Edinburgh, Strasbourg, Paris, Geneva, and others), as well as visits to famous European cities, following the English practice of the aristocratic Grand Tour. Other grounds to travel to Europe included taking up a diplomatic post or attending a spa for reasons of health. Women traveled, too, notably Ekaterina Dashkova (who went on to become the director of the Academy of Sciences) and Natalia Golitsyna (the prototype of Pushkin's Queen of Spades), the latter residing in Europe for seven years, at once to chaperone her daughters while they were adding the final polish to their manners and to rejoin her sons studying in Strasbourg and then Paris. There was no fixed itinerary travelers would follow, although most of them visited the German principalities, parts of France, and Italy. Quite a few made detours to the Low Countries, England, and Switzerland. The length of stays abroad was also variable, but more a matter of years than months, especially if study at a university was included. If they attended one of the European centers of learning, the elite were more likely to agree individual tuition with prominent teachers than to enroll in a program of study.

Many of these travelers kept diaries of their journeys, or else wrote extensive letters to their families back home to account for what they had seen and accomplished. The motivations behind these diaries were not always clear. Students were advised by their parents to consign their impressions to the page, both as a form of educational exercise and for future use (Berelowitch 1993, 199). Requiring travel accounts was also a way for parents to monitor the activities and progress of their sons, who were often supposed to send reports of expenditure back home. Although travel diaries were not initially meant to be published, they were often implicitly addressed to a notional readership broader than direct parents or family, but narrower than an anonymous "educated reader." In the diary of her journeys of 1783–1790, Golitsyna pleaded that it would be useless for her to describe the sites of Vienna or Paris, as everybody knew these cities well anyway (RGB OR, f. 64, k. 113, ed. 1, 20ob). The only extant copy of her journal is in her daughter's hand and was copied some time after their return to Russia, suggesting some degree of handwritten dissemination. Golitsyna was, in other words, writing for her set, for the benefit of elite society, those close to her family and those who might undertake a similar journey. This contrasts with Nikolai Karamzin's *Letters of a Russian Traveller*, which the author started to publish in 1791 and which aimed to reach a broader readership, as the author posits a reader less conversant with famous European sites (Karamzin 2003, Lotman and Uspenskii 1984, Schönle 2000; we will discuss Karamzin's *Letters* more extensively in our chapter on literature and focus here on a selection of travel accounts that were not written directly for publication). Aleksandr Kurakin's account of a journey he made in 1770–1772 after studying in Leiden was only published in 1815, and with a note from the "editor" indicating that Kurakin had found his account in his papers "by chance" and printed a few copies "for himself and his friends," without any authorial pretensions (Kurakin 1815, 1). Despite these protestations redolent of the widespread topos of modesty, the text indicates clearly that Kurakin had partially reworked his notes prior to publication. Perhaps he was

persuaded to publish his travelogue in light of the popularity of literary travel-
ogues in Russia in the wake of the publication of Karamzin's *Letters*. Similarly,
Fedor Rostopchin's account of a journey to Prussia in 1786–1788 was never
published in his lifetime, but was written or rewritten in 1792–1794, several
years after the actual journey, possibly as a response to Karamzin's description
of Prussia in his *Letters* (Ovchinnikov 1992). The writings of the elite thus
struck a middle ground between the domestic and the literary spheres.

A brief look at a selection of these travel accounts gives us an opportunity
to gauge the frame of mind of elite travelers. What were they interested in
during their journeys, and how did they see their standing in Europe? And
was travel primarily motivated by a pursuit of pleasure and entertainment, or
for other reasons?

Most writers commented on the nature of elite sociability in various
European cities. Rostopchin quipped that each of the festivities regularly
given by Russian grandees would have become an epochal event in Berlin. In
contrast, assemblies in the Prussian capital were modest and boring. They also
lacked dinner, the entertainment mostly limited to playing lotto (Rostopchin
1849, 1:86; 10:77). Golitsyna described elite gatherings in Vienna in similar terms (RGB OR, f. 64, k. 113, ed. 1, 22ob), while Kurakin complained
about the "phlegmatic" Dutch, who prefer home to public sociability and
spend their time in society playing cards (Kurakin 1815, 40–41). Moreover,
most travelers were surprised at the lack of pomp and ceremony at European
courts. Although they generally appreciated the absence of constraining etiquette, they could not fully stifle a sense of superiority in view of the relative
austerity on display. Only in Paris did Russian travelers find suitably sprightly
public events. The pleasures of sociability at watering holes were of course
of critical importance, but here, too, some faced disappointment. Ekaterina
Bariatinskaia left a devastating depiction of social life in Spa in 1791, where
French aristocrats on the run drowned their sorrow in ostentatious consumption. "Life in Spa," she wrote, "is so dissipated and noisy that instead
of restoring one's failing health, it is capable of destroying that of the most
vigorous people." And she expressed particular revulsion at the "pestilential
exhalations," "the sweat of desperation," emanating from the people thronging
around the gambling tables (RGB OR, f. 19, op. 5/2, d. 12, l. 75–75ob). The
pursuit of social entertainment thus hardly justified the journeys undertaken
by the elite, all the more so as in most cities, with the exception again of Paris,
theaters were found to be at best passable.

More important than the ability to gain access to foreign assemblies was the opportunity to measure one's prestige in foreign eyes, and more broadly to compare oneself to others. Kurakin argued explicitly that foreign travel provided a means of gaining a true knowledge of oneself by observing "the mutual proofs of consideration and esteem." It is only among foreigners, he went on, in commerce with people of all classes, that one "can shake the yoke of error and prejudice and evaluate what one is worth," as at home, one is blinded by one's name and habitual relations (Kurakin 1815, 95). For Golitsyna this confrontation with foreign views was primarily a matter of receiving confirmations of her distinction. She fastidiously noted all the attention foreign rulers lavished upon her: in Vienna, Paris, Brussels, and London, kings, queens, and assorted princes graciously bent all the rules of etiquette to make her feel welcome (RGB OR, f. 64, k. 113, ed. 1, l. 21ob, 66, 83ob, 112ob). Interestingly, she never asked herself why she deserved this attention and happily acted as the main beneficiary of such warm reception, her husband, who traveled with her, hardly figuring in her account. Visits to various courts thus offered an opportunity to gauge one's standing in the European limelight.

Travel to Europe straddled the divide between public role and private pursuit. If they traveled under their own name, members of the elite were in fact assuming a semiofficial role as representatives of the Russian court. Upon their arrival in a new city, it was usually the Russian ambassador who introduced them to the local society. Diplomats not only facilitated the social intercourse of the elite but also assumed a custodial responsibility over younger travelers. While stationed in Frankfurt, Nikolai Rumiantsev reported to Golitsyna about the doings of her sons, who stayed in the city to attend the coronation ceremony of Leopold II. He also advised them on their travel plans (RGB OR, f. 64, k. 100, ed. 57). Travelers willingly assumed the role of representatives of their country or ruler. On the occasion of the Russian victory over Turkey in 1791 at Yassy, Bariatinskaia gave a lavish festivity in Spa, despite her distaste for its frivolous public. Dressed in a "Russian costume," she staged an illumination representing the initials of the empress, enhanced by a (hapless) poetic encomium to her she had commissioned, while basking in effusive compliments received on account of Catherine's triumph (RGB OR, f. 19, op. 5/2, d. 12, l. 75).

Russian travelers did not feel completely free from the Russian court. In Genoa Bariatinskaia declined the offer of an escort of four noble ladies, lest accepting this honor would come across in Russia as undue arrogance (36).

Bariatinskaia had, in fact, a controversial reputation at court for being too francophile, and even in foreign lands, she felt somehow under the court's surveillance, or at least in its line of vision. Younger travelers were usually subject to control from the Russian capital, sometimes directly by the empress. Kurakin, for example, had to turn down Aleksandr Stroganov's invitation to come to Spa, as "we were dependent upon someone's orders and thus had to be unbending" (Kurakin 1815, 8). Nikolai Sheremetev's governor felt that it would be unseemly for him to socialize with Frenchmen given the tense relations between the French and Russian courts at the time (11). Traveling under a pseudonym (as Sheremetev did) was a common means of limiting social obligations, but even that did not permit fully to evade this kind of representativeness.

By and large, the Russian elite wore a patriotic hat as they visited Europe. Some travelers articulated pronounced national stereotypes. Denis Fonvizin's "Letters from France," addressed to Petr Panin but quickly disseminated in handwritten copies, put forward a pithy critique of the French and explicitly used the concept of "national character" (Fonvizin 1983, 289). In his satirical description of Prussian society, Rostopchin savaged the exasperating slowness of postmasters, the nearly sadistic carelessness of coachmen, the overbearing aristocratic pride of the Prussian elite, in spite of their straitened circumstances, as well as their stiff obsession with military rank and demeanor, at the expense of polite and witty conversation (Rostopchin 1849). Clearly, he had little sympathy for the Prussian way of life.

Yet Russian travelers did not uniformly condemn the moral makeup of the nations they visited. Some parts of Europe felt entirely germane, notably France, even during revolutionary times. As she was leaving Paris to return to St. Petersburg (by order of the empress, in fact, although she did not acknowledge that), Golitsyna stated that she had felt entirely at home in the city and had been received like a local (RGB OR, f. 64, k. 113, ed. 1, l. 122ob). Karamzin took a nuanced view of the countries he visited, finding some faults with each of them, but also praising some facets and perhaps hinting that only Russians succeeded in combining the best traits from different European nations. Traveling to Europe clearly helped buttress a sense of national identity, whether this was conceived in terms of distinctiveness and superiority, as in Fonvizin's and Rostopchin's travel notes, or as a demonstration of well-connectedness on equal terms, as Golitsyna and Karamzin implied.

But identification with Russia did not prevent the elite from also espousing nonofficial subject positions. In good sentimentalist fashion, the discovery of European landscapes and European art elicited modes of feeling that placed the individual on the margins of society. The ability to feel and to engross oneself in a scene prompted notions of distinctiveness based not on social standing, but on sensibility. After visiting the studio of Angelica Kauffmann, Bariatinskaia confessed that the artist's unpretentious manner would hurt her in society: "Many French people and unfortunately also Russians would be judges in front of whom she would pass as someone who lacks knowledge and wit, because they look at her superficially," she claimed (RGB OR, f. 19, op. 5/2, d. 12, l. 64). In contrast, she implied, only she was able to disregard the painter's unrefined conversation and appreciate her character. What she did not acknowledge in her diary, perhaps symptomatically, was that she commissioned several paintings from Kauffmann, including a family portrait (which now hangs in the Pushkin Museum of Fine Arts in Moscow). In this, she was, in fact, acting very much like other Russian grandees: Andrei Razumovsky, Nikolai Iusupov, Ekaterina Skavronskaia, Aleksei Naryshkin, and Ivan Chernyshev had likewise commissioned works from the painter in the same years, not to speak of the empress (Kauffman 1924, 154–163).

Sentimentalist rhetoric about the sublime pleasures gained from the contemplation of art and nature also coexisted with a more public-minded interest in political economy, which was characteristic of the times. Golitsyna and Kurakin criticized high taxes levied by princes and generally cast a keen eye on political structures, economic practices, public institutions, and social mores. Developing an extensive argument about the economic benefits of religious tolerance, a "state virtue which brings about general felicity," Kurakin blamed Catholicism for the economic decline of the once prosperous Antwerp (Kurakin 1815, 46–48). Golitsyna similarly underscored the enormous difference in wealth between Catholic and Reformed cantons in Switzerland, castigating the economic cost of maintaining numerous churches and monasteries. She also took a very dim view of direct democracy in central Swiss cantons, "the most disorderly popular government that can be" (RGB OR, f. 64, k. 113, ed. 1, l. 54–54ob).

Kurakin's economic analysis seems to have been informed by Adam Smith's views on the convergence of particular interests in free markets and the ensuing maximization of everyone's prosperity, as developed in *The Wealth of*

Nations, although Kurakin struggled to fit his notion of the aristocratic ethos within the liberal concept of self-interest:

> Labor belongs to all classes. The lord considers it his duty to contribute to the physical and moral good of his fatherland. The merchant takes care of all means which make commerce flourish; his speculations lead to the establishment in the state of a circulation of money, the sign of wealth and security. ... In a word, he raises his fortune while working toward that of others. The villager, in turn, contributes to the common happiness by spreading plenty in the kingdom. In this way, the three classes whose particular efforts seem to pursue different goals, work nevertheless together toward the same result, which is public felicity. Thus the common interest is a happy combination of particular interests. (Kurakin 1815, 107)

In this account, nobles do not pursue an economic self-interest, but an internalized commitment to the public good, which contradicts liberal economics. *The Wealth of Nations* was published in 1776, a few years after Kurakin's journey of 1770–1772, suggesting that this paragraph may have been added later, in preparation for the 1815 edition. Although Kurakin's attempt to draw on economic theory to justify the privileges of the nobility seems incoherent, it is significant that he charted Russia's future economic prosperity through the shedding of stereotypes (Kurakin 1815, 119) and that he imputed journeys with the power to foster this form of enlightenment through practical observation of others. There may be some echoes of Adam Smith's earlier *Theory of Moral Sentiments* (1759) in his views.

Golitsyna was also keenly interested in political economy, and she repeatedly commented on the relative prosperity (or poverty) of nobles and peasants alike in various places. In fact, she began her diary with a detailed description of the reforms she undertook on her own country estate before embarking on her journey, which consisted of spacing out *izbas* and farm buildings in the village to avoid the spread of fire. Over the course of her journey, she considered agricultural matters in considerable detail, describing the different techniques used in various places. Golitsyna's "hands-on" approach to estate management reveals a degree of civic-mindedness on her part. Although it certainly also pursued hedonistic aims, her journey to Europe enabled her to micromanage the European Grand Tour of her children and to learn about agricultural practices she could subsequently introduce on her estates.

Did the elite become politicized as a result of their journeys? The most dramatic example here is the young Pavel Stroganov, the son of Aleksandr Stroganov, who embarked on an educational journey through Europe with his tutor Gilbert Romme, the future Jacobin. While traveling, Pavel followed a rigorous educational curriculum designed by Romme in consultation with Pavel's father. Although devoutly religious and somewhat indolent, Pavel demonstrated versatile interests, including for technological matters such as watchmaking. Traveling through Switzerland, he described in detail the political system of various towns (RNB, f. 1278, op. 1, ed. khr. 346), but it isn't until he arrived in Paris in 1789 that he became more absorbed in politics, attending the National Assembly almost daily, even speaking twice at the bar, and briefly becoming a member of the Club of Jacobins before his father recalled him to Russia by instruction of the empress. Recent scholarship by A. V. Chudinov downplayed Pavel's revolutionary fervor (Chudinov 2007, 237–279), yet many around him, from the empress down, were concerned about his radicalization. It is clear from Pavel's letters that he supported the French revolution, saw Russia as a despotic country, defined his allegiance as directed to the people rather than the empress, and returned to Russia only out of filial duty, being greatly despondent about his ability to make a beneficial contribution to his country (Nicolas Mikhailovitch 1905, 1:188–195). Nevertheless, Pavel also admitted that he had no appetite for inciting revolution in Russia. More importantly, his flirtation with radical politics did not last. During the early years of Alexander I's reign, Pavel became a reform-minded but generally moderate member of his government.

Broadly speaking, the elite's exposure to the variety of political systems in existence in Europe did not by itself undermine its loyalty to the tsar and autocracy. Nevertheless, through travel, the elite became sensitized to issues of political economy and learned the language of comparative political analysis. There are signs that it developed a more nuanced and at times critical allegiance to Russia. Over time Kurakin became more militant in asserting his freedom as a courtier and was eventually banished from Catherine's court, although he continued to profess staunch loyalty to Paul I and eventually made a brilliant diplomatic career as Russian plenipotentiary. Bariatinskaia's ambivalence vis-à-vis the Russian court and polite society led to her restless peregrinations across Europe and in and out of Russia between 1790 and 1798, until she finally settled in Berlin. Upon return to St. Petersburg, Golitsyna successfully converted the cultural capital acquired by her children

into advantageous promotions and marriages for them. She hosted a successful salon, received many honors, and became a state-lady, although she also
devoted much time and attention to the improvement of the family country
estates. European journeys were not a transformative experience in the life
of the elite, but they consolidated certain identities, notably as self-confident
Russians, who gain authority and distinction from their cosmopolitan background, knowledge, and contacts and who think that they deserve morally
and intellectually to stand at some distance from the court (see Bekasova 2004
for an opposite view, emphasizing the transformative impact of study abroad).

Starting in the 1790s, sentimentalist literary discourse magnified the significance of travel, enlarging its meaning as a transformational ritual (Schönle
2000, 72–110). Karamzin conceived his journey as a way to collect memories that would then sustain life in more prosaic settings. At the end of his
Letters of a Russian Traveller, he famously waxed ecstatic at his collection
of memorabilia, the "notes, accounts, books, stones, dried plants, and twigs"
that made him richer than "all the Croesuses of the world," reminded him
of the places he visited, and would enrich the "*Chinese shadows* of his imagination" as he retired to his countryside cottage (Karamzin 2003, 456–457).
The poet Vasilii Zhukovsky thought that it was only by traveling to Europe
in the company of a friend that he would subsequently become a genuine
human being. "Traveling will be an important matter for me," he wrote,
"especially if I manage to go together with Merzliakov. Upon my return I
shall devote myself to literature. One has to become a human being, one has
to live not in vain, but with a purpose, and the best one can" (Zhukovskii
1959, 4:451–452). For Zhukovsky, traveling to Europe was an indispensable
stepping-stone to becoming an agent of his own destiny, a self-determining,
autonomous individual. Increasingly, a journey to Europe afforded the social
polish and the cultural baggage required to develop a sense of individuality
and to strengthen the habits of fashioning one's identity, sometimes in opposition to courtly norms and practices.

This sense of moral autonomy also could acquire ambiguous connotations
of cultural superiority. Andrei Turgenev, the leader of the Friendly Literary
Society, a group of young admirers of German Sturm und Drang literature to
which Zhukovsky and Merzliakov also belonged, left two diaries of his stays in
Vienna and visit to the Austrian Alps in 1802. In them he jotted down romantic descriptions of mountain landscapes, recorded his impressions from the
Viennese art gallery, the library and the philanthropic society, and conveyed

his feelings about the theater, where he attended the plays of Lessing and Iffland and responded enthusiastically to a production of Mozart's *Magic Flute* (IRLI RO, f. 309, f. 272, sh. 92–99, f. 1240). Describing the performance of the famous Viennese actor Johann Brockman as Odoardo in Lessing's *Emilia Galotti*, Turgenev proudly remarked that the Moscow actor Vasilii Pomerantsev played this role better. And yet, in order to explain Pomerantsev's advantages in his Russian-language diary, Turgenev had to resort to the German word *gedämpfter* (more reserved), as the Russian theatrical vocabulary seemed to him inadequate for such a comparison. This example illustrates in a nutshell how exposure to European cultures by and large helped Russians articulate their own superiority, while requiring the assimilation of European modes of linguistic and cultural expression.

Material Culture

Material culture was one of the main avenues of Europeanization, and journeys abroad provided an opportunity to acquire goods and artifacts that supported the adoption of a European lifestyle upon return to Russia, in particular with regard to interior decoration in urban mansions and country estates. Art, furniture, and books could be purchased more cheaply abroad than in Russia, so the elite went on shopping sprees while they traveled through European countries. The elite demonstrated their voracious appetite and encyclopedic interests in constituting sizeable libraries of foreign-language books on the most diverse topics, from belles-lettres to political, economic, geographical, religious, scientific, and practical literature. Ivan Shuvalov, Aleksandr Stroganov, Nikolai Iusupov, and others started to build famous art collections in the 1760s and 1770s. The latter's collection of books and paintings, which he began to assemble while studying in Leiden, was already drawing the attention of foreigners in St. Petersburg in 1778. He was on friendly terms with Antonio Canova and acquired a collection of paintings that featured six major works by Claude Lorrain, about ten Greuzes, several by Rubens, and one Rembrandt. The Swiss mathematician Johann III Bernoulli declared that this set of paintings exceeded other large collections in value and testified to the owner's refined taste.

Of course, the elite could continue their purchases following their return to Russia, as foreign merchants imported and sold fashionable luxury goods in the capitals, including art, furniture, fashion, and haberdashery (Berelowitch

and Medvedkova 1996, 187). The *marchandes de mode* who set up their bou-
tiques in St. Petersburg and Moscow became important purveyors of French
fashion. Information about new trends also came by way of visitors to the
capital, as well as through the circulation of foreign fashion magazines and
fashion plates. The painter Elisabeth Vigée Le Brun apprised members of
the court of the new classical style in vogue, drawing some rebuke from the
empress. The first Russian fashion magazine, lasting for three issues, was published in Moscow in 1791 under the title *Magazine of New English, French, and
German Fashion*. Its subtitle—"with the addition of descriptions of the way of
life, public entertainments, and pastimes in the most distinguished European
cities"—indicates that fashion was part and parcel of a broader attempt to
inculcate European styles of urban living.

Food and foodways also underwent transformation. By mid-century,
French and Hungarian wines became readily available, and Russian food
preparation came under the influence of German and subsequently French
cuisine, which is reflected in the import of culinary terminology from French.
The *Dictionary of Eighteenth-Century Russian Language* gives the following
dates for the first Russian occurrence of these French culinary terms: *cotelettes*
(1786), *blanc-manger* (1755), *béchamel* (1795), *caramel* (1796), and *crème*
(1765). Fresh produce was imported from Europe, along with Dutch cheeses,
Prussian butter, and bacon from Hamburg (Munro 1997, 33). This is the time
when thick sauces, sausages, and cutlets appeared on the table, introduced by
foreign chefs hired by the elite. As Catherine Wilmot commented in her recollections of her time living in Dashkova's household in the years 1803–1808,
in Moscow "everything is shocking for dinner that is not dress'd by a French
Cook" (Wilmot 1934, 216). Surprisingly, this is one area where the court
seems not to have set an example, as Catherine had little interest in fine food
and her court was reputed to have one of the worst kitchens in St. Petersburg
(Munro 1997, 33).

To help transform their everyday life in Russia, the elite hired foreign professionals—not only tutors and cooks, but also architects, gardeners, musicians, and doctors. They also imported machinery (threshing machines, distilleries, and the like), instruments, and vehicles (plows, carriages), as well as
plants, seeds, and animal species (merino sheep, for example). Keeping up
with changing fashions in carriages was a pricey means of displaying family
wealth and distinction. As he traveled to Berlin, Rostopchin was taken by surprise, and not a little disdainful, that no such fashion existed there, with the

result that old clunkers were still traveling the streets of the Prussian capital (Rostopchin 1849, 1:86).

How did this buying spree affect the mindset of the elite? Ostentatious consumption, as in other countries, was a way for the elite to differentiate itself from the lower classes, and it clearly magnified social disparities. But crucially, in this instance, it also implied participation in artistic networks and markets outside Russia, and it ensured access to the briskly developing knowledge of the world and to European ideas of beauty and propriety. Taken together, this practice of foreign purchases and imports, supported by extensive correspondence with agents, by personal contacts with well-placed individuals in various countries, and by the use of cross-border financial instruments, vastly expanded the elites' intellectual and cultural horizons. Through the transfer of various images and viewing contraptions, it created an entirely new visual culture. Suddenly, the landscapes of the Roman campagna or of the English picturesque countryside became readily accessible to the elite without even any need to travel. Catherine, who never traveled beyond the Russian empire after her arrival to Russia (except for a brief trip to Finland), "made imaginary voyages for which she required a number of albums and plates, gouaches, and drawings in the style of fanciful ruins by artists established in Italy" (Bondil 2006, 171). The landscape designer and agronomist A. T. Bolotov confessed to engaging in the following pastime on harsh winter days:

> Sometimes, following a traveler, I undertake faraway journeys in my mind, either on sea or on land, and with his help I learn many new things. With him I cross immense fields, betake myself into far corners of the world, contemplate countries, peoples, cities, and villages unknown to me. Maps and an atlas help me in this case. When I want to become more familiar with a famous city, which I had not had a chance to see in nature ... I take my perspective box, pull some drawings representing the famous streets, squares, buildings, and places of these cities, and looking at them through the lens, I move in thoughts into those places and watch them as if they were real. (Bolotov 1993, 192)

It is not simply that travel accounts and images imported from Europe fostered the practice of armchair traveling. Bolotov, here, indulges his taste for fiction, for living in imaginary worlds, which he can visualize with the help of clever optical devices. The painterly genre of the trompe l'oeil, widespread in interior decoration, similarly created spurious surroundings often modeled

after a stereotypical iconography like that of the Roman campagna. Through
its exposure to European arts and culture, the elite began to live in mental,
imaginary worlds, which compensated for the often unassuming conditions of
its actual surroundings or for the unpicturesque drabness of the Russian landscape. As we will analyze in greater detail in the chapter on the provinces, the
travel notes of I. M. Dolgorukov, who traveled through Russia and Ukraine,
show that this habit of mental vision taught the nobility to recognize a Roman
portico in the shape of a common ruin in the provincial town of Serpukhov,
or to assimilate a valley in Ukraine to the Vale of Tempe (Dolgorukov 1870, 4,
57). Catherine encoded the Enlightenment notions of transparency, visibility,
and power in her hyperbolic claim that from the Cameron gallery in Tsarskoe
Selo, she could see 100 *versts* (about 60 miles) around (Ekaterina II 1878, 540).
Vision, straddling the physical and the mental, was also a trope of power. In
this statement, Catherine actualized the notion disseminated in tragedies that
clear eyesight is the attribute of a great soul, itself the defining mark of a mag-
nanimous autocratic ruler (Levitt 2011, 98–104).

Landscape design represented an effort to bridge the gap between the mental world of a Europeanized landscape and actual physical nature. Catherine
invited the comparison between English gardens and her gardens at Tsarskoe
Selo: in the upper room of the newly reconstructed boat house, she ordered
to hang 166 painted engravings of English scenes and buildings brought
back by the brothers Neelov, as if to enable visitors to convince themselves
of Tsarskoe Selo's genuine English pedigree (Vil'chkovskii 1992, 154–155). In
keeping with picturesque aesthetics, the gaze could freely wander between the
original (the engravings, which served as models for garden designers) and
the copy (the gardens), testing their indistinguishability. In the gardens of the
elite, the allusions to foreign localities were created both by designing landscapes in recognizable styles and by the use of architecture. Petr Sheremetev's
Kuskovo near Moscow, for example, featured both a French and an English
garden, along with a Dutch and an Italian house. The Dutch house was surrounded by a Dutch garden, a canal, and some pavilions in the same style,
all of which aimed at conjuring up a sense of visiting the Low Countries. A
stroll through a garden like Kuskovo was thus tantamount to sampling various
European landscapes in one afternoon. In a poem describing the Masonic garden of Savinskoe, Dolgorukov praised its eclectic installations and inquired
"who knew how on a *desiatina* / to copy an extract of the entire universe?"
(Dolgorukov 1849, 147). Often, this bridging between mental vision and

material actuality was more a matter of denomination than physical resemblance. Calling a little hill Parnassus or Zion did little to create verisimilitude, but it helped nurture the illusion of living within global parameters. In short, the elite took to the habit of living in partly imaginary worlds, superimposing the physical settings of its daily life with mental views it procured from the art it beheld, the places it visited, and the landscapes it designed. Of course, indulging vicarious spaces in this manner also helped sustain the notion that Russia was neither divorced from nor inferior to Europe in visual amenities.

Social Practices

Among the social practices that shaped the Europeanization of the elite, theater, balls, clubs, Masonic lodges, and duels played a critical role in fostering the development of the upper nobility's corporate identity and defining its relationship to the ruler. These were all foreign imports—only theater existed before, albeit in a substantially different form. As will be discussed in the chapter on literature, French comedy theater at Catherine's court was a powerful mechanism to disseminate behavioral norms and emotional templates, all under the instigation and watchful eye of the empress in person. Through their plots, these comedies exalted exemplary demeanor and castigated moral foibles—bigotry, boastfulness, foppishness, and cowardice—while also eliciting certain patterns of response shaped by the cues given by the empress herself. Thus emerged an emotional community inflected by the behavior of the ruler. Theater became an indirect, allegorical way of managing conflicts between the elite and of censuring behavior that violated the norm. At the same time, theatricality stepped beyond the walls of the Hermitage theater. The elite brought theater to their mansions or country estates as a form of home entertainment, and they readily took on roles on this domestic stage. In a potent brew, the elite thus became at once the actors, subject matter, and public in a theatrical culture imported to a large extent from Paris but adapted to local manners. For the ruler, theater was a powerful mechanism to shape the norms of elite sociability.

Balls were introduced in Russia by Peter I as a way to foster sociability between men and women, and indeed sociability per se, as well as to emulate Western customs. Peter's so-called "assemblies"—social gatherings in private houses—were promulgated in 1718 by decree. As described in the law, they were intended both as a form of entertainment and a place to conduct affairs freely. What is more, the decree envisioned that assemblies would provide a degree of public transparency to social intercourse, serving as a place "to hear what is happening where." They instigated a form of public life, all the more so as they were open to people of various social standing, including non-nobles (PSZ 1830, vol. 5, no. 3246, p. 597–598). Although quasi-compulsory for the St. Petersburg nobility, the assemblies were described as informal and included a variety of entertainments from dancing to smoking to checkers (although no card playing). Yet the first memoir recollections of balls indicate that aside from dancing, men and women did not interact much with one another, as during intervals they congregated in two opposite groups and women sat "speechless" (Berkhgol'ts 1857–1860, 2:102). During the reign of Elizabeth, balls took on a more brilliant aspect as a form of court ritual unfolding according to an established protocol. By then the nobility had assimilated the skills needed for various dance figures and the strict etiquette associated with them. The sequence of dances was modeled after European practice and included the ecossaise, menuet, anglaise, allemande, and contredance, yet for good form, Elizabeth also introduced a Russian folk dance.

Balls were a ceremony of state, often given in honor of a dignitary, which the upper nobility of St. Petersburg was obligated to attend. Catherine continued the same practice, upping the ante in matters of opulence and brilliance, and showing a predilection for masquerades, which remained compulsory for the upper ranks. In parallel, balls moved into the mansions of the nobility, where they became a form of regular private entertainment, often involving lavish expenses. In Moscow, the Assembly of the Nobility (*Dvorianskoe sobranie*), founded in 1782, started to host weekly balls, strictly limited to nobles. From a state choreography, balls became a corporate institution of the nobility, which fostered the coalescence of a group identity, particularly in Moscow. Balls became one of the few permissible forms of collective existence (Lotman 1994, 91). The controversial introduction of the waltz in the 1790s—a dance that required prolonged physical contact between the dancers—reduced the sway of formal etiquette, allowing more freedom in movements as well as the discrete exchange of private communications between dance partners.

The new corporate sociability extended beyond balls and progressively emancipated itself from the court. Imperial gardens became places of entertainment as access to them was progressively relaxed, in particular when the monarch was not in residence. Wealthy aristocrats began to hold festivities in their gardens, open to a broad section of the "well-dressed" public. British residents in St. Petersburg founded the English club in 1770, followed by the Moscow English club twelve years later. Although initially patronized by foreigners, in time both clubs became regular sites of sociability for the nobility (Smith 1999, 78–85). Far from the court and inhabited by many retired or non-serving nobles, Moscow successfully invented forms and places of sociability distinct from court culture. Freemasons were especially active in importing civic institutions, particularly in Moscow, where they temporarily possessed a printing press, magazines, a philanthropic organization, and direct access to the university. This network was destroyed when Catherine grew suspicious of the activities of Rosicrucians in the early 1790s (Zorin 2016b), but noble sociability reinvented itself in the form of salons and literary societies at the beginning of the nineteenth century. After 1812, the Moscow English Club became a site of predilection for the nobility, a place where it could play cards, exchange opinions, and read the foreign press in a safe and exclusive atmosphere (Velizhev 2016a). The almost complete absence of public coffeehouses in St. Petersburg and Moscow points to the fact that sociability remained socially stratified and served more to consolidate corporate social identities than to facilitate urban integration.

The development of these forms of sociability also affected the intimate life of the elite. Already in Elizabethan time St. Petersburg society was shattered by a major scandal when an underground bordello was discovered, where young women mostly brought from Germany and the Baltic provinces provided high-ranking Russian nobles with sexual services and some form of pleasant and civilized leisure, very much in the spirit of French libertinage (Fedyukin 2017b; Roldugina 2016). In this instance, the assemblies instituted by Peter had turned into parties that hinged on cross-dressing and the transgression of social boundaries and sexual conventions (Roldugina 2016). During the reign of Catherine the Great, the court, at least in its upper reaches, began to flaunt its lax sexual morality more openly, setting an example that some noblemen were all too eager to follow. Accounts of men cavorting with serf girls or keeping a harem are numerous (Roosevelt 1995, 183–191). In 1799 Andrei Turgenev was deeply impressed by his conversation with young Count Sergei Vasilievich Saltykov, who told him that from the age of fourteen he kept "a *Mädchen.*" Following this revelation, Saltykov demonstrated to Turgenev his small select library, in which pornographic works such as *La foutromanie* by Gabriel Sénac de Meilhan were kept together with the works of Montesquieu and Boileau. Saltykov became later known in St. Petersburg for his sybaritic lifestyle and unique collection of snuffboxes and rare books (Zorin 2016c, 228). Notions of libertinism began to shape the behavior of certain nobles, and some interpreted Enlightenment rationality and naturalism as a license to adultery and child molestation (Marker 2000).

At the same time, noblewomen remained subject to the requirement to protect their innocence prior to marriage. Count de Brühl and the chevalier de Corberon, two foreigners living at the court of St. Petersburg in the late 1770s, commiserated about "the difficulty to form pleasant affairs. Young ladies speak promptly of marriage ... and always think that one wants to marry them as soon as one tells them an honest word" (Corberon 1901, 1:116). As a foreigner and a highly desirable fiancé, Corberon was, of course, not fully aware of all the intimate secrets of Russian families. For example, Russian literary history had for a long time cherished the romantic story of the marriage between the poet and architect Nikolai L'vov and Mariia D'iakova, which, according to legend, had been left unannounced for three years, because the parents of the bride would not agree to it, given L'vov's straitened financial circumstances. However, a recently published letter by L'vov to D'iakova shows that more than a year prior to her wedding, she had had a miscarriage; moreover, L'vov's friends and D'iakova's mother were aware of it. This discovery allows us to see this well-known romance in a very different perspective. One can hardly suppose that this story was absolutely unique; still, everyone concerned most evidently tried to keep it secret. The letter itself was preserved in spite of a clear instruction given by the author: "Brulés [sic] d'abord la lettre après l'avoire [sic] lue" (Burn first the letter after reading it; Lappo-Danilevskii 1997, 139). This example illustrates both the strength of the sexual morality to which noblewomen were subject and its violation in actual life.

When the new domesticity spreading in Europe reached Russia, it is again at the highest level that the sentimental notion of the family was put into practice and proffered as a model for emulation, notably through the careful self-presentation of Maria Fedorovna, the wife of Paul I. Maria Fedorovna displayed her commitment to the family in many ways, erecting monuments to her parents, husband, and children in the gardens at Pavlovsk, taking an active role in the education of her youngest son, and allowing visitors access to the family "home," thus developing an outright "scenario" of domesticity (Wortman 1995, 250–251).

Before the eighteenth century, dueling was a custom entirely alien to Russia. In the absence of a chivalric history, the first duels in Russia were performed by foreigners, to the dismay of local observers. Even the very notion of honor was a foreign import, which took a long time to set roots in Russia, despite being implied in some of Peter I's legislation. The social stratification of the nobility enshrined in the Table of Ranks and the rivalry between two concepts of nobility, by heredity or service, contradicted the main premise of the *point d'honneur*, namely the equality of all nobles in matters of honor. Social disparities among the nobility were such that, to many members of the estate, it seemed more important to defend their relative position in the hierarchy than the autonomy of the nobility as a self-regulating corporation. As a result, even in the second half of the eighteenth century, nobles tended to fight duels only with foes of equal or similar rank. Furthermore, the foreign origins of dueling also made it suspicious in some quarters. Peter III's interest in dueling, for example, was often portrayed as a consequence of his Prussian leanings. Nevertheless, the practice of dueling slowly penetrated the mores of the nobility and a few notorious cases occurred during the reign of Catherine the Great, which prompted her to reaffirm in a Manifesto on Duels (1787) the official prohibition already decreed by Peter I. In its extensive preamble, the manifesto made much of the fact that dueling was a foreign practice inimical to Russian ways. Dueling reached its apex during the reign of Alexander I, when it became a way for the nobility to adjudicate its internal conflicts, in particular to fight against upstarts close to the monarch, and thus also to affirm its moral independence from the court and the government (Reyfman 1999, 45–96).

Most of these social practices also represented opportunities to interact with foreigners. Foreign visitors to the Russian court were, of course, granted high-level access to balls, masquerades, and other ceremonies. Indeed, foreigners were one of the crucial audiences of court ceremonies. With the exception of the actual church service, over the course of the century official rituals such as the coronation increasingly adopted forms inspired by European models (Ageeva 2006, 170; Wortman 1995, 69–75). On the occasion of the birth of the future Paul I in 1754, the ceremony of congratulation of the mother in the official bedchamber was developed by the College of Foreign Affairs, revealing the international resonance expected from such rituals (Ageeva 2006, 185). Foreigners were of course also invited to the private homes of grandees. Count de Ségur noted the great hospitality given to him by the "brilliant societies" of St. Petersburg and in particular society's positive inclination toward the French (Ségur 1859, 1:345, 347). Prince Adam Czartoryski, who arrived in

St. Petersburg in 1795, wrote, "The society of St. Petersburg, in general, was brilliant, lively, and full of nuances. Many houses of various genres were open; everywhere one would fight for foreigners; the diplomatic corps and French emigration were setting the tone" (Czartoryski 1887, 44). Thus the social practices introduced by the tsars in the first half of the eighteenth century turned into fora in which Russian polite society mingled with foreigners, learning by way of social interaction about the latest fashions in vogue in Paris.

For Catherine the general reverence in which foreigners, in particular the French, were held in society went too far. In various ways she sought to resist the penetration of French fads and fashions. For example, she took an active dislike of princess Ekaterina Bariatinskaia after the latter returned from Paris to St. Petersburg, bringing with her all the polite graces she had acquired in the French capital (Corberon 1901, 2:51). However, when French aristocrats on the run from the revolution sought refuge in St. Petersburg, Catherine was keen to welcome them, as a demonstration of Russia's preeminence in European affairs. She offered these émigrés high positions at court, unwittingly setting off a kind of competition with the vernacular elite for favors. Emerging conflicts between Russian and French aristocrats, notably a high-profile duel, had the effect of consolidating the Russian elite's corporate and patriotic identity, yet again demonstrating how Europeanization ended up solidifying the elite's sense of its distinctiveness and autonomy (Evstratov 2016b). Thus the import of fashion and the general emulation of French manners turned into a tug-of-war between the court and noble society, the latter increasingly seeking to affirm its own values independently of court models, and in particular taking Europeanization into directions the court could no longer condone.

Reading

For the elite, one of the most powerful and least cumbersome ways to assimilate a European habitus was to join the republic of letters through reading, especially as reading habits and the settings of literature consumption began to change. The reading public for secular literature was narrow. Based on a study of subscriptions, A. Iu. Samarin established that the "active" reading public of secular literature in the years 1762–1800 consisted of 8,500 readers, mostly from the upper ranks of the nobility (Samarin 2000, 135–137). Calendars and almanacs, which had a broader appeal, had the largest print run, about 30,000 per year in the 1790s, but they contained mostly religious instruction and practical advice (Marker 1985, 191). On the basis of print runs and available sales figures, Gary Marker concluded that the reading public favored entertaining tales and instrumental literature such as edifying fables or practical guides to everyday life, rather than abstract, philosophical works. With the exception of *Candide* and *La Nouvelle Héloïse*, the major works of European Enlightenment in translation were a commercial flop (201–211).

It would be important, for our purposes, to distinguish between various interpretive communities subsumed in the figures Marker used, but limited evidence makes this impossible. The elite, of course, also collected and read books in their original languages, which is not captured in the figures cited by Marker and Samarin. The low demand for Enlightenment philosophy in Russian translation may be attributable to the fact that interested readers read these works in the original. In his brief confession, Fonvizin noted that his father "had not had the opportunity to enlighten himself with study ... at least he read only Russian books," the implication being that a well-educated person read works in the original language (Fonvizin 1983, 246).

As will be discussed in the chapter on literature, belles-lettres in Russia were initially introduced by the state as a top-down technique to fashion the attitudes and views of its elite servants. In the initial stages, literature was received in a collective manner. Odes to the ruler were recited in public, for example during assemblies at the Academy of Sciences, although they were also printed and disseminated to the audience to facilitate understanding. Theater was of course performed, rather than published, at least initially, and the collective response to the staging was critical to its impact. In a first attempt at dissemination, Russian playwrights—notably Denis Fonvizin, who was known as an excellent reader—recited their plays aloud before gatherings of nobles. After a successful reading to the empress of his first satirical play, *The Brigadier*, Fonvizin was invited to make the round of aristocratic houses to entertain the society in attendance with his comedy. His public success, of course, was predicated on initial approval from the empress.

Modifications in European reading practices are difficult to trace. The German scholar of print culture Rolf Engelsing advanced the notion of a "reading revolution" taking place around the 1750s, when readers switched from "intensive" to "extensive" reading. "Intensive" readers, for Engelsing, were those who read the same few books they owned over and over again, in order to seek reassurance and confirmation of what they already knew, and thus to consolidate their identity, while "extensive" readers went out into the

world in a ravenous way to read everything they came across, in the hope of
finding ways to enhance their lives, to acquire new knowledge, to experience
new emotions—in short, to invent new identities (Engelsing 1974). The evidence to support this typology is limited at best, although David Hall found
evidence of a similar "revolution" taking place in New England (see Darnton
1990, 165). Robert Darnton rejected this typology, believing that the huge
popularity of Rousseau in the eighteenth century can serve as an example of
the continuation and even reinforcement of the practice of intensive reading,
albeit with a different object. Darnton emphasized the rise of a specific culture
of reading created by Rousseau, which consisted of personal identification
with the protagonists and the author to the point of "throwing oneself'" into
the text with complete abandon, aiming to fashion one's life as if it belonged to
this fictional world of rarefied emotions (Darnton 1985, 250–251). This mode
of reading required an intimate contact with the book and called for reading
in specific settings outside the confines of polite sociability, notably in nature
or in the privacy of the home, as a way to "ingest" the book more intensively.

Whether the same developments obtained in Russia, or, more importantly,
how broadly they affected reading practices there, is difficult to ascertain.
Certainly the large and eclectic collections put together by the elite in the
second half of the eighteenth century indicate voracious and versatile interest, compatible with Engelsing's "extensive" mode of reading, but much more
research is required to ascertain how many of these books were actually read.
We can gather some clues about reading practices from depictions of reading
in literature and from treatises on reading. In a passage of his brief confession, referring to the 1750s, Fonvizin described scenes of reading aloud in
his family, during which both father and children would take turns reading
(Fonvizin 1983, 250). In his comedy *The Minor*, the virtuous character Sofiia
is depicted reading Fénelon's treatise "On the Education of Girls" (1687;
Fonvizin 1983, 115). Significantly, she is reading on her own initiative and by
herself. Furthermore she reads, in a self-reflective manner, an abstract treatise on the education of girls like herself. Of course, we may not simply infer
that this scene represents actual reading practice of the time. What we can
say, however, is that Fonvizin encoded and promoted the idea that reading is
an activity conducive to the creation of the interior, reflective self and to the
cultivation of virtue.

In his short essay "On the Benefit of Reading Books" (1767), A. T. Bolotov
delineated the semiautobiographical story of a nobleman whose interest in

books was sparked by listening to tales. He learned literacy by copying books, then read Fénelon's *Télémaque* over and over again, which eventually stimulated his curiosity about the world. To feed his thirst for discovery, he moved on to all sorts of books, including vast numbers of German adventure novels, through which he acquired substantial knowledge in history, geography, and national customs. It is, however, when he discovered a Russian translation of Johann Adolf Hoffman's *Zwei Bücher zu der Zufriedenheit* that reading turned into a life-changing experience for him. This book, as he put it, "brought him out of his sleep and opened his eyes to the world," inculcating in him a passion for didactic literature that "taught him to know himself, to discover his vocation, and to secure his well-being" (Veselova 1999, 362). He then abandoned novels and took up philosophical books, which he read "not like others read, but with attention and deliberation, and by comparing various situations to himself, detecting his own flaws, and beginning to reform himself, so that a year later he was hardly recognizable. He had, so to speak, changed completely." This transformational experience, which taught him the means to lead a virtuous life, compelled him to retire from the army to his village and to seek ways to make himself useful to the state there.

Bolotov's little essay nicely encapsulates various modes of reading described in scholarly literature, from intensive to extensive reading, and from light-hearted entertainment to reading as moral introspection. However, the conversion experience Bolotov describes takes place independently of Rousseau and in the context of exposure to didactic literature variously inflected by Christian and Masonic ideas (see our chapter on religion for more examples of religious conversions prompted by the reading of foreign books). The practice of strengthening moral conversion and edification through the recurrent reading of instructional and spiritual literature was widespread in Masonic circles, especially among the Moscow Rosicrucians (Zorin 2016b). We can hazard the conclusion that in Russia, the mode of transformational reading for self-knowledge and moral guidance, which Darnton described on the basis of an avid reader of Rousseau, drew on a much broader array of spiritual literature, from Fénelon to German pietistic instruction to Masonic treatises. The reception of Rousseau and the modes of reading he rhetorically pressed upon his readers were thus refracted through this larger body of instructional literature of various religious types, which colored the perceived meaning of his works.

Rousseau's impact was, of course, profound. His *Rêveries d'un promeneur solitaire*, for example, were responsible for a new genre emerging in the 1780s, the "Promenade," which celebrated the act of reading in the bosom of nature, a setting perceived to be more conducive to interiorization than reading in public. The young Ivan Bariatinsky displayed typical identification with the author of the *Reveries*, very much in the reception mode described by Darnton. Writing to an acquaintance who had lent him this book, he confessed, "I don't know of a reading which better suits my character, which touches and stirs my soul more, and which makes me better enter into the sad and difficult situation of the author.... He pulls tears out of me and I succumb to the illusion that my crying alleviates at least half of his misery, forgetting that death has stopped them all" (RGB OR, f. 19, op. 5, d. 117, l. 2ob). The notion that the aim of reading is to enter into emotional, sympathetic communion with the author is characteristic of the literary paradigm promoted by Rousseau. More broadly, the relationship between fiction and reality, which Rousseau had so skillfully blurred in his *La Nouvelle Héloïse* as a way to enhance everyday life emotionally, became the object of anguished concern, with writers and readers obsessively ascertaining their indistinguishability. In Karamzin's *Letters of a Russian Traveller*, the traveler repeatedly compares sites of sublime nature with literary descriptions thereof, as if to verify, if not enhance, his emotions through simultaneous reading and gazing, as well as providing his readers with a primer on appropriate and fashionable emotional templates.

This type of reading was by no means confined to Russia, indeed it was typical for the European public at the time of the emerging cult of sensibility. By the end of the eighteenth century, each culturally significant part of everyday life had its own European classic, which set an appropriate mode of emotional response and thereby inflected behavior. The European public learned how to fall in love while reading *La Nouvelle Héloïse* and *The Sorrows of Young Werther*, how to go to the countryside with James Thomson and Rousseau, how to visit cemeteries with Edward Young and Thomas Gray, and how to escape from the world with Johann Georg Zimmerman.

In Russia, this type of relationship between literature and its audience was even more pronounced, as the role of literature as a manual to stimulate correct feelings was greatly strengthened by the efforts to assimilate the new Western culture. Russian authors did not try to disguise their imitative strategies. On the contrary, they made all their borrowings explicit and declarative. The authority of famous foreign writers buttressed their own legitimacy as instructors of sensibility. Translating indispensable books was not enough, especially as a significant part of the Russian readership was francophone anyway. It was no less important to give appropriate and adaptable examples for following the models set out in those texts, as if to give keys to them. Karamzin's *Letters of a Russian Traveller*, which he started to publish in 1791 in his journal *The Moscow Review*, demonstrated a panoply of emotional and behavioral patterns. The nearly universal success and long-lasting influence of Karamzin's travelogue was caused not so much by its encyclopedic breadth, as by the feeling of intimacy he established between European cultural treasures and the Russian reader. The traveler recorded his conversations with Kant, Wieland, Herder, and Lavater; recounted his visits to the main European memorial sites such as Rousseau's grave in Ermenonville or Westminster Abbey; conveyed his impressions from German and Parisian theaters; described iconic natural scenery like the Rhein waterfall or the Swiss Alps; and most importantly, demonstrated how to react to all these sites, texts, people, and events.

In the courtyard of the hotel of M. Dessin in Calais, where thirty years earlier Sterne had started his journey to France, the Russian traveler exchanged memorable quotations from Sterne's *Sentimental Journey* with a French officer and witnessed an Englishwoman reading the very same book, the Irish novelist's chef d'oeuvre (Karamzin 2003, 375). The Russian traveler, French officer, and ravishing English lady constituted a cosmopolitan emotional community centered around one particular text. Even more daringly, in a lodge at the Parisian Opera, Karamzin, to judge from his account, taught the arrogant French the most sensible and fashionable way to listen to music, namely to absorb oneself in the performance without interrupting it with applause. This new pattern of listening had just been introduced by Glück, and the young Russian made a point of demonstrating to backward Parisians the appropriate way to enjoy *Orfeo and Euridice* (Johnson 1995, 53).

On his return home, Karamzin created a stir and a name for himself by publishing in *The Moscow Review* his story "Poor Liza," the tale of a poor peasant girl seduced by a nobleman and committing suicide after he abandoned her. The story itself was a variation on motifs borrowed from Samuel Richardson, Rousseau, and Sterne, but the author, in his usual manner, introduced it as a personal recollection, presented through a double narrative perspective: the repentant seducer tells his story to the narrator, who himself conveys it to the readers, showing them the right way to empathize. Poor Liza's imaginary grave near Simonov monastery in the vicinity of Moscow became a place for sentimental pilgrimages. In 1796, a separate edition of the story appeared with an engraved frontispiece depicting the monastery and the pond where Liza perished fictionally, surrounded by birches where the elegant public etched inscriptions on the bark of the trees. The engraving was accompanied by the following explanation:

> Not far from the walls of the Simonov monastery on the Kozhukhov road there is an ancient pond surrounded by trees. In their fervent imagination readers see poor Liza drowning in it, and on almost all of these trees inquisitive visitors have expressed in various languages their feelings of compassion toward the unfortunate beautiful girl and of respect for the writer of her story. (Karamzin 1796)

The editor specifically mentions the multilingual character of the inscriptions on the birches. One of them, written in Italian—"Non la connobe il mondo mentre l'ebbe" (The world did not know her when she was in it)—serves as an epigraph for the story. Italian was not one of the languages Russian nobles were supposed to know, but this line from Petrarch was immediately recognizable to an educated Russian reader because it had already served as an epigraph for *La Nouvelle Héloïse*. Rousseau's novel and Karamzin's story were thus united under the same emotional pattern of nostalgic sigh over an unknown beauty who had left this world. What allowed poor Liza to be perceived by Russian readers as a real peasant from a village outside Moscow was precisely that she merged with the characters of European sentimentalist novels. The emotional grammar of contemporary European literature allowed Russian nobles to understand themselves and shape their identities; more than that, thanks to its dissemination—the story was republished seven times in the first ten years and was also shared in handwritten copies (Zorin 2016c)—the story also helped to bridge the gap between the fully Europeanized elite and the broader layers of provincial nobility.

As a result of the spread of such forms of interiorization, the elite literary field began to show cracks. The theatrical culture promoted by the court continued to play a large role in the lives of the elite, both in the capitals and on their country estates. Aleksandr Kurakin built a special pavilion in his garden, the so-called Receptacle of Eternal Feelings, which housed his archive and to which he retired for reading, but he used the same building to host theatrical shows he put on for his visitors (Dolgorukov 2004–2005, 1:397). But in Rosicrucian quarters, a debate arose on the psychological and moral harmfulness of acting: the question was whether performing in plays was appropriate for young society women, given that it taught to feign emotions (Zorin 2016b, 209). A contradiction was beginning to emerge, if only tentatively, between the culture of interiority, fostered by didactic and introspective reading, and the theatrical culture that had pervaded the life of the elite in Russia and allowed the collective forging of emotional patterns under the instigation and watchful eye of the empress. Sentimentalist literature explored in different ways the interactions between individual subjects, noble society, and the ruler, fostering a degree of critical self-consciousness, while also providing a distinctive idiom that solidified the elite's corporate identity, encouraged its autonomy from the court, and conferred a veneer of European respectability.

By and large, in Russia, the import of sentimentalist literature fostered social stratification. The French, German, and English writers who provided this set of emotional templates for the Russian noble elite were dealing with the task of creating new national literatures that could be read and emulated across social boundaries. In Britain, Karamzin noticed that English servants were reading Richardson's novel *Clarissa*. In Russia, the impact of European literature was more exclusive—it provided a unified (and unifying) cultural paradigm for the educated public and at the same time reinforced cultural and consequently social boundaries between this public and the rest of the population. The sentimentalist culture that in Western Europe was successfully challenging the cultural domination of the ancien régime and assisted in the social integration of national culture (Denby 1994, Maza 1997) became in Russia one of the defining components of the noble elite's identity.

This brief survey of some of the major ways in which the elite came into direct contact with Europe indicates that Europeanization produced complex effects. It paradoxically strengthened the elite's pride in its Russianness, yet without erecting a dichotomy between Russia and the West. Members of the elite drew patriotic pride from their country precisely because they participated in networks of interaction and exchange with European elites and shared in the linguistic and cultural capital of their European counterparts. It is only as Europeans that they felt Russian, which explains why until Napoleon's invasion of Russia they had few scruples to express their patriotic identity in a non-Russian language. Contact with Europe inspired energetic efforts to reshape or enhance material culture with the import of goods and artifacts from Europe, but it also fostered a propensity to indulge in fictions or to satisfy oneself with token marks of Europeanization, thus sustaining life in a kind of alternative reality at once domestic and European.

Even though Europeanization was initiated by the court and expressed in the form of new social practices mandated from above, it generated forms of social intercourse that helped the elite consolidate its corporate identity as distinct from court society. The upper nobility embraced the opportunity to socialize with European visitors to Russia and emulated their manners, but it also resented having to compete with them for favors dispensed at court. Thus, in the end, European forms of sociability gave rise to ambivalent feelings of cosmopolitan interconnectedness and corporatist retrenchment. Reading habits produced even more differentiated relations between the elite and the court. While theater had been a major technique of social engineering deployed by the ruler, which allowed the shaping of behavior and emotion from above, the emerging practice of individual silent reading afforded the elite access to European literature and fostered the internalization of a whole gamut of emotions. Literature became a primer in sensibility restricted to the educated reading public, thus opening a deep gulf between the elite and the people, while allowing members of the elite to explore subject positions that buttressed their sense of uniqueness and individuality. Bolotov's decision to retire from military service as a result of his moral conversion induced by reading Western didactic literature exemplifies the ways in which the consumption of European literature complicated the elite's relations to the court and the bureaucracy. To analyze in greater detail the fluid interrelations between the court and elite society, the next chapter will describe the elite's position in court society, the sway of conventions, and the emotions the elite experienced as it fought to protect its position in the court of public opinion.

3

. . . .

COMMERCE WITH POWER

The Elite at Court

What Is a Court?

How do we define a princely court? This, in itself, is a controversial question, as in their relations with society, courts often cultivated a studious and politically expedient ambivalence and porousness. A court is defined in the first instance as the residence of the king, queen, prince, or princess. This residence, usually a palace or castle, hosts a community of people of various ranks and titles, who are either employed in service to the ruler or visit to express their respect, attend courtly entertainment, or discharge some business. The people admitted to court mingle also among themselves, forming a complex, variously structured network of social relations gravitating around the ruler and subject to the ruler's interventions (Adamson 1999, 7). Courtiers, when they are in the semipublic realm of the court, generally adopt a heightened degree of conventionality in their behavior and attire, in keeping with the etiquette required at court. Body language, dress, and speech are often meticulously calibrated to conform to the prevailing norms of the court and to convey both distinction and deference (Duindam 2003, 161–163). This formality, which reaches its apex in such rituals as the *sortie* of the ruler—the procession when the monarch comes out of the chambers to attend church, for example—may produce the impression that court life is a tightly choreographed spectacle in which courtiers enact various more or less prominent roles, depending on their ranks and titles.

The overall function of this solemn pageant, enhanced by a display of opulence, has traditionally been construed as a manifestation of the prestige and power of the ruler or ruling dynasty, aimed at public opinion domestically, but also internationally, to impress the rulers of rival kingdoms and empires. However, princely courts may assume many additional roles. They are a way for monarchs to shape their relations with the serving nobility, upon which they depend to administer the realm and which they seek to control. They are an arena for the inculcation of social norms, as well as moral values. They are often the place where policy decisions are formulated or political decisions made, in a semi-informal relationship with grandees who come to audiences to weigh in upon issues or to plead their case. And, beyond such pragmatic considerations, they are also a place where the authority of the ruler is not only reaffirmed but also endowed with a sacred aura, variously "borrowed" from religion, which may become an end in itself (Adamson 1999, 27–32; Duindam 2003, 318–320; Geertz 1980).

Scholarship on European princely courts has undergone a revisionist revival in the last twenty years. While under the influence of Marxist historiography the study of princely courts had been marginalized as a pastime for nostalgic monarchists, Norbert Elias's *The Court Society*, written in the early 1930s but not published until 1969, demonstrated the centrality of princely courts in shaping society in the early modern period. In recent decades, many of Elias's conclusions have been significantly revised. Although his analysis comprises many astute descriptions of the conventions of court society, his main premises can no longer be upheld. Elias conceived of the princely courts as a transitional social formation pointing toward the development of the modern state in that it subjected human behavior to a rigorous "civilizing process," which led to the interiorization of certain rational behavior patterns. According to him, the court is the place where, by way of the prevailing etiquette, external compulsion (*Fremdzwang*) was transformed into internal self-discipline (*Selbstzwang*; Elias 1983, 92). In political terms, this meant that absolutist rulers used the rising importance of the court to subjugate the nobility, strip it of its power base in the country, restrict its political autonomy and economic self-reliance, and make it fundamentally depend on the ruler for its subsistence. Thus, in keeping with the premise of absolutism, princely courts fostered a process of centralization that eventually underpinned the rise of the modern state.

It is now recognized that the relationship between the monarch and the nobility was often more mutual than antagonistic and that monarchs depended on the nobility as much as, if not more than, the nobility depended upon them (Adamson 1999, 15). Furthermore, the direct line of evolution between feudalism, court society, and the modern state has become much more complex and messy than Elias envisioned. Clearly it will no longer do to conceive of court society simply as a precursor to the nation state. The premise that court ceremony is no more than a form of "propaganda" (or "rhetoric" in a milder version of the same argument) to indoctrinate the nobility has yielded to a much greater sense of the multiple functions of rituals, including as a liturgy that finds an end in itself. Finally, as they dismissed the centrality to Elias's account of Versailles during the reign of Louis XIV, scholars have revealed the wide diversity of practices across European courts, and even the multiplicity of courts within one realm, as members of the ruling house, members of junior blood lines, or even grandees hold their own courts and develop their own following through the dispensation of patronage. All of this undermines the very foundation of absolute power. The effort to exhume concrete historical data about the size, practices, customs, finances, and power of various European courts is far from complete, but already we have gained a much more sophisticated idea of issues as critical as the relations between princely courts and organs of government in various realms (Duindam 2003, 6–12; Adamson 1999, 16–17).

The scholarly study of the Russian court in the eighteenth and nineteenth centuries has made much headway. Ol'ga Ageeva studied the court as an institution, focusing on the complex implementation of court ranks, court offices, and rituals. Paul Keenan examined the impact of the court on sociability in St. Petersburg in the first half of the eighteenth century (Keenan 2013). Richard Wortman did pioneering work in analyzing the representational strategies of the court, in particular the ways it shaped the image of the ruler and fashioned "scenarios of power." The Petrine court has drawn particular attention (Zitser 2005), but we also have well-informed studies of the nobility that pertain to its role at court in Catherine's age (de Madariaga 1994). Much more work needs to be undertaken if one wishes properly to assess the relations between the court and the nobility, the court and government structures, and even things as basic as the determining role of such social conventions as the order of precedence, the behavioral etiquette, and the honor code. And in order to evaluate the distinctive nature of the court of the Russian tsars, it will also be necessary to frame this discussion within a broad European context.

We cannot presume to address all of these aspects in this chapter, but in keeping with our emphasis on the processes of Europeanization of the elite, we will try, after a basic description of the Russian court during the reign of Catherine the Great and of its specifics on the background of European courts, to reconstruct how it felt for a member of the elite to attend court in light of its conventions, as well as how foreigners perceived the goings-on at court. The Russian court will emerge as an arena for the expression of raw emotions, to an extent often surprising to foreigners. Emotionality does not necessarily mean uncontrolled spontaneity, however. The court of St. Petersburg also required a knack for fine calibration of behavior and presupposed, for success, that one deploy a complex repertoire of emotional and behavioral practices, again to the great astonishment of visitors. The court was also an arena in which the elite had to compete with the presence of foreigners, who often commanded high prestige. These impositions created some resentment among the elite, which encouraged attempts to seek alternative sources of identity and forms of sociability outside the court hierarchy.

The Court of the Russian Tsars

Peter the Great initiated the process of creating an imperial court that resembled the major European courts and could compete with them. The Table of Ranks, implemented in 1722, established a unique system of precedence valid across Russian society, which conferred advancement solely on the basis of service and aimed to supersede other hierarchies, including those based on family lineage (de Madariaga 1994, 339). This table contained three separate, although interrelated, hierarchies of military, civil, and courtly ranks. Courtly ranks were listed last, suggesting perhaps that Peter saw them as least important and prestigious. In preparation for publishing the Table of Ranks, models of estate offices and of the nomenclature of ranks were consulted from various European princely courts (Ageeva 2006, 69–71). For higher ranks, it was the Prussian terminology that was adopted. The use of foreign terms probably aimed to endow the office holders with status comparable to Western elites and comprehensible to them. And even though the structure of ranks could be mapped over offices that existed in Muscovite Russia, the new terminology served to break with received custom and thus deflate any claims of entitlement by elite families based on their prior status (72–77). Over the course of the century, the courtly ranks in the Table sustained several modifications, as rulers were not fully satisfied with a system that had perhaps been adopted hastily. In general, the tendency was to confer a higher rank to court offices than before (relative to military and state ranks) and to create more court ranks, thus boosting both the prestige of court service and the number of office holders (81–123).

In addition to the Table of Ranks, Peter also introduced hereditary titles borrowed from Europe—counts, barons—which, however, had no incidence on the order of precedence. Prior to Peter, only the title of prince had been in existence in Russia as hereditary title, and, as it referred purely to lineage, it was not a title that could be awarded. The existence of these new titles, albeit lower in prestige than high rank or ancient princely title, conferred to the court a veneer of European comparability (de Madariaga 1994, 339). For example both Peter and Catherine II used the title Prince of the Holy Roman Empire to reward favorites (Peter put forward Aleksandr Menshikov and Dmitrii Kantemir, while Catherine nominated Grigorii Orlov, Grigorii Potemkin, and Platon Zubov). These nominations, which had to be approved by the emperor of the Holy Roman Empire, served, as it were, to "plug" the Russian elite into the system of European titles.

In keeping with the revival of knighthood orders in Europe, Peter also introduced chivalric orders to Russia, the first of which, the order of St. Andrew the Apostle, was created in 1698. While it was conferred "to some in recognition of their fidelity, bravery, and various services rendered to us and the fatherland, and to others to encourage all manners of noble and heroic virtues," it also had a patriotic religious dimension, expressed in its motto "To faith and fidelity" and in the fact that St. Andrew was the patron saint of Russia (Shepelev 2004, 352). Several more orders named after saints in the Orthodox calendar were established over the course of the century. If initially the order of St. Andrew was restricted to candidates already belonging to the highest ranks, when its statute was finally adopted during Paul I's coronation in April 1797, it automatically conferred the third rank to its holders.

Taken together, the newly instituted ranks, titles, and orders introduced over the course of the century created a system superficially similar to hierarchies of lineage, distinction, and merit in Europe. This system empowered rulers with a complex and differentiated set of awards that could be used to foster patronage relations and would command prestige abroad. Yet the defining role of the Table of Ranks, in its linkage to service rather than lineage, together with the Orthodox veneer of chivalric orders, also ensured that there was enough distinctiveness, both in structure and symbols, to tie the elite to the will of the ruling tsar and underpin a sense of patriotic pride, if not national identity.

The size of the Russian court is a matter of definition and contention. The court can be defined narrowly as consisting of the ruling family and the people who hold courtly offices, including those serving in the lower ranks, to the exclusion of the numerous servants. Over the course of her reign, Catherine appointed 103 chamberlains and 123 chamber junkers. In 1775 she published an edict according to which only 12 men in each of these two court ranks would receive a salary, as only they were expected to be continuously present and discharge their service responsibilities. In a staff roster of 1796, there were 26 chamberlains and 27 chamber junkers listed (Volkov 2013, 26–27). And although these numbers rose steadily over the course of the century, they remained small. In 1768, the ranked staff, men and women, comprised 104 persons, with an additional 1,165 servants (Ageeva 2008, 202). However, this risks mischaracterizing the nature of the court, as during Catherine's time the first four ranks of the military and civil hierarchies enjoyed direct access to the empress and took an active part in court affairs and rituals (de Madariaga 1994, 350). Nor are foreign diplomats and other fashionable foreigners included, despite being among the key participants and witnesses of court proceedings. And the issue is further complicated by the fact that the distinction between genuine office and honorary rank was not always very clear. Chamber junkers, for example, often continued to serve in the guard regiments. Courtly ranks could serve as honorific offices that allowed a quick rise in the ranks without requiring actual service at court.

A broader calculation of the size of the court would encompass all those who were expected to attend court during its ceremonies, but this group varied greatly, as the inclusiveness of court events ranged from the select few invited to Catherine's Hermitage theater to all nobles belonging to the eight highest rungs of the Table of Ranks on dynastic festivities (coronation days, name days, etc.). For court days, balls, and masquerades, it was more typical to invite nobles from the four or five highest ranks, which in Catherine's times would amount to 300–400 persons, still a far cry from the 2,120 *officiers* of the inner *maison* estimated at the court of Louis XIV in 1699 (Duindam 2003, 302), while on regular days, dinners would host no more than 10–25 people (Ageeva 2008, 206).

Access to the inner chambers of the court was variable. It was in the nature of the court to operate a system of gradual degrees of access to the monarch, manifested not only in the relative and changing exclusiveness of court events, but also in the very architecture of the palace, where a system of successive chambers allowed calibrating physical proximity to the ruler with rank. Although this system seems to presuppose the rigorous implementation of court regulations, in fact, more often than not, it enabled the ruler to confer distinction by overriding the order of precedence. Deviations to the regulations were a convenient means to show favor to one person or clan, and they serve as a reminder not to set too much store by formal criteria of belonging. Given this system of concentric circles and the habit of suspending protocol, drawing a line around the presumed boundaries of the court becomes somewhat arbitrary. Nevertheless, despite a rapid rise in number and opulence over the course of the century, the Russian court remained modest by the standards of Versailles, albeit less so in comparison with Vienna (where the Hofburg was too small to accommodate significant numbers of guests; Duindam 2003, 179).

This did not prevent the court from organizing lavish displays of opulence—for example, by hosting "public" feasts for the "nobility and merchants," which in 1767 accommodated 1,500–2000 participants, and later up to 8,000. Such events aimed precisely at taking the brilliant display of the court outside its walls (Ageeva 2006, 234). Georgi described masquerades with 4,000 invited guests—"hence it is not difficult to take part in them," as he put it—where foreigners could not help but "marvel at the reigning magnificence and fine taste, not only in the decorations of the halls [of the palace], but also in the attire and headgear of men and women, bedecked with insignia and precious jewelry, gold and silver-threaded clothes, etc." (Georgi 1996, 159). Georgi worked at the Academy of Sciences as he prepared the Russian translation of his statistical analysis of St. Petersburg in the early 1790s, and in his depiction of the city, he clearly reflected an official view. His description captures the fact that foreigners were among the intended audience and witnesses of court festivities.

Daily life at court was punctuated by the schedule of the empress. Although reports conflict in the details, one can work out the general course of the day. Count de Ségur, the French ambassador, reported that she would rise at 6 a.m. and devote the early hours of the day to working with her secretaries and ministers (Ségur 1859, 1:323; however, Ludwig von Cobenzl reported that she would rise at 7 a.m.: Cobenzl 1901, 15). From the diaries of her personal secretary A. V. Khrapovitsky we learn that this is the time she would receive reports from the perlustration of domestic and international post, which helped her stay abreast of public opinion in town and monitor (as well as punish) any offence to her dignity. Around 11 a.m. she would proceed to the ritual display of her toilet, during which she gave audience to those with the highest level of access (Cobenzl 1901, 15). Dinners were held early afternoon and remained mostly a low-scale affair, in small circles, where the etiquette was proscribed (Ségur 1859, 1:323). In the afternoon the empress would either retire to her chambers to read and receive her favorites (Cobenzl 1901, 16) or pay social visits to small circles (Ségur 1859, 1:333). The early hours of the evening were devoted to sociability at court with music and card play as mainstays. The empress would then retire between 8 and 9 p.m. without supper.

The order of the day, of course, changed on festive days, which were numerous, as they included dynastic celebrations (name days, coronation days, wedding days, accession to the throne days, etc.), religious feasts (Christmas, Easter, and other Christian holidays, including some saints days, as well as christenings, not to speak of Sundays, which usually involved a procession to church), victory celebrations, likewise celebrated in church, as well as celebrations of the chivalric orders, including foreign ones (Ageeva 2008, 208–214). By the early 1790s, there were altogether fifty-nine days reserved in the year for religious, dynastic, or chivalric celebrations (Georgi 1996, 158). In addition, there were biweekly court days, weekly balls and masquerades, and regular theater evenings, usually twice a week, although these entertainments stopped during fasting weeks. The higher the rank, the more events one was expected to attend. Count de Ségur complained that "what struck me as excessively magnificent and tiring, was the large number of obligatory festivities, not only at court, but also in society" (Ségur 1859, 1:334). Ségur would also have been invited to the parties held by grandees, and he mentioned the tedious custom of paying visits to those celebrating their name days. All of this made for a breathless social circuit. There were seasonal variations to this pattern. The empress typically spent summers in her country residence at Tsarskoe Selo, where the etiquette was reduced and sociability more spontaneous (1:386). In the last years of her reign, in the autumn and spring, the empress often resided in the Tauride palace, where social events were more restricted and intimate (Czartoryski 1887, 94). The peak season for grand formal events was hence in the winter, when the empress resided in the Winter Palace.

Court life had both a secular and a religious content, the latter constraining the extent of its complete Europeanization. By Catherine's accession to the throne, the order of ceremonies for dynastic events was already firmly established. Signal rituals such as the coronation had both religious and secular dimensions, and while the core of the religious ceremony, dictated by the church, had remained more or less stable, it was the secular parts that had changed substantially during the first half of the century, along with the collection of tsarist regalia that were worn and displayed. Modifications aimed mostly to bring the ritual closer to European models, removing links to Byzantium, incorporating references to the diverse components of the Russian empire, and reflecting the order of precedence of the Table of Ranks, while the ensuing merrymaking became ever more elaborate and protracted (Ageeva 2008, 169–170; for a description of the ritual see Wortman 1995, 113–120). Ageeva makes the point that by the time of Catherine's coronation, only Russian precedents were used, and there was no need to turn to foreign models, as the Europeanization of the ritual was taken for granted (170). In 1748 the Office of Ceremonies conducted a comparison among European courts of the protocols regarding access given to foreign emissaries at court. According to Ageeva, the result of this exercise was the discovery that whatever protocol the Russian court adopted, it could always find a European precedent, so that the Europeanized credentials of court ceremonies were averred (Ageeva, 2006, 239).

Nevertheless, despite the secular dimensions of courtly entertainment—the balls, masquerades, theater, music, illuminations, and fireworks—the court carefully retained an overall Christian Orthodox context, expressed in rituals such as coronation, christenings, weddings, and funerals, as well as in prayers and processions associated with declarations of war and victory celebrations. Foreign princesses had all to be baptized into the Orthodox faith before they could wed members of the tsarist family. Eventually the court even refused reciprocity in this regard: during negotiations about the prospective marriage of Grand Duchess Aleksandra Pavlovna to the King of Sweden Gustav IV in 1796, Catherine, keen to impose her imperial prerogatives over a "mere" king, insisted that the bride be given confessional freedom—that is, allowed to retain her faith—which sank the intended alliance.

Within the context of Europeanization and the obvious desire to burnish Russia's reputation abroad, continuing to profess Orthodoxy was hardly a trivial matter, as many foreigners had little patience for the Orthodox faith. We can get a sense of how Orthodoxy was seen in foreign eyes from prince Adam Czartoryski—admittedly not someone favorably disposed to the Russian court—who witnessed the christening into Orthodoxy of Princess Juliane of Saxe-Coburg. He described her baptism as a highly humiliating process, Orthodox ceremonies being close to paganism and entirely oriented toward "external pomp." "It is a theatrical representation derived straight from idolatry," he commented acidly (Czartoryski 1887, 86).

The tension between secular and religious content in festivities at court and beyond sometimes came to a head. The grand festivities given by Potemkin upon his triumphant return from the war against Turkey in the spring 1791 shocked a great many because they took place during Lent. As one witness wrote, "The wise and enlightened of this world were laughing at piety, which they saw as a vulgar superstition and rusty antiquity" (Kir'iak 1867, 675). The festivities themselves were devoid of any Christian dimension and seemed, according to the same witness, to express relish in the secular, mechanical production of marvel without any larger aim but to instill wonder. For Derzhavin they were a synesthetic monument to Catherine, presented as a military victor and goddess descending from the Olympian heights (Derzhavin 1864).

By and large, the Russian court aimed at least for parity and comparability with European courts, when it did not indulge in bedazzling and overpowering displays of opulence, while insisting on a degree of cultural and religious distinctiveness. And even if it affected an overall Orthodox Christian ceremonial framework, it did so without kowtowing to religious authorities or even necessarily paying due respect to religious sensibilities.

Behaving at Court

How can we assess the extent to which etiquette and protocol ruled over the life of the upper nobility at court? One of Catherine's first decisions when she acceded to the throne was to issue an edict on 15 August 1762 "On the duties of court cavaliers" (PSZ 1830, vol. 16, no. 11645, p. 54–5), which prescribed the rank, wages, dress, deportment, and duties of chamberlains and chamber junkers. The edict aimed to regulate the duties of court chamberlains during stately occasions, such as where they would stand during ceremonial dinners and who would serve the empress. Instructions for chamber junkers were less precise, their brief being to "serve Her Imperial Majesty, to the extent that Her Imperial Majesty deigns to instruct them." For both ranks, the edict sought to ensure their constant availability at court to execute orders from the monarch. "Court cavaliers in service are to be constantly at court and never to absent themselves," the edict stipulated sternly. One can perhaps already detect a certain ambivalence in this edict between the urge to codify behavior explicitly and that of demanding unconditional obedience to anything the empress might fancy—that is, between a well-ordered and a despotic political regime.

Many conventions were implicit and transmitted by way of example, in particular in the case of gestures. Czartoryski quickly understood that thanking the empress for a favor required a genuflection (Czartoryski 1887, 77). Hostilities between rival clans had, of course, to be concealed at court. James Harris, a British earl in attendance, was astonished by the self-control required of Potemkin and Aleksei Orlov, two arch-enemies, as they played cards with the empress. "It is beyond the power of my pen to describe to your Lordship," he wrote, "a scene in which every passion that can affect the human mind bore a part; and which were, by all the actors, concealed by the most masterly hypocrisy" (Harris 1844, 210). Politics was banned from all private discussions, at court and in society, even if only to praise the government. "Fear had given the habit of prudence," Ségur reported (Ségur 1859, 1:357). Likewise, no one dared to utter an ill word of the empress, even foreigners and notorious gossips and mudslingers (Czartoryski 1887, 49). There were books one could not read in public. Grand Duchess Elizaveta Alekseevna, the wife of the future Alexander 1, had to be rescued in the nick of time when she left a copy of *La Nouvelle Héloïse* lying in her apartments just as a party was to pay a visit in her absence (Golovine 1910, 114).

Some elements of etiquette were stipulated in law, which does not necessarily mean that they were internalized by the elite. For example, in the first two years of her reign, Catherine felt it necessary to remind everyone in two edicts that under no conditions should petitions be presented directly to her. Instead they should be handed to relevant instances such as the Senate (PSZ 1830, vol.

16, no. 11606, p. 17–18; PSZ 1830, vol. 16, no. 11858, p. 293). Some sartorial matters were regulated formally, with varying success. An edict issued in 1782 ruled that ladies attending court should not wear "any trims made of fabric larger than 2 vershoks [about 2.5 in]." Furthermore "it would please her majesty ... if ladies could observe simplicity and moderation and refrain from using any items which gain value only from their novelty" (PSZ 1830, vol. 21, no. 15556, p. 713). A further edict regulated the kind of fabric courtiers were allowed to wear on holidays and normal days (PSZ 1830, vol. 21, no. 15569, p. 726–727). The practice of regulating sartorial conventions by decree reveals the importance that was accorded to external appearance as well as, perhaps, the ruler's inability to obtain full compliance.

The unstated target of such regulations was Parisian fashion, as Grand Duchess Elizaveta Alekseevna discovered when she proudly wore a dress designed by the painter Louise Vigée Le Brun, who had recently arrived from Paris, only to earn a disdainful cold shoulder from the empress (Golovine 1910, 106–107). Imports from Paris were automatically dubious. Corberon reported that when she returned from the City of Light all imbued with French manners, princess Bariatinskaia met a cold reception: "Princess Bariatinskaia was not appreciated, as she spoke too much of Paris and one does not approve of disadvantageous comparisons. The empress found these fashions ridiculous" (Corberon 1901, 2:51). Yet society remained well inclined toward the French (Ségur 1859, 1:357). And in fact, according to Ségur, the dress code resembled that of Versailles, erring on the side of formality, which although impractical, "encouraged decency, gallantry, nobility of manners, and civility" (Ségur 1859, 1:333). While Catherine sought to cultivate a measure of sartorial self-restraint among her subjects, which she thought behooved the dignity of the Russian court, society was more prone to indulge the extravagance of Versailles. Although she welcomed foreigners at court, hoping that their presence would burnish her reputation, she expected foreigners to adjust to Russian ways and to show some loyalty. The general tenor at court was patriotic, and Catherine steadfastly fought against received notions of the superiority of French culture and mores. In contrast, Czartoryski noted that in society "foreigners were everywhere in high demand. Diplomats and the French emigration set the tone" (Czartoryski 1887, 44). For society, the imitation of French manners and rubbing shoulders with Parisians were not simply a form of cultural appropriation, but also a way to assert symbolically a degree of autonomy from the monarch.

Courtly conventions were frequently honored in the breach. Catherine's habit of picking favorites from the ranks of the guards and giving them a meteoric rise is, of course, the most egregious and famous example of derogation of protocol. But more prosaic nominations to various roles and distinctions likewise fell victim to court politics, or simply to the whims of the empress, who could make decisions without regard to considerations such as length of service and merit. Thus Saltykov bemoaned that he was passed over for advancement for the sole reason that he was serving at the court of Grand Duke Paul (Garnovskii 1876, 15.1:21). Ladies-in-waiting were dismayed when it was the youngest among them, Princess Orlova, who was awarded the order of St. Catherine in 1777. On this occasion, Corberon described the atmosphere of the court as "a chaos of envy, pettiness, and desire" (Corberon 1901, 2:187). This pervasive resentment was clearly encouraged by the lack of ordered procedure in matters of advancement and distinction. At times, Catherine seemed to hesitate between merit and length of service in awarding decorations, choosing to refer the matter to her favorite instead of making a decision. Such was the case, for example, for Alexander Suvorov, whose military success Catherine hesitated to recognize with the award of a ribbon, lest older officers would resent his distinction (Garnovskii 1876, 15.3:473).

Signs of favor elicited hostility from other courtiers, suggesting that they were engaged in bare-knuckled competition for attention and favors. In her memoirs Dashkova lamented the fact that her privileged access to the empress created many an enemy for her (she would have preferred monetary awards to the distinction of access), and she begged the king of Sweden not to award her the cross of the Order of Merit, lest it attract even more animosity toward her (Dachkova 1999, 175). Foreigners likewise succumbed to this pettiness. Corberon, in his own account, was the butt of envy among foreign representatives, as "for unknown reason" his access to court was much higher than that of his counterparts from other countries (Corberon 1901, 2:188).

There were also, in the lives of courtiers, events and places where the etiquette was explicitly suspended. These included evenings at the theater in the Hermitage or dinners and afternoon walks at Tsarskoe Selo. On these occasions, the empress would cast off her mask and expect the same from her courtiers. Here is how Ségur characterized the atmosphere at Tsarskoe Selo in the summer: "The complete freedom, the joyful conversation, the absence of boredom and constraint could have led me to believe, had I turned my eyes from the imposing majesty of the palace of Tsarskoe Selo, that I was in the country seat of a most pleasant lady" (Ségur 1859, 1:386). Catherine skillfully played with the innocence and spontaneity suggested by the habit of holding games in her gardens at Tsarskoe Selo. Dashkova railed against the "ignominious hypocrisy" at the heart of this theatricalization of a countryside idyll. These sudden suspensions of etiquette resembled what is now called code-switching, except that they were governed less by the context of interaction than by the demands and expectations of the ruler. Even when the etiquette was banned, courtiers were expected to follow prescriptions. Guests invited to the intimate gatherings at the Hermitage were greeted with a placard enjoining them to "leave all hats, walking-sticks, and ranks outside the door; don't have a sullen expression; don't get overly excited and don't argue" (Smith 1999, 46). Thus the requirement for informality in fact strengthened the courtiers' subjection to the vagaries of monarchical preference.

Courtly practices radiated into society. Catherine's favorites adopted court rituals and set up their own small courts, which commanded equal authority and startled foreigners. Czartoryski described in colorful details the *levée* of Count Zubov, which took place every day at 11 a.m.: "A huge crowd of petitioners and courtiers of all ranks congregated to attend his toilet. The street was full of carriages with four or six horses, exactly like at the theater." He went on to describe the throng of people, including generals and "the first dignitaries of the empire," rubbing shoulders to place themselves advantageously in a semicircle around the count, so as to make their bows and attract his gaze, in the hope of drawing attention to themselves and being allowed to speak to the count (Czartoryski 1887, 57–59). This ceremony was timed to take place at the same time as Catherine's equivalent procedure, to which only the highest ranks were admitted. This example of behavioral mimicry was not merely a result of Zubov's vainglory. Grigorii Orlov, almost two decades earlier, had adopted a similar practice. Wishing to thank him, Corberon attended Orlov's levée and was astonished at the scene he witnessed: "I entered a cabinet full of people, who waited for the levée of the prince. It was a real court, of which we have no idea in European countries. Our princes of the blood and our ministers receive in full dress and give audience with the respect one always owes to the public. Here Asiatic mores have retained the sluggishness of oriental despotism, and each man in position receives the national public with magnificence and indolence; it is perhaps less haughtiness than habit" (Corberon 1901, 2:113–114). Corberon's rhetoric is, of course, characteristic of Enlightenment binaries, but it is nevertheless worth noting the dismay he expresses at this ritual, and his observation that it owes less to the vanity of the prince than to social custom.

Commerce with the same person required different degrees of formality depending on the context, to the point of requiring at times profoundly demeaning behavior. Czartoryski was astonished that at the same levée "the first dignitaries of the empire, the most illustrious names, the generals commanding our provinces, in front of whom everybody trembled," all these exalted personalities were bowing their heads in abject humility in front of the grandee, and were "leaving without receiving any glance from him or were posted like a sentry while he changed his costume sprawled out in an armchair" (Czartoryski 1887, 58). Along with such settings, there were somewhat ambiguous situations in which the etiquette was intended to be relaxed. While having regularly to attend Zubov's levée to press his case, Czartoryski was also invited to after-dinner gatherings with the favorite, where "one was supposed to be admitted to a kind of familiarity, which resembled a gathering of friends. The favorite would appear in frock-coat, more nonchalant than ever. He would invite visitors . . . to sit down and would spread himself comfortably in an armchair or settee" (71). Zubov seemed to excel at imitating Catherine's clever use of etiquette shifts, and Czartoryski clearly registered his unease and lack of familiarity at this custom.

The jockeying at court for access and favors created rivalries among court clans that extended into society. Court society was divided into different groups called the "party" of this or that grandee (Garnovskii 1876, 5.2:262; 16.5:715). Conventions of patronage required that clients displayed total loyalty to their patron. It was inappropriate or risky, for example, to pay a visit to a patron's rival (16.5:30). Indeed, the suspicion of duplicity in the battle among court clans was pervasive, such that to preserve the trust of one's patron, one had carefully to avoid any public signs suggesting familiarity with his enemies. At times the need for secrecy went so far as to require the assumption of spurious identities in correspondence (15.3:482). Corberon observed that contrary to Paris, conventions of patronage had fragmented social life: "What is quite particular is that they [members of society] communicate little among themselves. Each house has its own coterie and does hardly depart from it; you don't see, even in the largest houses, the same ebb and flow of people one experiences generally in Paris" (Corberon 1901, 1:330).

Foreigners were also surprised that duels served to entrench the fragmentation of society. As we saw briefly in the introduction, duels were an imported social convention, especially among officers, which the court sought to abolish. They offered a mechanism for the nobility to affirm its values and resolve its conflicts outside of court intervention and of the government's judicial system, thus implicitly asserting the nobility's independence, a notion the court could not but discourage. Men of high rank refused to fight duels with lower-placed officers. Corberon and the prince d'Anhalt, both foreigners, agreed that contrary to the practice in Europe, where duels could be fought among nobles of unequal rank, the stupendous inequality of Russian society created by the government undermined the notion of the "point d'honneur," the defense of one's corporate dignity (Corberon 1901, 1:111). Noblemen's relative position on the Table of Ranks mattered more to them than the defense and demonstration of their intrinsic nobility. Such supercilious adherence to rank among the upper nobility can be construed as a reaction to the social mobility fostered by Catherine's favoritism, and more broadly by the Table of Ranks.

At the highest echelons of court life, sexual mores were surprisingly lax, contrary to the stricter sexual morality prevailing in society, as we discussed in the previous chapter. The reports of sexual dissolution in the life of Catherine, in the imperial family, and at court are numerous (Harris 1844, 233–234; Corberon 1901, 1:230, 283). Czartoryski observed that no one took offense at the "depravation" of the empress (Czartoryski 1887, 47) and noted with surprise that the empress and Count Zubov could be seen in négligé in the early hours of the morning without anyone being disconcerted by this, neither actors nor bystanders (89). Catherine didn't waste too much effort maintaining the appearances of propriety. While it is impossible to evaluate whether extramarital amorous frolicking was more pervasive at court than in society, one may point to a different regime of openness and publicity. While in society affairs had to be conducted with discretion, the tolerance for open displays of illicit desire at court was clearly much higher, which resulted in widespread gossip about affairs involving high-placed individuals.

A case in point is the behavior of Platon Zubov, who openly courted Grand Duchess Elizaveta, the wife of the future Alexander I, while also remaining Catherine's favorite. Czartoryski described what can only be termed a public performance of erotic longing, which Zubov enacted at court, while also signaling lassitude with his obligations as Catherine's favorite (Czartoryski 1887, 72). While society, in Czartoryski's account, had little patience for Zubov's ambiguous and slightly daring game, Zubov enlisted the help of his clients to arrange "chance" encounters with the grand duchess, where he could express his yearning to her. According to Golovina, who, as Elizaveta's unofficial chaperone and protector, was implicated, Alexander was fully aware of Zubov's infatuation—indeed, seemed naively to encourage it. In her account, the court split into different clans, including one supporting Zubov's aims and another distrustful of Golovina's friendship with the grand duchess (Golovine 1910, 65). Elizaveta was at once embarrassed by the attention and overcome by a *"douce jouissance"* (67), as, according to Golovina, she had not found with Alexander the intimacy she was taught to expect from her husband, their relationship being no more than fraternal (68).

Golovina strikes a somewhat defensive tone in her memoirs, pleading complete probity in allowing the grand duchesse's friendship for her to blossom, and also claiming the support of the empress. Her obfuscation barely conceals the fact that Elizaveta's attachment to her had reached an intensity that could seem troubling to bystanders, notably to the party of her mother-in-law, Maria Fedorovna. The extraordinary love letters Elizaveta wrote to Golovina, which referred to a moment of total intimacy the two shared on 30 May 1795, when, as she put it, "I gave myself over to you completely," suggest that such suspicions were not completely unfounded (Nicolas Mikhaïlowitch 1909, 407–426, quotation on 417). To put it differently, in this *ménage à quatre* between Elizaveta, Alexander, Zubov, and Golovina, some of which was played out in public view, what unfolded was a battle over the soul of the grand duchess. Catherine, true to form, was fully aware of Zubov's passion for her daughter-in-law (Nicolas Mikhaïlowitch 1909, 412), and so was Alexander of Elizaveta's infatuation with Golovina (417). Indeed, maximum transparency toward one another, despite the prurient and political eye of society, seems to have been one of the unstated yearnings of all participants in this sentimental drama.

What interests us here is not so much the details of these intricate relations as the fact of their public visibility. Other affairs involving the ruling family and high-level courtiers were equally talked about. Count Andrei Razumovsky's relationship with Paul's first wife was public knowledge, although Paul himself was kept in the dark (Corberon 1901, 1:230). Konstantin Pavlovich's abusive and unfaithful relationship with his wife was in the public domain (Golovine 1910, 118). And if Catherine put an end to Zubov's infatuation with Elizaveta, then Alexander seemed to encourage Czartoryski's yearning after her, giving him unfettered access to his wife (112–113). The fact that Aleksandr Bezborodko kept a harem and "trialed" young Italian women to assess their suitability was widely known (Garnovskii, 1876, 15.2:245). When he was ridiculed for it, he reportedly retorted maliciously that "at least I have the power to shape them, which husbands can't do with their wives, although they know that they are w . . ." (15.3:488). Orlov, in turn, was rumored to have selected four young graduates from the Smolny Institute for his own pleasure (Corberon 1901, 1:283). Aleksandr Mamonov's infatuation with Dar'ia Shcherbatova, at a time when he was still Catherine's favorite, drew much attention (Garnovskii 1876, 16.5:8; 16.6:211). And of course scrutinizing the ups and downs of Catherine's relations with her favorites was a beloved pastime. In the case of the dismissal of Semen Zorich, for example, Harris observed that "both court and town are occupied with this event alone" (Harris 1844, 200).

Such comments about private life can be fodder to the mill of clan rivalries, and not all of them may be entirely reliable, but this does not diminish the fact that court society involved constant mutual snooping for outward signs of favor, distinction, and infatuation, as well as the dissemination of rumors to undercut the public reputation of rivals. Not for nothing did Garnovsky use the concept of "the public" to describe the intended audience of such gossip-mongering and opinion-shaping. In comments such as "the public largely blames Petr Lukich in this matter," he seemed to refer to the views of a fairly homogenous community, implying that there is a degree of commonality in the group of people who observed and judged doings at court (Garnovskii 1876, 15.3:492). He also related Catherine's deceitful attempts to shape the opinion of this community, corroborating the sense that the "public" is self-consciously construed as such by its members. The notion of public, of course, presupposes a degree of publicness, and the continuous chattering fed on the absence of genuinely private space at court. Ultimately, this shared intelligence of sentimental affairs also served to define the boundaries of this community of insiders, despite the dissensions among them.

Raging Emotions at Court

The lax sexual morality on display at court casts some doubt on Elias's idea that court society is the arena where self-discipline becomes internalized. One of Elias's central ideas was that court society encouraged a specific kind of rationality, defined as the exclusive pursuit of prestige, which entailed tight control of passions and a judiciously "calculated and finely nuanced behavior."

Above all, court society demanded complete restraint in expressing any sort of interiority and affect (Elias 1983, 111). Depictions of the Russian court hardly confirm these ideas. Indeed, observers of court affairs paint a world in which feelings are running wild at all levels and in which social actors see little advantage from holding back their emotions. Instead, the display of feelings becomes part of the spectacle enacted by court society.

Khrapovitsky's spare notes in his diary depict an empress who responds heatedly to much of what happened under her watch. She can be "angry for three days" (Khrapovitskii 2008, 31), speak "with heartfelt gratefulness" (35) or "almost through tears" (67), "cry" (numerous times, e.g. 36, 142, 185, 211), "be bored" (40), show "visible anxiety" (58), "embarrassment" (59), "sudden bitterness" (67), look "somber" (69) or else "joyful" (72). Sometimes she "can't hold back her tears" (99). Indeed, in particular critical moments, such as when her relationship with Mamonov unraveled due to his love for Shcherbatova, she retired for a day or two, and Khrapovitsky jotted down that "I wasn't asked on account of her tears" (142). On this occasion, Garnovsky wrote that "rivers of tears flowed here and later in her chambers" (Garnovskii 1876, 16.7:401), while Ségur, more restrained, wrote of an "anger and despondency unworthy of her" (Ségur 1859, 2:163). Yet, when she then drafted a letter to Mamonov, Khrapovitsky was invited to correct her punctuation, suggesting again that she saw no reason to keep the tremors of her heart from external view (144).

Many observers commented on Catherine's flares of passion and dejection, which happened in plain sight. Garnovsky noted, for example, that during festivities on the saint's day of Alexander Nevsky, Catherine was "sombre and cried after dinner" (Garnovskii 1876, 15.2:247). There was talk of Catherine being beaten by Grigorii Orlov and complaining to others in tears about his behavior (Corberon 1901, 2:89). Garnovsky also described an episode in which Mamonov sought to humiliate Catherine for her loyalty to Bezborodko, the scene ending with Catherine's complete capitulation and her "crying through the night" (Garnovskii 1876, 15.2:262). Potemkin's callous indifference to Catherine's requests for regular news about the course of the war against Turkey also left her in tears (15.3:497). At times, courtiers tried to dispel her gloom with comedies and other entertainments, but to no avail (16.6:225). And even Catherine's writing of comedies did reportedly little to dry her tear ducts (16.6:228). Conflicts between rival parties at court could leave Catherine "chagrined," "highly miserable," and "lonely" (Corberon 1901, 2:370). Her attempt to reconcile Aleksei Orlov with Potemkin ended

in her "bursting into tears" (Harris 1844, 215), although witnesses also suspected some outpourings of emotion to be disingenuous (Corberon 1901,
1:248). Ségur attributed Catherine's emotionality to her cosseted existence:
"Catherine experienced what happens to all people continuously favored by
their good fortune: the slightest annoyance turns for them into real sorrow"
(Ségur 1859, 1:426). Of course, on many occasions, the empress behaved with
much composure and dignity, as scholars have emphasized (Madariaga 1981,
356). What matters here is not the extent and frequency of any lachrymose
outbursts, but the fact that public rhetoric about her tolerated, if not fostered,
the image of a vibrant, emotionally restless person, rather than that of a hier-
atic, aloof, and calculating monarch.

Nor was Catherine alone in displaying such emotionality. Men were likewise reported to be crying. Count Petr Sheremetev, who was then a senator,
shed tears as he confided the vagaries of his heart to a Frenchman (Corberon
1901, 1:120). Mamonov cried profusely when he disclosed to Catherine his
love for Princess Shcherbatova, and then to Garnovsky, when he implored him
to plead Potemkin for his protection, as he feared revenge for the offense he
gave to the empress (Garnovskii 1876, 16.7:400). And prior to this falling-out,
he could take to his bed for days, or pretend to be ill, when he felt that the
empress was directing her favors elsewhere (16.6:216). Women were equally
emotional. When her son was provoked into fighting in a duel, Dashkova
intervened with an entirely inappropriate letter to Mamonov, full of "wailing,
sobbing, and thirst for revenge" (15.3:491). When Paul and Maria Fedorovna
left on their journey to Europe in 1781, they feared that this journey was a
thinly disguised form of banishment. "It is impossible to express the agitation
of the grand-duchess," Harris reported. "On taking leave of her children she
fainted away, and was carried speechless into her coach.... The grand-duke
was nearly in the same state," he added, while Panin, their faithful courtier,
was struck with seizure and delirium following their departure (Harris 1844,
454, 470). Commenting on such high-octane court culture, Corberon noted
that "they tear one another apart, slander each other, and as one Russian told
me, there is no transition point between the most contradictory movements
of the heart: one switches from the rapture of pleasure to the darkest hatred"
(Corberon 1901, 1:247).

What shall we make of such depictions of court society? Foreigners registered their surprise at the intense feelings running rampant at the court of the
Russian tsars. And reports by Russians largely corroborated these accounts.

Whether they were evidentially correct in all instances or not, the prevalence of such emotion-laden accounts is itself a historical fact. Commentators did, of course, partly gain their information by hearsay, so we can assume that what they write reflects the way the court talked about itself. And such collective self-representation by courtiers was bound to affect the way they felt and acted. Courtiers saw themselves engaged in a highly emotional and conflict-laden battle for standing at court and prestige beyond. They viewed their empress not as a neutral arbiter of their destinies, nor as a sacred being who towered above them in splendid inapproachability, but as an individual endowed with immense powers, yet liable to the same kinds of mood swings, idiosyncratic preferences, and emotional needs they experienced themselves. In this highly personalistic culture, most of them developed ostentatious affection for their monarch, although they knew that they could not count on her friendship to endure forever, regardless of the vicissitudes of fortune. The sense of instability, which we have documented elsewhere, loomed very large at court (Schönle 2016b). This had only partly to do with Catherine's mood swings, although they certainly played a role. Corberon may not have been too far off the mark when he commented that "her character follows the mobility of her soul; swept by the impression of the moment, she seems incoherent with herself when she does not follow the quick slope of her passions," adding that she is "less devious than inconstant and fickle" (Corberon 1901, 1:365).

The instability of court society also stemmed from the ambivalent and fuzzy nature of conventions of rank and etiquette, and even of the law. On the one hand, rank was everything in Russian society, and individuals undertook enormous efforts to ensure their prompt ascent on the Table. Yet on the other hand, rank was also strangely insubstantial and swiftly cast aside. The behavior of Bezborodko one day in October 1787 is a perfect example. As Bezborodko came to the palace to deliver his regular report to Catherine, he arrived at a moment when her favorite Mamonov, a member of the opposing clan, was in attendance. Bezborodko, who was then privy councilor, on the third rank, with a distinguished career in foreign affairs behind him, lost his countenance, his voice, and ultimately his face in the presence of the favorite, eleven years his junior, who was then, as a major-general, lower in rank and had only recently been plucked from obscurity (Garnovskii 1876, 15.3:479). Czartoryski was astonished that young men from the guards, "people without any personal merit," nominated as chamber junkers, enjoyed unfettered access to court, while officials and generals discharging "real service" struggled to draw attention to themselves in the throng of the antechambers (Czartoryski 1887, 83). At court, service hierarchies were at an unfair disadvantage against dashing youth, and even grandees knew of their vulnerability and trembled before favorites. The ambiguity between a regulated and a despotic exercise of power we detected earlier in Catherine's first legislation on court duties indeed profoundly affected the life of the court elite.

The St. Petersburg Court in a European Context

How distinctive was the Russian court on the background of its European counterparts? While the many differences between various European courts make it difficult to generalize, we can at least point to certain specific features in Russia that affected the lives of courtiers, in particular in comparison with the court of Versailles. Given the table of equivalences between military, civil, and court ranks in Russia, the fault line between *noblesse de robe* and *noblesse d'epée*, characteristic of Versailles, played little role in Russia. The potential conflict between an ancient, locally rooted nobility with credentials that hark back to distinguished military service and a rising caste of civil servants had been largely settled by Peter's reforms and the introduction of the Table of Ranks. As distinct from Russia, many offices in France could be purchased, and subsequently passed on to descendants, thus escaping from the control of the king. It was extremely difficult for a king to remove someone from office (Adamson 1999, 16). It is clear that the kings of France had much less leeway in appointing and dismissing members of their entourage than the Russian tsars, who controlled all appointments to the upper rungs of the hierarchy, and thus could elevate and fire courtiers at will.

Relatively speaking, and bearing in mind the flaws in the very notion of absolutism briefly discussed above, the Russian court was more "absolutist" than even the court of Louis XIV. Of course, Catherine was careful enough to extend golden retirements to the grandees she wanted to sack, but dismissals could be very abrupt, with immediate and consequential effects in terms of public prestige. When Mamonov was fired, everyone at court promptly abandoned him, and only Ségur, in his own account, mustered the decency to pay him a visit. Catherine praised Ségur publicly for that courage, upbraiding "the cowardice of those who hurried away precipitously from a man they had once courted and idolized" (Ségur 1859, 2:164). It is as if, in professing indulgence and magnanimity toward outcasts, Catherine wanted to counteract the moral consequences of the flexible system of patronage she had created, or else as if she claimed for herself alone the right to exclude individuals from court society. In any case, owing to the monarch's significantly wider prerogatives in appointments, instability at court was much more acute in Russia than in France, even if one accepts Elias's claims that the preference of the monarch also played a role in fashioning the public reputation of subjects in Paris (Elias 1983, 90–91).

Elias contended, with some justification, that Louis XIV ruled by pitting court clans against one another, but he had in mind the competition for access and influence between social orders such as the epée and the robe. Catherine likewise balanced clans against one another, but these were informal patronage networks, rather than social orders, and thus groupings much more liable to change as they were not rooted in social structures. Given possible switches of allegiance—Garnovsky's letters are full of discussions of the likely faithfulness to Potemkin's clan of various members of the court—a climate of perennial suspicion arose between courtiers, which compounded the instability inherent in court society. Furthermore, Catherine's way of offsetting one clan against the other could be erratic, as it was often based on tactical decisions made on the spur of the moment, and could entail a fusing of her private desires with reasons of state. In contrast, Duindam plays down the importance of patronage in European courts as "rulers were interested above all in maintaining a dignified and undisturbed ceremonial at court" (Duindam 2003, 214). Foreign diplomats at the St. Petersburg court lamented the extent to which decisions about alliances with foreign countries were affected by the competition between grandees and favorites at court. Commenting on Catherine's most recent change of favorite and the instability that ensued, Harris wrote "Such, at this instant, is the face of the Court; it may change before my letter is finished. I shall attempt to get as quick and as accurate intelligence as possible on these subjects, because, unfortunately, they influence too much the political system of the country" (Harris 1844, 202).

For the elite, there were huge opportunities to grasp at court. Gaining the trust of the empress could result in many advantages, even if impermanent ones. Czartoryski was surprised that Aleksandr Stroganov, supported by his bond with the empress, enjoyed a tacit right to free speech at court, even in her presence (Czartoryski 1887, 153–154). The opportunities for material gain were likewise immense. Enabled by the land wealth of the Crown, including that resulting from the partition of the Polish–Lithuanian Commonwealth and the annexation of territory in the south, Catherine was in the habit of making large grants of land to her supporters, including to foreigners, no doubt in part in the hope that her munificence would convert into increased power for herself. The opportunities for quick social advancement were enticing, and were made more crucial by the Table of Ranks, which compelled scions of high-placed families to start their ascent from the bottom of the ladder. Although rulers always used personal favors as part of their toolkit, compared to other courts and relatively speaking, Catherine availed herself of such means to a much greater extent than did rulers in other European courts, and did so with considerable success in securing consent to her rule.

The result was that despite its risks, the Russian court proved a great magnet, including for foreigners. Indeed, the prominent role of foreigners attending court in one or the other capacity was another distinguishing feature of the court of Catherine. In the overall context of a general Europeanization of court manners, for Russians, the openness of the Russian court meant that in the competition for privilege and prestige, they had to jockey for positions with people from abroad. This did not fail to result in considerable ambivalence regarding strangers, who were both models for imitation and competitors for resources. Catherine—herself, of course, originally a German princess—managed this relationship very carefully. When during his exile Charles-Philippe (count d'Artois, the brother of Louis XVI and future king Charles X) briefly visited St. Petersburg, Catherine appointed him with a court for the duration of his stay. When he made ready to leave, she discreetly bestowed upon him gifts he could award to his courtiers (Bashilov 1871, 200).

Patriotic pride remained very much part of the court's self-presentation, while xenophobic hostility persisted in latent form and could come to the surface in moments of specific conflict (Evstratov 2016b). For the elite at court, Europeanization meant participating in a world of triple, if not quadruple, standards. They imagined themselves as equals to their European counterparts, and many displayed the requisite cosmopolitan graces to prove the point. And in cutting a European part, they sometimes set themselves against the more sober deportment Catherine expected from her subjects. At the same time, they witnessed the privileged access many foreigners received at court, and competed with them in the social arena. And finally, they also shared in an ideology, which began to emerge from Catherine herself, about Russia's superiority over other countries in terms of wealth, military power, and spiritual vocation. Thus as Europeanized nobles, they cut a path through a complex web of ambiguous norms and ambivalent feelings, all predicated on the simultaneous pursuit of European credentials and Russian distinction.

The views of foreigners on courtly behavior corroborate the distinctiveness of the Petersburg court. While there are many accounts of the pleasantness and distinction of manners at court, foreigners also expressed surprise on the one side at the rigidity of the etiquette and on the other at its frequent violations. As we saw above, rituals such as the levée of the ruler or favorite were clearly excessive for most foreign observers, as they rested on a performance of despotic arbitrariness and presumed radical social inequality between ruler and subject. Foreigners were astonished by the humiliation of high-ranking individuals, the fragmentation of society, the need continuously to defend one's social standing, and the importance of minor differences of rank and prestige. One common denominator behind these observations is the perception that the nobility lacked moral autonomy and security in its interactions with the monarch or her favorites. Of course, these depictions tapped into the stereotype of Russia as a despotic country and may have been colored by it. But there is enough corroboration in domestic literature not to dismiss such descriptions outright. Foreigners were startled by the rampant emotionality of the court and its ostentatiously lax sexual morality at the highest level. The raw feelings flaring at court and disrupting courtly propriety suggest that the degree of rational self-control Elias imputed to court was even less internalized in St. Petersburg than elsewhere. Yet it would be reductive to contend that Russian courtiers were simply less proficient in enacting conventions of politeness. For what is even more characteristic, and equally surprising to external observers, was the sense that behavior conventions were situationally differentiated. Ruler and grandees alike required different levels of formality from the same interlocutor depending on the moment and the setting. While all cultures display some context-based variation in degrees of formality, it is notable that foreigners visiting the Russian court were startled by its magnitude. Performing adequately such fine-grained code switching required considerable skill and adaptability. Characteristically, foreigners tended to perceive such requirements as an additional form of humiliation, but for Russians this fragmentation of social propriety was merely a way of being at once European and Russian.

The public roles required from the elite were thus highly differentiated, which counteracted the attempts of courtiers to unify their performance and buttress a subjective sense of self. Crucially, these roles did not necessarily require the suppression of emotion, contrary to what Elias thought. On the contrary, displays of emotion could serve as manifestations of loyalty and devotion, and thus be encouraged. Proficient as they may have been at enacting social conventions, the elite did not necessarily give their full assent to these complex social games, which they increasingly perceived as debasing. As the following chapters will illustrate, partly in response to the hegemony of courtly manners, the elite attempted to carve out spaces of interiority protected from the intrusion of courtly politics, while continuing to act out its requisite public roles. By the time of Catherine the Great, the "civilizing process" which Peter had initiated (to return to Elias's terminology), resulted not simply in the alleged internalization of the elite's devotion to the monarch and the rationalization of its subjective world, but in the development of a complex repertoire of emotional and behavioral practices, which the elite deployed tactically to cut a path between its public commitments and its subjective aspirations.

Of course, the court did not enjoy complete monopoly over fashioning the subjective selves of the elite, as religion, education, and literature—none of which the court entirely controlled—also provided powerful models of behavior and emotions that the elite could assimilate selectively. In the following three chapters we will thus examine each of these spheres in succession, aiming to map out the ways in which the elite developed its mental world by in turn adopting, ignoring, resisting, sidestepping, and deflecting injunctions coming from the court and its rulers.

4

. . . .

THE QUEST FOR TRUE SPIRITUALITY

The eighteenth century in Russia has been alternatively described as an age of Enlightenment that brought with it secularization, leading to the spread of Voltairianism and free thinking, as an age of mysticism marked by powerful spiritual quest and interest in esoteric teachings, and also as a time of deeply embedded Orthodox piety (Zaborov 2011, Faggionato 2005, Kirichenko 2002). One can easily find strong arguments to support all these positions, but the main problem is to trace the dynamics in the interplay of these tendencies in the same period, among the same social groups, and even in the minds of the same people. With rare if notable exceptions, the majority of the Russian elite were still attached to the everyday religious practices of their forefathers, trying to reconcile them with secular lifestyles and an enlightened worldview, while those who had significant spiritual interests often tried to find answers in the works of European mystics and rituals of Masonic lodges. This chapter will deal with the logic of this complex mixture.

Orthodox Conversions and Western Inspiration

In 1791 the most famous Russian eighteenth-century satirist, Denis Fonvizin, started to write his *Openhearted Confession of my Deeds and Thoughts*—an intimate autobiography modeled on Rousseau. Fonvizin was not yet fifty, but as he suffered several strokes and was semiparalyzed, he could hardly speak and knew that his death was approaching. Acute suffering brought about a deep religious conversion. According to a popular story, he used to sit in the church of Moscow University addressing entering students: "Children, take me as an example, I am punished for freethinking, do not insult God by your words or your thoughts." It is not clear to what extent this evidence should be trusted, but the intensity of his repentance of the sins of his youth is beyond any doubt. In his previous essay *The Deliberations of the Vanity of Human Life*, Fonvizin thanked Heaven for humbling him by depriving him of his vital organs and thus of his ability to sin. He also started the *Confession* with a quotation from the Psalms declaring his intention to reveal all the lawless deeds he committed in his lifetime.

   Given this stated intention, the story of his conversion he tells in the *Confession* sounds at best dubious, and not only because he failed to get rid of his powerful satirical mood and playful disposition, which are seemingly incompatible with such a solemn venture, but even more so in the way he treats sacred topics in it. The unfinished *Confession* ends with the author's first religious awakening. It happened in 1769, when young Fonvizin, who had preserved some piety in his heart but was nearly seduced by corrupt and freethinking friends, met senator and amateur philosopher Grigorii Teplov, who helped him find the path of Christian virtue. Teplov told Fonvizin about a debate between two guard officers he happened to overhear. One of them shouted that he knew for certain that there is no God, because Petr Chebyshev had told him this in a Gostinyi Dvor shop. The officer assumed that Chebyshev had first-hand knowledge of the matter, as at that time he served as ober-procurator in the Holy Synod, the civil clerk in charge of the spiritual affairs of the empire. Teplov thought that Fonvizin needed more reliable sources and advised him to read Samuel Clarke's refutation of materialism published in 1705 under the title: *A discourse concerning the being and attributes of God, the obligations of natural religion, and the truth and certainty of the Christian revelation. In Answer to Mr. Hobbes, Spinoza, the author of the oracles of reason, and other deniers of natural and revealed religion* (Clarke 1998). Fonvizin ordered the book in a French translation published in 1728 in Amsterdam (Clarke 1728) and was so impressed that he decided to translate it into Russian. However, he was discouraged from doing so by Teplov, who told him that such a venture would never be approved by the Holy Synod, referring to the fate of the translation of another even more famous product of Newtonian cosmology—Pope's *Essay on Man*. The translation by Nikolai Popovsky had been heavily censored by church authorities, and in order to make it conform to Orthodox doctrine, Bishop Amvrosii had inserted in it some rhymed lines of his own making. Fonvizin still prepared a digest of Clarke's treatise and, more than twenty years later, intended to attach it to his *Confession* for the instruction of the "well-disposed reader" (Fonvizin 1959, v. 22:102–104).

This episode is extremely revealing. In order to satisfy their spiritual quest, two educated nobles who most definitely consider themselves Orthodox are in need of a work by a British rationalist, Anglican priest, and ardent Newtonian, who was later accused by the Convocation of the Church of England of anti-trinitarian beliefs. Moreover, they feel impeded in their religious pursuits both by the primitive Voltairianism of their peers and the rigid dogmatism of the official church. Paradoxically, these two extremes converged in the person of Petr Chebyshev, an atheist occupying a high-ranking position in the Holy Synod. It is clear from the text of the *Confession* that Fonvizin's feelings of alienation from the church hierarchy persisted until his death even as his own religious faith grew more ardent and passionate.

Fonvizin's case was, of course, exceptional. A renowned satirist, he tried to combine in his *Confession* the feeling of deep repentance with his lifelong inclination for comic writing. Yet the story of Andrei Bolotov, whose piety and memoirs were much more traditional, unfolded very much along the same lines. According to Bolotov, he was since infancy attached to God and the Holy Revelation. Nevertheless, during his military service in Königsberg, he started to read German philosophy, which planted deep doubt in his soul and set off a spiritual crisis, during which he was for several weeks "burning as if on fire or in the midst of torture," praying on his knees and imploring the Creator for help. The supporting hand came from the same source as had, previously, the seduction: foreign books. In one of the local bookshops, he found by chance a sermon by Christian August Crusius, which finally set his mind at rest. As Bolotov put it: "I felt as if the greatest mountain had powerfully fallen from me and the blood that was boiling in me came at the end of the book to the most pleasant tranquility" (Bolotov 1870–1873, 2:62–64).

Orthodox Churches, and even Russian books, were most likely not available in Königsberg, though a military priest should have been present. But Bolotov, in any case, needed a confirmation of his faith from "the same great philosopher, whose works he had already studied and for whom he had already felt the deepest reverence" (62). He did not fail to notice that the sermon that saved him was "not so much theological as philosophical" (64). A Pietist philosopher and pastor considered to be one of the early precursors of Kant, Crusius finally turned Bolotov into a confident Orthodox. The situations described by Fonvizin and Bolotov are in many ways typical of the relations between the church, the state, and the educated nobility after the dramatic changes introduced by Petrine reforms. They show the roundabout ways in which the elite buttressed its Orthodox faith by way of inspiration drawn from Western religious philosophy as it failed to find spiritual sustenance in the practices of the church.

The Logic of Secularization

As in most traditional societies, Russian culture was religiously oriented. This does not, of course, mean that Russians were exceptionally pious: the notion of "Holy Rus," the alleged uniquely spiritual nature of Russians, gained traction only significantly later (Cherniavsky 1961). However, the Orthodox Church and its doctrine lay at the foundation of all spheres of national life—the law, ethics, politics, art, domestic economy, and so on needed religious legitimacy to be accepted by the population. The role of religion in national life was especially important, as during two and a half centuries after the fall of Kiev to Tatar dominance in 1240, it was the only basis of identity for the majority of Russians. This perception was reinforced by the so-called doctrine of Moscow as the Third Rome, which regarded Muscovite princes as the sole protectors and guardians of eastern Christianity. The fall of Constantinople to Turks in 1453 preceded Russia regaining its sovereignty from the Golden Horde in 1480 by no more than a quarter of a century, leaving Russia the only independent Orthodox power in the world. A century later Russia was granted permission to establish its own patriarchate, which quickly became the richest and most powerful in the Orthodox world.

The centrality of the church in the national life and culture was shattered in the mid-seventeenth century in the course of a religious schism, which started in 1653 (Bushkovitch 1992). In many ways, the purification of the

Church Slavonic translation of the Holy Scripture and of the ritual, practices, and morality of parishioners initiated by church reformers was akin to the Western Reformation, but unlike in the West, the modernizing segment of the believers stood on one side of the divide and the religious zealots on the other. The state took upon itself the burden of violently pushing the reform through and of persecuting those who clung to the Old Belief, such as bishop Avvakum, the author of the first autobiography ever written in Russian. By crushing and pushing into exile the most religious segment of the population, the official church undermined its own roots and legitimacy. As Patriarch Nikon, the leader of the reforms, accepted the nomination as head of the Russian Church, he procured from Tsar Alexis the promise never to interfere into ecclesiastical affairs; and, in the absence of the tsar from Moscow, Nikon de facto ruled the country. However, after the success of the reforms, he dared to quarrel with the tsar and was dismissed from his position, defrocked, and banished to a remote monastery. As a result, the position of the church dramatically weakened, which significantly facilitated the secularization policies introduced by Peter the Great.

After the death of Patriarch Adrian in 1700, which roughly coincided with Peter's return from his European Grand Tour, the tsar did not give his permission to anoint a new patriarch, choosing instead to put in his seat an acting patriarch who would be easier to control. His choice for the post was Stefan Iavorsky, an educated monk from Kiev who received his religious education in Poland and was rumored to have strong Catholic sympathies. Using admittedly anachronistic terminology, one can say that Stefan was definitely a Westernizer, but the Westernization he believed in was based on the culture of the Polish baroque. However, as Peter himself veered toward Protestantism, his relations with Stefan became strained, and the leading role passed to Feofan Prokopovich. Feofan also came from Kiev and had studied in the Roman Jesuit College, before wandering on foot through Europe and attending lectures at the Universities of Leipzig, Halle, and Iena, precisely at the time when Pietism began to take root in these institutions.

Iavorsky was never promoted to the position of patriarch. Finally in 1721, with the ideological and institutional help of Prokopovich, Peter abolished the patriarchate altogether, replacing it with the Holy Synod, the collective body of highest bishops, whose practical dealings were to be coordinated by an ober-procurator, a secular clerk appointed by the emperor. His personal beliefs were not an issue in such an appointment. Petr Chebyshev, whom

Fonvizin had mentioned, served as the ober-procurator of the Holy Synod in mid-eighteenth century. Later, in the beginning of the nineteenth century, Alexander I appointed his closest childhood friend, Prince Aleksandr Golitsyn, to the same position. Golitsyn's attempts to decline the appointment on the grounds of his utter disbelief in God were not seen by the emperor as a convincing argument (Filaret 1906, 215).

Peter's Protestant sympathies also manifested themselves in his deep dislike and suspicion of monastic life. He believed monasteries not only to be utterly useless for the country, but also potentially dangerous, as they could become the breeding ground of discontent and grumbling. He ordered monks not to keep pens and ink in their cells, thus eliminating the possibility of the development of learned monasticism, and forbade admitting healthy people under the age of forty as nuns and monks. In a way, he aspired to turn monasteries into some sort of social security network. Nearly a hundred years later, when a young Moscow noble girl named Varvara Sokovnina decided to take the veil, her mother told her that a convent "is a place only for the blind, lame, and disabled" (Zorin 2016a, 309). In order to admit her as a nun, the authorities of the convent had to forge documents making her on paper twenty years older than she was in reality. Peter's antimonastic policies were continued by Catherine II, who early in her reign secularized the lands and the peasants belonging to the monasteries, thus depriving them of economic power and making them dependent upon subsidies from the treasury. Both white clergy (the priests) and the black one (the monks) became reliant on state financial support. The number of priests and lower clergymen was fixed by state regulation, and those considered redundant were regularly transferred to the poll tax–paying estates or drafted as soldiers (Freeze 1977). The church lost the last vestiges of its independence and became part of the state bureaucratic machine, a role it has continued to play throughout the imperial, Soviet, and post-Soviet history.

No less consequential was the Petrine reform of the alphabet, with the introduction of the new letters modeled on Latin ones, and the emperor's repeated insistence on the use of spoken Russian in written and published texts. The traditional alphabet and Church Slavonic were kept for the publication of the Holy Scriptures, prayer books, and religious literature, and the Holy Synod retained a monopoly in this sphere. Still, Church Slavonic gradually became marginal in the lives of the cultural elite, and the church as a whole became culturally ghettoized, especially as new generations of nobles were losing direct contact with Orthodox written culture. In the same *Confession*

Fonvizin wrote that, having formed "the strong intention to practice himself in thinking about God," he took with him "the Russian Bible and, in order to better understand it, took the same book in French and German as well" (Fonvizin 1959, 2:100). He needed foreign editions of the scriptures to make the Slavonic text fully intelligible to him.

In 1757, the Russian poet and scientist Mikhail Lomonosov, who was the son of a fisherman and studied at the Slavo-Greco-Latin Academy in Moscow, wrote an article *On the Benefits of the Church Books in Russian Language*. His own mastery of Church Slavonic was superb, and he very much admired the Slavonic idiom. However, he believed that the main importance of Russian Church books was in preserving the old language so it could serve as a rich lexical resource for the high style of the new poetry he tried to create on Russian soil (Lomonosov 1957). For him church books were to be legitimized by their linguistic and cultural value. While the official language of the Orthodox religion was gradually losing its importance in the life of the elite, the great poet was reintroducing it by means of the newly emerging secular literature.

Peter's secularizing aspirations were, however, limited to the upper echelon of society. He wanted to Europeanize the elite, but he needed the church to facilitate contact between the throne and the majority of the population. The imperial manifestos about the succession to the throne, declarations of war and peace, recruitment drafts, and new taxes were to be read to parishioners in churches during Sunday services. Other than the reading aloud of necessary proclamations from the altar, illiterate peasants had no means of learning what the state wanted from them. "The common people [*narod*] having by staunch perseverance preserved the beard and the Russian coat, it was satisfied with its victory and looked indifferently at the German way of life of its shaved boyars," Pushkin wrote in his *Notes on Russian Eighteenth-century History* (Pushkin 1962–1965, 8:125). To a lesser degree, the same could be said about literate tax-paying social estates such as merchants and craftsmen, whose everyday life was still highly traditional and revolved around church service. Thus, Orthodox religiosity became one of the chief factors reinforcing existing social and cultural divisions within society.

The Nobles and the Clerics

The clergy did not have to pay taxes; however, their economic and social status, their cultural traditions, and their beards made them closer to the lower estates than to the higher ones. While eighteenth-century English novels describe situations in which village priests together with local squires constitute the cream of provincial society, in Russia priests had no place in the close circle of the landlord and would most likely be served meals together with the family servants.

Elizaveta Ian'kova (born Rimskaia-Korsakova), who left extensive memoirs about the life of several Russian noble families over five generations, begins her memoirs with a story she obviously considered to be funny. In the middle of the eighteenth century, her grandmother had to host in her house countess Shuvalova, the member of one of the richest and most influential families in the country. She chose to invite the priest's wife for this dinner and bade her to eat whatever she pleased. Deeply impressed by such unexpected generosity, the woman ate the whole fish prepared for dinner before it was served, leaving only the head and tail for the other guests, including the countess. When in utter confusion the priest's wife confessed her faux pas before the laughing guests, another fish was served, much bigger than the previous one. The story turned into a practical joke to entertain the guests at the expense of the priest's wife, who was totally unaware of minimal rules of polite behavior. Ian'kova, who wrote her memoirs a century later in order to celebrate the patriarchal mores of Russian provincial nobility, wrote wryly that "Jesters and fools were common at that time." She recollected that her grandmother usually referred to the woman she invited as "the priest's simpleton" (*dura popova*; Ian'kova 1989, 10–12). This type of social attitude did not change much over a century. When Ian'kova's family in the 1790s moved to their village estate, she was disgusted by the footwear worn by the priest and two other clergymen, which she thought damaged her floors. For a long time, she also could not get rid of the odor they left behind. Ian'kova presented them with a pair of boots each, for which they were immensely grateful (78–79). Ian'kova's family was immensely rich, but one witnesses the same disdain of Orthodox priests even lower on the elite pecking order, including in the countryside.

As usual, the exceptions are especially revealing. Trying to praise the parish priest Illarion, whom he loved from his childhood and with whom he enjoyed conversing, Bolotov found it necessary to stress that he was "completely different in character from other priests and had great superiority over them, as he was much more intelligent and behaved with measure, dignity, and stature" (Bolotov 1870–1873, 2:154). Bolotov recollected that he appreciated talking to

Illarion and was dependent on him for local news, but of course did not need any spiritual guidance from him.

The situation was slightly different in the southern regions of Little Russia (current Ukraine), because Ukrainian Orthodox priests were significantly better educated than their Russian brethren. The poor Ukrainian noble Grigorii Vinsky, who was born in eastern Ukraine and educated in the Orthodox Collegium in Chernihiv and the Mohyla Academy in Kiev but who spent most of his adult life in Russia, believed that the better education of priests in his native land made the people there more religious. According to him, "All Little Russians were strongly attached to religion, as the local priesthood was quite enlightened and they all knew the most important parts of canon law and the church service well" (Vinskii 1914, 24–25). However, speaking about the corporal punishment he had to endure during his school years, even Vinsky could not conceal his disdain of the clergy in general: "Oh, damned priesthood, where have you not made evil?" (8).

This attitude was highly typical of Russian educated society, which looked at the clergy from the other side of the major cultural divide introduced by the Petrine reforms. The white and to a lesser extent black clergy shared with the peasantry the same stigma of being perceived as uncivilized and illiterate, yet without the social and cultural excuses that were magnanimously provided for the peasants. In his poetic *Tale of the Priest and his Workman Balda* (1830), written at the time of his infatuation with Russian folk culture, Pushkin portrayed the peasant servant as highly intelligent, cunning, and cruel and the priest as stupid and greedy. Several years earlier, Pushkin liked to tell a (most likely invented) story about his planned escape from exile on the eve of the Decembrist uprising. According to the poet, he decided to head to St. Petersburg and, without official permission, leave his family estate, where he had been assigned to residence. However, as he encountered a series of bad omens, he was persuaded to turn back. Inevitably, one of these omens was a clergyman whom he had met on the road (Nemirovskii 2004, 189–190). Whether truthful or not, this story says a lot about the place of the clergy in the mindset of the Europeanized elite.

Everyday Religiosity

For the majority of Russian nobles of the period, it would be wrong to deduce from this attitude any sort of freethinking or even religious indifference. No

doubt freethinkers existed, and some members of the elite indulged in impi-
ous, libertine, or even plainly blasphemous behavior. Fonvizin tells in his
memoirs about a society formed in the 1760s around the young playwright
Prince Fedor Kozlovsky, "the main preoccupation of which consisted in blasphemy" (Fonvizin 1959, 94). And Anna Labzina describes in her memoirs her
first husband, Aleksandr Karamyshev, who considered his sexual exploits as
an act of rejection of God (Labzina 2001). However, while not unique, such
practices were hardly widespread and usually encountered universal condemnation. Fonvizin recalls, probably with some benefit of hindsight, that even
in his freethinking youth he was appalled by blasphemy, and Teplov, who
helped him regain firm footing in his Christian beliefs, condemned atheists
and enjoyed joking about priests at the same time.

The overwhelming majority of Russian nobles, except the richest and most
highly placed, were still attached to traditional piety. Despite being intensely
disgusted by her village churchmen, the same Ian'kova still found it necessary
to invite them regularly to her house and could not envisage not performing
essential rituals. She was brought up in a family that had a functioning house
church, which was hardly unique among the richest nobles. She also made
regular pilgrimages to holy places in order to kiss relics (Ian'kova 1989, 250,
252). In the same manner, Bolotov, deeply amazed to find an intelligent priest
who knew how to behave, at the same time was careful to keep icons in every
room of his house. And the first thing he did when he returned from military
service to his country estate was to prostrate himself before the holy images
(Bolotov 1870–1873, 2:239). In general, the memoirs, letters, and diaries of
Russian nobles abound with mentions of habitual religious practices, which
were performed in good faith. Such practices constituted a part of their daily
routine. Indeed, the unfolding of the day was organized by daily services, and
the year cycle revolved around religious holidays and fasts. Church rituals
were especially meaningful; they accompanied the most important events of
life, such as engagement or marriage, as well the births and deaths of loved
ones.

The memoirists, letter writers, and diarists who depicted such practices
in highly emotional terms cannot be described as exceptionally devout. For
example, the diary of Stepan Zhikharev is deservedly popular among historians of early nineteenth-century Russian culture because the diarist was
addicted to the theater. He recorded his impressions about hundreds of performances staged in Moscow and personally knew all actors and actresses.

Needless to say, this type of activity was not approved by the church, but Zhikharev engaged in it without feeling that it compromised his religious zeal. Church services are mentioned in his diary less often than visits to the theater, but from the existing records, it is clear that he attended them regularly and with unwavering religious feelings. In April 1805 Zhikharev writes, "Never in my life will I forget the minute when the bells of Moscow churches announced the arrival of Easter," and he reports feeling incredible "spiritual elevation" during the general prayer. In September of the same year he visited the Trinity monastery in Sergiev Posad and "looked, listened and prayed from [his] full heart" (Zhikharev 1989, 1:71, 122). In the same manner, in the mid-nineteenth century the elderly Anna Pavlova (b. Sokovnina) nostalgically recalled her vigorous youth, when she had enough strength to endure a full night of standing during the night service as well as full days of playing cards (OR RGB, f. 18, k. 30, d. 6, p. 19). Pavlova does not see any contradiction between these occupations, which is especially remarkable as her elder sister Varvara Sokovnina took the veil and became the abbess of a convent (Zorin 2016a).

In a way, everyday piety and the more or less exact observance of church rituals was the default position for a Russian noble of that period. These practices provided the majority of nobles with a sense of stability and continuity in their lives, which sustained the feeling of belonging to the family, thus confirming their noble status. Bolotov specifically mentions that he was happy to pray before the icons that were used by his ancestors (Bolotov 1870–1873, 2:239). Church services gave believers a powerful feeling of returning to their innocent childhood—and at a time when sentimental nostalgia for the lost childhood was growing, this emotion became especially powerful and important. Zhikharev purposefully organized his visit to the Trinity Monastery to follow exactly the pattern established when he was taken there for the first time by his mother (Zhikharev 1989, 1:123).

Even the slightly unintelligible language of the service elicited powerful childhood memories; except for the scions of the richest and most established families, most nobles usually learned to read in Russian from churchmen, using the Psalms, the Orthodox Menalogion compiled by Saint Dmitrii Rostovsky, and other basic Church Slavonic books. All these texts closely associated either positively or negatively with the earliest stage of an educated noble's life, the time they left behind never to come back to. "He is finishing the Prayer book and with God's help will start soon to read the Psalms," sarcastically says one of the characters in Fonvizin's comedy *The Minor*, about a sixteen-year old ignoramus who does not deserve his nobility. Thus, regardless of state-sponsored secularization, everyday religiosity, in particular in the sense of the routine performance of rituals and practices, remained a mainstay of Orthodox piety as well as the underpinning of the sense of being Russian.

Between Pious Peasants and Blasphemous Foreigners

Church rituals gave the nobility the feeling of a sort of spiritual unity with their peasants, which became important in difficult periods. Bolotov recalls the common service celebrated in his village at the time of the plague of 1771, stating that he did not think either he or his peasants ever prayed with such zeal (Bolotov 1870–1873, 3:35–36). Church services became the ideological pillar of national unity during the Napoleonic wars in the first decades of the nineteenth century. Zikharev left a lot of evidence about the outbreaks of general fervor during the campaign of 1806–1807. He witnessed some of them in the theater, when the educated public was hysterically applauding, stamping, and shouting "bravo" at patriotic tirades in Russian tragedies, and others in churches, where the same people were praying together with the members of the lower estates (Zhikharev 1989, 2:54, 92 a.o.). The famous description in *War and Peace* of a service celebrated in the Kremlin in 1812, during which Natasha Rostova suddenly felt her deep inborn Russianness, is based on many memoirs of contemporaries. Among others, Ian'kova, who was already in her forties, writes about the rapture she experienced during this service (Ian'kova, 2001, 121).

For Russian nobles abroad, the Orthodox Church was a symbol of Russianness connecting them with the motherland. The letters of Aleksandr Bulgakov, who served at the Russian embassy in Naples, to his brother Konstantin, performing the same service in Vienna, are full of sarcastic remarks about the rites and beliefs of local Catholics. Bulgakov makes fun of the old superstitions and ignorance he perceives in the vernacular traditions and enjoys writing about the theater, balls, and his infatuations with both aristocratic women and ballet dancers. Still, he is happy to keep Lent, together with other Russians, an opportunity provided to him by the presence of "our priest" on board a Russian military ship (Bulgakovy 2010, 1: 65).

In this context, it is hardly surprising that freethinking was usually perceived as a product of foreign influence, and specifically of reading Voltaire and other French philosophers. Vinsky, who condemned the "ignorant hatred toward all things foreign" that had taken root among Muscovites, at the same time believed that foreign books were to be blamed for the decline in religiosity. According to him, the slackening of faith, for example the failure to keep fasts, which initially was noticeable only in the houses of grandees, now began to spread to lower levels of nobility. He mentions in particular the nonobservance of some rituals and disparaging comments about the clergy and even about church dogmas. Vinsky blames here the close connection with foreigners and the publication of the works of Voltaire and Rousseau in translation (Vinskii 1914, 47). It is worth noting that, like many others, Vinsky is trying to find the causes of his own moral degradation as he was accused of forging official documents and sentenced to exile.

The famous Russian mystic Ivan Lopukhin, whose book *On the Interior Church* is arguably the only philosophical treatise written by an eighteenth-century Russian writer that acquired some international reputation, recalls how in his youth he enjoyed reading Voltaire and Rousseau and even endeavored to translate a digest of Holbach's *Système de la Nature*. Having completed his work, however, he felt "indescribable repentance" and could not sleep until he destroyed his manuscript. He regained his inner balance only after writing a refutation of contemporary materialists and later prepared and commissioned translations of Western didactic and theological literature.

However different their character, education, and background, Lopukhin described his conversion in the same way as Bolotov and Fonvizin. It was quick and sudden, it constituted a return to the basic rules of piety they learned from their childhood, and it did not require any guidance by priests or existing church institutions. In the same manner, as she described in her *Autobiography* the milestones of her decision to join the convent, Varvara Sokovnina never mentioned a single clergyman or Orthodox thinker, preferring to speak about François Fénelon and Edward Young. The only Russian who provided her with some sort of spiritual guidance was the sentimental writer Nikolai Karamzin and his essay *The Village* (Zorin 2016a). Sergei Glinka, who recalls experiencing a kind of moral and spiritual epiphany in church, constitutes a rare exception. His memoirs were written decades later, when the author had already turned into an ardent Russian nationalist and militant traditionalist. Furthermore, in this case, this transformation was caused by a marvelous recital of religious hymns by the composer Dmitrii Bortniansky (Glinka 2004, 56). Even Glinka never claims that a single official churchman played a role, however minor, in his spiritual progress.

A debate among two prominent authors is symptomatic of educated society's views of piety. In 1847, in a different historical epoch, the prominent Russian critic Vissarion Belinsky, in his famous letter to Gogol accused his favorite writer of betraying the cause of progress and civilization. One of the main points of his accusations was Gogol's reverential attitude toward the Orthodox Church:

> Our clergy is held in universal contempt by Russian society and the Russian people. About whom do the Russian people tell dirty stories? About the priest, his wife, his daughter, and his hired man. Is not the Russian priest regarded by everyone as a symbol of gluttony, avarice, sycophancy, bawdiness . . . ? The Russian people . . . have too much common sense, lucidity, and firmness of mind, therein may be the pledge of their future historical greatness. Religious feelings have not taken root even among the Russian clergy, for a few isolated, extraordinary individuals given to a quiet, cold ascetic kind of meditation, prove nothing. (Raeff 1966, 256)

Gogol, who was predictably incensed, drafted an answer, in which he tried to refute this argument, among others:

> What can I say about your harsh remark that the Russian peasant [*muzhik*] is not inclined to religiosity . . . which you make with such self-confidence as if you dealt for a long time with Russian peasants? What can one say, when the answer is given by thousand churches and monasteries covering Russia. They are built not by the gifts of the rich, but by small tributes of the poor. (Gogol' 1978, 7:301–302)

As is typical for the debate between Westernizers and Slavophiles, the notion of "the Russian people" is used here as a rhetorical tool deployed to support ideas and prejudices of the debaters from educated society. Gogol was convinced that Belinsky, the son of a provincial doctor (and the grandson of a priest himself), who had spent all his life working in the capitals as a literary proletarian, could not claim any first-hand knowledge of Russian peasants. Belinsky's perception was evidently shaped by Pushkin's *Tale of the Priest and of His Workman Balda*, to which he refers in his tirade. However, residing in Italy, the son of a petty Ukrainian nobleman, Gogol did not have any more exposure to the "Russian people" than his interlocutor and was reproducing the mythical image of Holy Rus'. It is known that in the eighteenth century the number of churches increased dramatically, and at least in Moscow it is nobles who funded nearly two thirds of the new constructions (Smolich 1994–1997, 1:279). In all likelihood, in cities and towns that unlike Moscow did not have a significant number of rich merchants, the proportion of nobility-financed construction would be even higher. Similarly, the building of village churches was often supported by noble landlords.

Leaving aside the difficult question of popular piety (Zhivov 2010), one can say that the two authors were speaking about different things. For Belinsky, religiosity is defined by the attitude toward the clergy and the moral character of the clergy as an estate, while for Gogol it is equated with spirituality and devotion. Russian educated society, to which both of them belonged, largely preserved its traditional piety, but did not rely for it on the institutionalized church and its members.

Masonic Mysticism and Orthodox Piety

In 1796, shortly after his accession to the throne, Emperor Paul I asked Ivan Lopukhin whether it was appropriate to award orders to the representatives of the higher clergy. Lopukhin answered, "To the true Church of Christ, such honors that feed vanity are, of course, inappropriate. However, the hierarchy of the church is more a political institution, so such distinction could be given to award and encourage its members, who cannot be considered truly spiritual." The emperor fully agreed with this assessment (Lopukhin 1990, 75). To compensate for the absence of spiritual guidance, Lopukhin elaborated his theory of the interior church. According to this doctrine, everyday piety, church attendance, strict observance of rituals, fasts, and rules were essential for any citizen of the state. However, this "visible church" constituted only the outer part of the Christian temple, necessary to prepare the believers for "the most correct and efficacious organization of spiritual exercises for the inner service of God" (Lopukhin 1997, 89). It was the effort to reach the depth of the interior church that constituted the utmost essence of the spiritual life of any true devotee. The outer churches with their rules and customs could be and were different in different jurisdictions, and good citizens were supposed to follow unwaveringly the practices of the church to which they belonged by birth. In contrast to this, the interior church was the same for all Christians and was the only one that gave wisdom, knowledge, and guidance to its members (Lopukhin 1997).

The members of the interior church could be Orthodox, Protestant, or Catholic; however, they would be able to recognize one another and pursue together the quest for the only true enlightenment. Lopukhin wrote that his "gates to wisdom" consisted of *Des erreurs et de la vérité* by Louis-Claude de Saint-Martin, one of the leading esoteric thinkers of the eighteenth century, a Roman Catholic by denomination, and *Vom wahren Christentum* by Iohann Arndt (Lopukhin 1990, 20), a late sixteenth, early seventeenth-century Protestant theologian accused of heresy in his lifetime by his Lutheran peers. Lopukhin's treatise on the interior church was published in 1789 in French and immediately became popular within the European esoteric community. One of the leading European mystics, Karl Eckhartshausen, personally corresponded with the author about it (Faivre 1969, 222–225).

Lopukhin's teachings loosely belonged to Freemasonry, one of the main European spiritual movements of this period, which was rapidly spreading in Russia in the second half of the eighteenth century. Masonic societies appeared in Russia under Peter the Great, but for a long period their membership consisted only of British expatriates in Russia, their immediate environment, and select dignitaries and aristocrats of the highest rank (Collis 2012). In the middle of the century, however, Freemasonry reached wider layers of nobility, initially in the capitals, and eventually in the provinces as well. Due to their exclusive character, Masonic lodges initially served likewise as elite clubs, useful for social networking necessary in a country where patronage constituted the main if not the only route to promotion and enrichment. A lot of early lodges functioned very much like elite clubs with dining, drinking, and card playing. According to later instructions, the members of the brotherhood should beware not to turn their meetings "into feasts to Bacchus as it is common by ill will in many Masonic lodges" (Vernadskii 1999, 109). Still, the esoteric quest and mystical worldview provided by this movement, along with its ideal of moral self-improvement, matched the spiritual aspirations of many Russian nobles, who could not find answers to their questions in the official church. While direct conversion to Catholicism, which in the beginning of the nineteenth century became rather popular in small circles of the highest aristocracy, especially among women, meant becoming a renegade and eventually cutting one's ties with the native country (Tsimbaeva 2008), the lodges provided nobles with a type of alternative spirituality compatible with traditional Orthodoxy.

Theses tendencies were especially pronounced in the activities of the Brotherhood of the Rose Cross active in Moscow in the 1780s and again later, in the early nineteenth century. The Rosicrucians, the most exclusive, hermetic, and esoteric part of the Russian Masonic community, developed a specific ideal of secular sainthood, based on the renunciation of material riches, philanthropy, and the quest for wisdom. Ivan Lopukhin, the scion of one of the wealthiest Russian families, donated all his money as charity to the poor and died on the verge of poverty, burdened with enormous debts. He dedicated his life to service in a court of law, always trying to protect those he deemed innocent and to soften the punishment of the guilty, and arguing against capital and corporal punishment. Semen Gamaleia, another Mason, renounced career and family pursuits and spent his life translating the works of Jacob Boehme, whom the members of the Rosicrucian brotherhood revered as the source of highest wisdom. When he resigned from service, Catherine offered Gamaleia a gift of three hundred serf souls, which he declined, claiming that he struggled to cope even with one soul, his own, and did not need three hundred more. Gamaleia did not have a home and stayed on the estate of Nikolai Novikov, the de facto leader of the Rosicrucian brotherhood. Novikov himself was endowed with the powerful charisma of a religious prophet. When in 1792 he was sentenced to fifteen years of confinement, his doctor, Bagriansky, voluntarily followed him to the cell in Schlüsselberg Fortress. During the famine of 1787, Novikov convinced the rich merchant Grigorii Pokhodiashin to donate the enormous sum of 300,000 rubles for the relief of the hungry. Pokhodiashin spent his entire huge fortune on charity and died in deep poverty under the portrait of Novikov. In short, a form of alternative religious asceticism took hold of a segment of the elite influenced by Masonic literature.

The number of members of the Rosicrucian order was small—there were around forty brothers engaged in practical Masonic works and around eighty preparing for such practice in the so-called "theoretical degree of Solomon sciences" (see Kondakov 2012, 309–313). And yet its influence was considerable. The order established a significant level of control over two main Moscow educational institutions—Moscow University and the Noble Pension at Moscow University. It also ran charity schools for the children of poor nobles. Novikov leased the letterpress of Moscow University and embarked on a publishing venture that dramatically increased the number of books in print that were available in the remote provinces. He and his associates also launched several periodicals, including the first Russian magazine for children. He established charitable hospitals and grain warehouses for the hungry. According to the doctrine of the interior church, the publishing activities of the Society had three layers: the university press specialized in books for the general public; the press of Ivan Lopukhin published books for Freemasons generally; and the secret press in Novikov's house—for the select few belonging to the Rosicrucian order. Andrei Bolotov, who was deeply suspicious of Freemasons and categorically rejected Novikov's efforts to enlist him in the Masonic society, still gladly cooperated with him in the publication of his agricultural magazine. The commercial terms proposed by Novikov were much more beneficial to Bolotov than anything he could aspire to from his competitors (Bolotov 1870–1873, 3:859). All these activities enabled Rosicrucians to involve in their activities many people who never belonged to the lodges.

Not surprisingly, Catherine, who saw Freemasons as Prussian agents and suspected them of trying to recruit the heir to the throne (the future Paul I), decided to put an end to these activities and explicitly forbade all secret meetings. In 1785, deeply suspicious of Masonic mysticism and especially of its activist variety practiced by the Moscow Rosicrucian brotherhood, Catherine ordered the Moscow city commander, Count Bruce, and Moscow's Archbishop Platon Levshin to inspect the print production of the Freemason presses led by Novikov. The results of this inspection proved relatively benign—only six books out of several hundred titles Novikov edited were found to violate the monopoly of the Synod for religious literature. Dissatisfied with such lenience, the empress not only launched a campaign against Freemasons by writing a cycle of comedies ridiculing them, but also ordered the university authorities not to extend Novikov's lease of the press when it expired in 1789. Other publishing enterprises of Moscow Rosicrucians also had to close during the anti-Masonic campaign pursued by the empress, which resulted in the arrest of Novikov and the eventual closure of his publishing venture.

Nearly at the same time, the German directors of the Rosicrucian order decreed a "syllanum"—that is, temporarily suspended the activities of the order in Russia. Notwithstanding this double prohibition, Moscow Rosicrucians continued the meetings of the higher degrees and of the preparatory theoretical degree. They valued their quest for truth so much and were so confident of their loyalty to the throne and to the Orthodox Church that they decided to defy both the laws of the country they lived in and the discipline of the order to which they belonged. During the investigation, Lopukhin and Novikov based the strategy of their defense on the innocence of their hearts and purity of their intentions.

The Charismatic Leaders of the Church

Writing about the religious indifference and ignorance of the Russian clergy, Belinsky singled out "a few isolated and exceptional personalities distinguished for such cold ascetic contemplation." While the overwhelming majority of Russian clergymen were mostly held in contempt or at best condescendingly accepted by the noble elite, a few spiritual authorities of the church were deeply esteemed and had a significant following among the nobility. Bishop Tikhon Zadonsky of Voronezh maintained an extensive correspondence with dozens of mostly nobles, providing them with spiritual advice and guidance (Kirichenko 2002), and Moscow Metropolitan Platon (Levshin), who earlier provided religious education to the heir to the throne, Grand Duke Paul, was highly revered by the Moscow public, including the members of aristocratic families (Papmehl 1983; Wirtschafter 2013). Arguably, the cleric who occupied the most prominent place in the spiritual life of the educated part of society was Archimandrite and later Metropolitan Filaret, the disciple of Platon, who once said about the young preacher: "I write like a human being and he writes like an angel" (Ponomarev 1868, 518). Shortly before Napoleon's invasion of Russia, Filaret became close to Prince Aleksandr Golitsyn, the personal friend of Emperor Alexander, who coordinated the religious policies of the empire. By that time Golitsyn had converted from a Voltairian atheist into a fervent believer. During the war he built a house church in his St. Petersburg palace, and Filaret's sermons there attracted the empire's highest dignitaries and became one of the ideological pillars of Russian foreign policy. Later, in the reign of Nicholas I, Filaret managed to keep some sort of moral independence as Moscow metropolitan, and in 1861 he drafted the imperial manifesto about the abolition of serfdom.

Needless to say, these and some other influential religious figures belonged to the highest echelons of the Russian Church. The cultural, educational, and social gap between, on the one side, this small group of metropolitans, bishops of large provinces, and members of the Holy Synod and, on the other, lower church officials was immense. In many ways the elite of the church was closer to the elite of the nobility and state bureaucracy than to the lower ranks of their own estate. In 1763, during the secularization of monastic property, only one of the members of the Holy Synod, Metropolitan Arsenii Matseevich, dared to voice the general dissatisfaction of the rank-and-file clergy. He was immediately demoted by his peers in the Synod to the status of an ordinary monk and subsequently defrocked and sent to prison.

What is more, some spiritual leaders of the Russian Church were also inspired by European mysticism, which made their teachings attractive to religiously inclined nobles. Tikhon Zadonsky was strongly influenced by German pietists and even more so by Arndt's book *On True Christianity*, which had reoriented Lopukhin from French materialism toward Freemasonry. In turn, Lopukhin revered Tikhon, whose portrait he kept on his estate in Savinskoe together with the portraits and busts of Boehme, Fénelon, Eckartshausen, and Rousseau. While some conservative Russians viewed Rousseau as a dangerous freethinker, Lopukhin valued him as a powerful opponent of Voltaire and the Encyclopedists.

There were strong spiritual affinities between Rosicrucians and the elite prelates in the capitals. When Catherine in the beginning of her campaign against Moscow Rosicrucians instructed Platon to assess Novikov's Christianity, he gave a glowing review. Platon wrote to the empress that he could only pray that not only in Moscow "but in the whole world there would be more such Christians as Novikov" (Longinov 1867, 262). A year later, an infuriated Catherine made Platon and all the members of the Holy Synod attend the performance of her comedy directed against the Freemasons, during which the highest ranking church officials had "to laugh like madmen and applaud as loudly as they could" (Ekaterina II 1878, 374). Evidently, the leaders of the Russian Church wanted so much to show their loyalty to the monarch that they failed to behave with the "measure, dignity and stature" appreciated by Bolotov in a village priest. After the death of the empress, once the leading Rosicrucians were again in favor, Platon resumed his friendly relations with them and enjoyed spending time with Lopukhin and Ivan Turgenev. Platon and the mystics were attracted to each other by the power of their spiritual quest, which put them apart both from the majority of educated nobles and the majority of the clergy.

Filaret's case was especially revealing. In his sermon at the consecration ceremony of Prince Golitsyn's house church, he preached that the "curiosity to see the consecration of the visible temple would be in vain if at the same moment we did not think about the consecration of our inner, invisible temple" (Filaret 1812, 2–3). The connection with Lopukhin's ideas about the interior church was so evident that later Filaret had to exclude this sermon from his collected works. However, in 1812, the select audience was so impressed by the sermon that, in violation of church traditions, Filaret had to repeat it.

The success of the sermon was due to the fact that it ideally expressed the new vision of Alexander's foreign and religious policy. After his conversion, Golitsyn, the ober-procurator of the Holy Synod, who was at the time the emperor's spiritual mentor, had become not so much a practitioner of traditional Orthodoxy as a sort of ecumenical mystic. Filaret, the most popular and influential Russian cleric of the period, shared his vision and aspirations. They both took leading positions in the Russian Bible Society, which was tasked with translating the Holy Scriptures into the vernacular languages of the empire, bringing it closer to the literate population. Alexander Etkind and, more recently, Elena Vishlenkova have interpreted the Protestant origins of the Russian Bible Society patronized by Alexander as a symptom of the august intentions to convert Russia to some form of Evangelical Protestantism (Etkind 1996, Vishlenkova 2002). However, such presumed plans would not only have been impractical; they directly contradicted the letter and spirit of the doctrine of the interior church that inspired the emperor and his advisers. According to Lopukhin and his European teachers and peers, changing the religious affiliation one was born into was useless and even dangerous, as the strict observance of the outer rites was the only path that could eventually lead the believer into the inner temple. At the same time those who have already joined this sacred spiritual circle were to look for their brethren among members of the other Christian denominations. In this spirit, after the victory over Napoleon, Alexander concluded the so-called Holy Alliance, aiming to unite the Orthodox emperor of Russia, the Lutheran king of Prussia and the Catholic emperor of Austria in a joint triumvirate of Christian rulers. None of them, of course, was ever expected to change his original religious affiliation.

Paradoxically, the attitude of mystics toward the church of their native country was strikingly similar to the attitude of the majority of the profoundly secularized educated nobility. Orthodox rites, practices, and traditions were meticulously followed and respected, as they provided the daily and yearly routines necessary for personal integrity, which also allowed the French-speaking and European-looking elite to feel their Russianness. However, both the church as an institution and its clergy, with the exception of several eminent personalities, were regarded with a mixture of condescension and contempt. The Russian elite overwhelmingly considered itself Orthodox, but saw Orthodoxy as something distinctly inferior to either the secular culture of contemporary Europe or Western esotericism.

These attitudes took final shape after Alexander I renounced ecumenical mysticism as an official policy in 1824, after the downfall of Golitsyn, and even more explicitly in the 1830s, when under Nicholas I, the doctrine of Orthodoxy-Autocracy-Nationality was established as an official ideology. Within this ideological framework, Orthodoxy was proclaimed as one of the main pillars of the empire, but it was understood instrumentally as a national religion preserving historical continuity and old traditions. The founder of the doctrine, the Minister of National Education Count Sergei Uvarov, was entirely francophone and also strongly influenced by German romantic nationalism. As appropriate for a person of his rank and stature, he strongly despised the Russian clergy responsible for the dissemination and maintenance of national religion. One of his French witticisms about the clergy was especially popular among St. Petersburg high society. According to Uvarov, "this caste is like a sheet of paper thrown on the ground—however much it is trampled, one is unable to crush it" (Buturlin 1901, 411). This officialization of the historical church led to a final loss of prestige in the eyes of the nobility and the emerging intelligentsia educated in the new secular schools and universities, and even in the church seminaries.

It is clear that already by mid-eighteenth century, the ruler and the government were aware of the moral and spiritual failings of the church, in particular its inability to guide the moral development of the elite. Instead of seeking to reform the church, which, as stated above, was needed for communication with the lower classes, Catherine shifted responsibility for forging the moral and spiritual character of the elite to new institutions, created and controlled by the state, at least in their initial stages. As we will argue in the next chapter, entirely new educational institutions were created with the explicit aim of bringing about a fundamental transformation of the moral makeup of the elite, while a secular literature, as we will see in the subsequent chapter, was deployed to correct the foibles and inflect the manners of the reading public, a broader segment of the nobility. In both instances, the elite eventually succeeded in either sidestepping or appropriating these institutions for itself, thus asserting its independence from government control. In the nineteenth century, the role of spiritual leader guiding the development of the nation and capable of challenging the authority of the omnipotent state passed to literature.

5

WRITING ON THE TABULA RASA

Educational Theories and Practices

Russian educational policies during the long eighteenth century were based on a shared belief among officials that the state and not the family should be responsible for the education of children. Thus, the existing scholarship in the field is mostly focused on the institutional history of Russian education, covered in several seminal works (Black 1979; Dixon 1999, 150–155; de Madariaga 1979). This chapter will tell the story of *Bildung*, the project of a radical regeneration of the nation inherent in the educational practices of the period, and will highlight their intended and unintended consequences.

We will show that the rapid proliferation of educational institutions and the improvement of educational standards brought forth tensions between utopian aspirations and limited resources, between universalist and socially distinct paradigms, as well as between the need to create a fully Europeanized elite and the fear of foreign influence. The nobles interiorized these goals, as the possibility of enhancing the social status and career prospects of their off-spring increasingly depended on their educational achievements, while at the same time wishing to preserve control over the upbringing of their children and therefore resisting the ambitions of the state to direct the education of the elite.

The idea of Russians being completely remade by a reforming tsar had already emerged during Peter's reign and had rapidly become a rhetorical cliché (see Rogov 2006). According to Chancellor Gavriil Golovkin, this is the period when Russia was "brought from nonexistence into existence." Prince Antioch Kantemir, one of the founders of new Russian poetry, wrote that Peter's decrees "suddenly made us a new nation." However, neither Peter nor his immediate successors regarded institutions of formal education as important tools in shaping future Russians. As he prepared his subjects for their new duties, Peter focused on their skills, to the extent of prohibiting illiterate nobles from marrying, as well as on outside appearance, customs, and manners. He needed rapid results and preferred to send a select few to be educated abroad. The schools that rapidly spread during Peter's reign were mostly designed to fill specific gaps in practical skills in the military sphere and were, as a rule, initiated not by the monarch or his close associates, but by "administrative entreprisers," as Igor Fedyukin aptly called them (Fedyukin 2017a). These self-declared educationalists were mostly of foreign origin and tried to establish their credentials with the Russian court by initiating new educational establishments.

During Peter's reign and immediately afterward, the noble elites were not too interested in sending their children to schools either, strongly preferring home schooling. This situation began to change with the creation of the Cadet Corps in 1731. The new school exclusively accepted noble children, who underwent preparation for a military career appropriate to their social estate and were awarded ranks at the completion of their studies. Even while the number of young people who could benefit from the new opportunities was limited, the corps gradually evolved into one of the major cultural institutions of the new capital. It hosted the first Russian amateur theater, which opened in 1749 with the performance of the tragedy *Khorev*, written by Alexander Sumarokov, himself a graduate of the school. The play was such a success that Empress Elizabeth ordered it to be repeated at court. In 1757 the Corps was given a license to open a press to print manuals, textbooks, and didactic materials, but the establishment rapidly became one of the most important venues for the publication of all sorts of books, including translated novels, dramas, and opera libretti (for a catalogue, see Shamrai 1940, 311–329). Failing to attract many children from the upper echelons of the Russian elite (Rjéoutski 2013), the Cadet Corps provided unique promotion perspectives and social connections for the offspring of the lower and middle nobility, thus enhancing the prestige of formal education, all the more so in that it had also become a significant cultural institution.

Building a "New Race"

It was the Manifesto on the Freedom of Nobility, issued in 1762, that established a clear connection between noble privileges and formal education. While granting the noble elite freedom not to serve and to travel abroad, the manifesto made education in the Noble Cadet Corps obligatory for all male nobles coming from families possessing less than one thousand souls (PSZ 1830, vol. 15, no. 11444, p. 912–915). This clause demonstrated the growing perception of the throne that only truly educated nobles could have the necessary zeal for service to the monarchy, but it was never implemented, as the Cadet Corps were simply not able to admit such a mass of pupils. As Simon Dixon has noted, even in 1825, after more than a century of significant educational progress, more "than four fifths of Alexander's state council had no formal education" (Dixon 1999, 153) and were still schooled at home according to the financial circumstances and the perceived needs of the family.

Catherine the Great initiated a policy of massive education of the Russian elite on an unprecedented scale, by far surpassing even the aspirations of Peter the Great, whose steps she claimed to follow. Unlike most of her predecessors, the new empress regarded education not only and not primarily as a tool for preparing her subjects for state service, but as a way toward the moral and social regeneration of the whole country and primarily of the nobility. Early in her reign, she convened a legislative commission to grant new laws for Russia based on her famous *Instruction*. The failure of this enterprise supported her conviction that "laws are useless if the morals are corrupt," as she stated in one of the first issues of her didactic magazine, *Vsiakaia Vsiachina* (*All Sorts of Things*; Vsiakaia 1769, 9).

Across Europe, in the eighteenth century education had become a central concern. Locke's notion of the *tabula rasa* of the human mind and his ideas about human perfectibility, expressed in his "Some Thoughts Concerning

Education" (1693), raised the stakes as they implied that one could fashion the human mind as one wished. One cannot overstate the influence of Rousseau's *Emile* (1762), in which the author laid out his views on raising a "natural" man and promoted nondisciplinarian pedagogical methods. The second half of the eighteenth century saw a flowering of treatises on education, and many Russian writers intervened on this subject.

Catherine entrusted the development of a national educational system to the elderly grandee Ivan Betskoi, the illegitimate son of Prince Ivan Trubetskoi. Betskoi traveled extensively in Europe and studied the educational practices accepted in major European countries. In particular, he tried to adapt Locke's and Rousseau's pedagogical ideas to Russian soil. He wrote new statutes for all educational institutions—some yet to be inaugurated, others, like the Cadets Corps, to be completely reorganized. In March 1764, Catherine confirmed Betskoi's *General Guidance for the Education of Youth of Both Sexes*, in which he envisaged a total change of the nature of Russians. He believed that Russia "needs to overcome the prejudice of centuries and give a new upbringing and a new existence to the nation" and that there is only "one remedy remaining" to achieve this goal:

> to produce first by means of *education* a *new race*, so to say, or *new fathers and mothers*, who would be able to put in the hearts of their children the same correct and sound rules which they themselves had received, so their children would pass them on further, and so they will go from generation to generation to future centuries. (Maikov 1904, Appendix, 8)

This change of goals of educational institutions had practical consequences. First, it implied firm age requirements: a child accepted to one of the new schools had to be no older than five or six years old and was to be kept there until seventeen for girls and twenty for boys. Betskoi thought that it would be "unreasonable to believe" that after that age it would be possible to correct morals that are already corrupt. Secondly, new schools were to function as boarding schools. In them children were to be subject to complete isolation, being forbidden to go home for vacation, and kept away even from closest relatives, who were allowed to visit pupils only during specially assigned days and in the presence of their tutors (Maikov 1904, Appendix, 7–8).

This "golden cage" regime was based on a deeply pessimistic assessment of the moral condition of the current Russian elite, matched by an equally radical optimism about human nature in general. This perception shows the influence of Locke's ideas of the child as a *tabula rasa*. Even more important to Betskoi was the Rousseauistic utopia of total regeneration of humankind through education, to which he gave a specifically Russian twist. According to Timothy O'Hagan, Rousseau believed that "public institutions of schools and colleges were irredeemably corrupted" and that "the only solution was to withdraw both pupil and teacher from society, and conduct the experiment in isolation from it," namely within the family (O'Hagan 2007, 56).

Betskoi's logic was equally radical, but in a way opposite. He wanted not to supplement or replace bad public institutions by reformed family practices, but in the first instance to break the tradition of dysfunctional home education by creating a network of closed schools. He envisaged creating a new generation of fathers and mothers, who would emerge from these schools and would infuse true values in the souls of their future children. Current nobles were characterized by Betskoi as "beastly and furious." We find an echo of this strategy in Fonvizin's play *The Minor*, in which Sophia, who educated herself reading Fénelon, had literally to be saved by force from her distant relatives, whose surname, Skotinin, means "beastly." The utopian scope of Betskoi's project went far beyond the imagination of Rousseau or other European thinkers, who could not rely on the support of an absolute monarch for the implementation of their ideas. Russia was also in a better position to launch such a visionary project, because its new schools were to be built from scratch.

The Cadet Corps, the only existing noble educational institution, was also put under Betskoi's supervision. By dramatically lowering the age of admission, Betskoi shifted the focus from educating officers to the total moral and spiritual reformation of the noble elite. The parents of enrolled boys were to sign a pledge that they were not going to interfere in the educational process. During her visit to Smolensk, Catherine agreed to enlist in the Cadet Corps the three sons of the local landowner Nikolai Glinka. Having later heard from him that his wife had "wept and pleaded him to keep one of the sons for herself," the empress answered with "tender smile": "Am I not a mother for them?" and generously deigned to accept Glinka's nephew as a substitute for one of the sons. After several years in the Corps, when their father came on a visit, the Glinka brothers recognized him only with considerable difficulty (Glinka 2004, 44, 73).

Bonds of kinship were to be replaced by symbolic adoption into the extended family of the monarch, in keeping with the personalistic mode of governance Catherine espoused. The younger boys studying in the Cadet Corps were taken to court weekly to play with the grandsons of the empress, Grand Dukes Alexander and Konstantin (Glinka 2004, 52). This type of upbringing was intended to afford the young students the sense of belonging to the highest echelons of power, to shape their identity, and to structure their loyalties.

Living in this kind of hothouse could not fail to produce a specific mindset among the pupils, notably a combination of idealism and practical inability. The romantic writer Sergei Glinka, one of Nikolai Glinka's sons, who spent twelve years in the Cadet Corps, devoted numerous pages of his memoirs to a eulogy to Betskoi's virtues and noble heart. Still, he admitted that as an "old eighteenth-century cadet" he "started to think about what life looks like only at the sunset of [his] life." "We all lived without knowing what it was," he wrote (Glinka 2004, 53). He recounted life stories of the radical idealism of the cadets with a characteristic mixture of pride and dismay. According to Glinka, one of them, trying to act like an ancient Roman, went to visit his sick brother walking over a frozen river without proper clothes. Having predictably fallen ill, he made his way back in time for his turn of duty but eventually died from fever, accompanied by the universal lament of his peers (78). Whether accurate or not, Glinka tells this story without condemning the reckless behavior of the cadet, who risked his life for no obvious reason. On the contrary, his narrative reveals reverence and admiration.

The transformational nature of Betskoi's projects is especially evident in his persistent interest in female education. As long as the main goal was to provide pupils with skills necessary for service, the state could limit its efforts to male schools, but when the focus shifted to reforming human nature, educating girls became equally important, if not more so. As the life mission of a nobleman was to enlist in military service, usually far from his estate and his family, it was a wife's duty to bring up children and to plant the first seeds of virtue in their souls.

One of the first establishments founded by Betskoi was the Imperial Educational Society for Noble Girls, later known as the Smolny Institute, which was founded in 1764 immediately after the publication of the *General Guidance for the Education of Youth of Both Sexes*. Smolny was modeled after the famous Saint-Cyr, a school for the girls of French noble families opened at the end of the reign of Louis XIV according to the recommendations of François de Fénelon (see Cherepnin 1915). The institute was located outside

St. Petersburg, separate from the court but not far from the city borders, so that the empress, the members of the august family, and the grandees, especially Betskoi himself, could regularly visit the girls, follow their success, and attend their examinations and performances.

The ties between the imperial palace and the Smolny Institute were exceptionally close. Catherine exchanged letters with Aleksandra Levshina, who was supposed to circulate imperial messages among the other girls. Glafira Alymova, another Smolny pupil, wrote that Natal'ia Alekseevna, the first wife of heir to the throne Grand Duke Paul, became her best friend and regularly visited her in the institute. At the first graduation ceremony in 1776, the best pupils of the first intake were awarded a Gold Medal of the First Degree and the Golden Monogram of Catherine the Great and were assigned the position of lady-in-waiting at court.

The isolation of the girls from their families was even more severe than that of their male peers at the Cadet Corps. The regulations of the Educational Society openly stated that "the parents of the girls and their other relatives are free from any concern about them from the moment of their admission until graduation" (Betskoi 1774, 9).

In 1780 Levshina, a graduate of the first intake of the Smolny Institute, pleaded Catherine for permission to marry. In her letter she wrote that accepting her to the institute, the empress had "benevolently" ordered her uncle and her father to forget they have a niece and a daughter (Maikov 1896, 347).

Alymova's memoirs indicate that she clearly saw the connection between the chosen educational method and the intention to create people having "characters of their own"—that is, following not the customs and traditions of their families and social milieu, but rules and direction given in their youth:

> I shall try to demonstrate the wisdom of the empress. She placed the institute outside the city to keep the girls from the world until fully developed reason and moral principles deeply rooted in their hearts would be able to protect them from bad examples. Like many others, I was endowed by nature with good inclinations but their sound development was solely the result of education. Nothing can be firm in high society, customs everywhere prevail over rules. One meets there only monkeys and parrots, but you will not find original characters that make one person different from another in the same way their faces do not look alike. However, the girls educated in our institute stand out from this uniformity, each one had a character of her own. Their originality, so often mocked

by many, had a very good side. They made excellent wives. They had to struggle against existing prejudices about their education, which they met even in their own families, and against general ill will. In most cases, they were acting honestly and defended their principles. Very few deviated from the direction given to them. (Rzhevskaia 1871, 5–6)

Predictably, the relations between the young women formed in the institute and high society were fraught. Alymova's own spectacular biography shows an impressive example of the difficult negotiations required between the rules her upbringing instilled in her and court life. For a quarter of a century she managed to navigate her way in the tense environment of the court of Grand Duke Paul, preserving his trust without jeopardizing her relations with his wife, who suspected her of romantic relations with the grand duke. After the death of her husband in 1804, she overcame the resistance of her family, society, and the court and married a man of common origin who was also significantly younger. Alymova complained about the hostility with which *smolianki*, the graduates of the institute, were treated in high society.

There is a lot of evidence to substantiate this claim. Several sources quote a popular poem circulating in St. Petersburg proclaiming that Betskoi had grown and brought into society "a hundred silly chickens" (Glinka 2004, 47). However, opposite views were also often expressed. Prince Dolgorukov, the scion of one of the most aristocratic Russian families, wrote in his memoirs that having become used to dealing with Smolny graduates, he

> was charmed by their upbringing, simpleheartedness, the virtuous inclinations of their souls, and their common sense. They did not use pretense or deceit, were always open with everyone and never showed any coquetry in their behavior. When I was thinking about marriage, I always wanted to choose a graduate of Smolny monastery, who would be poor and not of an aristocratic lineage. It seemed to me that there could be nothing more unpleasant than to enter a major house through your wife. (Dolgorukov 2004, 1:122)

Dolgorukov married poor *smolianki* twice. In order to realize his dream and marry his first wife, Evgeniia Smirnaia, he had to overcome the considerable resistance of his parents, who were finally swayed by the charm of innocence and sincerity of their would-be daughter-in-law. Likewise, Sergei Glinka tells in his memoirs the story of one of the graduates of the institute. Before making family visits to a highly important female relative, she was told by her mother all sorts of nasty things about the society lady, to the extent that upon arrival, she refused to greet such a dishonorable person (Glinka 2004, 47). This story looks very much like a literary anecdote, but it clearly reflects the reputation of Smolny alumnae as too good for this world. Some of the contemporaries regarded this quality as a sign of stupidity, others, like Dolgorukov, as purity of heart, but both sides were able to understand Betskoi's intentions and believed that he had achieved his goals.

For Rousseau, the necessity to reform the educational system derived from the tectonic shifts in the social environment that were severing the link between the circumstances of one's birth and one's future life. All people, notwithstanding the estate to which they belonged, should be educated as universal human beings and prepared for unexpected changes in their life trajectories. Rousseau took social mobility as a given. Betskoi, on the contrary, wanted to reinforce the existing social structure through education. Apart from the institutions for nobles, he founded a Commercial School and a School for Commoner Girls (*meshchanskie devushki*), giving each estate a distinctive education. And the institutions he inaugurated for the education of the nobility represented a compromise between the radical vision of a new universal human being and the ideal of the accomplished courtier. Betskoi instructed his associates about the age when universal natural education had to give way to teaching appropriate manners and the child ceased to belong to nature, instead becoming a member of polite society:

> We can agree that boys until the age of 15 and girls until the age of 12 would be regarded as children and allowed to run even barefooted— they should be only instructed to maintain cleanliness appropriate for their health. However, after that age, from the very morning and until going to bed, they should be dressed properly, so that they acquire habits necessary for public life that would serve them after graduation. (RGIA F. 759, inv. 10, f. 349, 16ob.–17)

In short, notwithstanding its sources in the educational theories of Locke and Rousseau, the education dispensed in the new institutions designed by Betskoi aimed to forge socially differentiated types of behavior and thus to reinforce the existing social structure, while transforming the moral character of the subjects of the Russian empire.

Foreign Educators and Patriotic Education

The total isolation of the pupils implied that an enormous responsibility lay upon the shoulders of their teachers. According to Betskoi, the initial choice of "teachers and especially of the heads of the schools" determined the future of the "first generation of the new race" (Betskoi 1774, 13). In the land of his "beastly and furious" contemporaries, it was all but impossible to find people who deserved such a task—Betskoi had not only to rely on Western educational ideas and institutional patterns, but also on imported cadres. Madame Sophie de Lafont, a French Huguenot, was put in charge of the Smolny Institute for thirty years. According to Alymova, she was "a mother, a guide, a friend, and a patron" for the girls, who strove to follow her "advice and instructions" (Rzhevskaia 1871, 13–14).

In the Cadet Corps the situation was in many ways similar. Patriotic upbringing was especially important in an institution that was supposed to produce the military leadership of the country. Nevertheless, Betskoi started his reforms of the Corps by appointing as director the naturalized Greek General Purpur, who was later replaced by the naturalized Scot Count Balmain. The golden days of the school started with the appointment of Count Anhalt, who had previously served in the armies of Prussia and Saxony. Anhalt, who combined a characteristic veneration for Roman virtues with sentimental inclinations, became the director in 1786, at a time when Betskoi was already out of favor, but in his memoirs Glinka clearly presents his tenure as a direct continuation of Betskoi's tradition.

The governors who directed the students' reading and their instructors in military training were also French. French, and the teaching of foreign languages in general, were at the center of the curriculum. French and German were considered indispensable languages, and Latin, English, or Italian could also be taught. The cadets enacted roles in French tragedies and read French newspapers. However, this francophone education was meant to instill patriotic feelings in the hearts of the cadets. Anhalt deeply admired Frederick the Great, the Prussian king against whom Russia fought in the Seven Years' War, yet at the same time he gave the students their first ideas and impressions of Russian greatness with examples from Russian history, as well as instilling in them the practice of courtesy toward the Russian people, their social inferiors. Glinka wrote:

Hardly any foreigner traveled across Russia more than he did. Russian history was still in its infancy among us and we could get some information about the Russian nation from the examples and the words of count Anhalt. He loved and respected the Russian people very much and always praised their clever and quick understanding and brave spirit. Our guards in the dorms, classes, and entertainment halls were retired Russian sub-officers, and every day we saw how charitably the count treated them. (Glinka 2004, 80)

Contrary to the usual accusations against the corps that its graduates were better versed in writing poetry and acting on the stage than in military skills, a significant number of its alumni became heroes during the Napoleonic wars (Lappo-Danilevskii 1904, 58). The Cadet Corps, with its francophony and reverence for ancient heroic virtues, became a cradle for the enhancement of patriotic ideals.

It is only during the Napoleonic wars that linguistic nationalism became strongly associated with patriotic feelings. Aleksandr Shishkov vociferously condemned the francophony of the Russian nobility, turning it into a sort of political accusation. Glinka himself renounced his former European aspirations and became one of the proponents of fervent Russian romantic nationalism, agitating in 1812 on the streets of Moscow against the French. Yet among the educated elite, his views remained fairly marginal and quickly lost steam once the initial patriotic mobilization in the wake of Napoleon's invasion abated. The elite continued to be fully conversant in French, which did not prevent it from developing equal proficiency in Russian, while different generations of writers, from Nikolai Karamzin to Alexander Pushkin, proceeded to equip the Russian language with the same functional versatility that the French language already had.

Breaking the Regime of Isolation

The Smolny Institute and the Cadet Corps could afford to be entirely closed off from everyday life, because they accepted limited numbers of pupils and dispensed an emphatically elite education. The country also needed educational institutions that catered to a broader segment of the population. Moscow University, founded in 1755 by Ivan Shuvalov, the favorite of Empress Elizabeth and a major patron of many cultural and educational projects, immediately became and still remains the leading educational institution in Russia. Moscow had a better chance of attracting students than the new capital, as it was significantly more populated and located closer to the major provincial cities possessing significant noble communities. As the graduates of the Cadet Corps and other military schools were immediately enlisted in the army and were reluctant to continue their education at the university, two gymnasia (secondary schools), one for nobles and another for commoners, were opened to prepare young people for university studies. The Russian poet and scientist Mikhail Lomonosov, who served as an expert for Shuvalov, said that "a university without gymnasium is the same thing as a field without seeds" (Lomonosov 1957, 10:508). An additional gymnasium was also opened in 1758 in Kazan. Unlike the Moscow ones it lasted only for a year, but it nevertheless played an important role in the history of Russian literature, as Gavrila Derzhavin studied there, and the year he passed in the gymnasium significantly influenced his education and career.

To lure the nobles into sending their sons to the gymnasium, they had to be convinced that their offspring would be treated in a special way. By no means was their life supposed to be lavish or even minimally comfortable, but it had to be different from the lifestyle of the commoners. As the university did not have the facilities to maintain a different curriculum for noble pupils, apart from teaching them basic military skills, dancing, and French, the distinction was established through everyday practices. The nobles wore a special uniform, their desks were covered with cloth, and they ate from faience with silver utensils. Even their breakfast buns were prepared from different grain.

However, the effect of these measures was not sufficient to attract nobles, and as a result, an exclusive Moscow Noble Boarding School was inaugurated in 1778. Even here the budget was significantly lower than in Petersburg schools, so the everyday life of the students was somewhat ascetic (Dmitriev 1998, 72–73), but the school rapidly acquired necessary status. In the 1760s, Shuvalov needed to pressure Prince Mikhail Dolgorukov to convince him to enlist his son Ivan in the university gymnasium instead of sending him abroad; in contrast, in the 1790s and 1800s, Ivan Dolgorukov readily put all his three sons in the Noble Boarding School (Dolgorukov 2004, 37, 631).

We have only anecdotal evidence about the level of education in these schools. The famous Russian playwright Denis Fonvizin, who entered the gymnasium immediately after its foundation, recalled in his memoirs that during the grammar examination, the teacher gave students helpful prompts about conjugation and declination by pointing to the buttons on his camisole and caftan. At his geography exam, Fonvizin was awarded the highest mark by honestly admitting his absolute ignorance. The memoirist wryly commented that his answer could be praised "in the class of moral philosophy, but not of geography" (Fonvizin 1959, 2:88). Due to his satirical temperament, the memoirist might well have embroidered upon the reality. The education he received served him well: after finishing the gymnasium and studying for a year at the university, he embarked on an exceptionally successful career. In his famous comedy *The Minor*, he showed himself to be an ardent opponent of home schooling.

Both the Noble Boarding School and the gymnasium grew rapidly. The majority of nobles were much more interested in the lower levels of education, seen as necessary preparation for civil and military service, than in the more specialized knowledge taught at the university. While the number of university students nearly quadrupled between 1760 and 1787, from 30 to 118, the number of pupils of the secondary schools increased more than twelve-fold—from 82 to 1,010 (Liubzhin 2000, 38). There is no exact data about the social origins of these students, but there is very little doubt that if we exclude commoners from the count, the difference in the dynamics of growth of the gymnasium and the university would be even more striking.

Moscow University was more socially diverse than the Cadet Corps, and the lifestyle of students was significantly less secluded. The student body consisted not only of boarders who were supported by the University, but also of self-paying students and free auditors who lived at home or rented apartments, but attended classes. The public resonance of the university was much more far-reaching than that of the educational establishments located in the imperial capital. While life in St. Petersburg was dominated by the court, in Moscow the university played a role neither the Cadet Corps nor the Smolny Institute could aspire to. Some of the university courses were open to the public, and one of the students later wrote disapprovingly in his memoirs that the appearance of ladies distracted young people from their studies (Timkovskii 1874, 24).

The university aimed to prepare students for both military and civil service, but its success in the latter was mixed. Military ranks continued to constitute the main goal of the young men belonging to the elite, which left the civil service, with the exception of the diplomatic corps, to uneducated representatives of lower estates. The best university students were promoted to the first officer rank, and this promotion constituted their main incentive. Il'ia Timkovsky drew a slightly ironic portrait of the motivation of his classmates:

> Look at this young man during the day of the university annual award ceremony. With what joyous agitation does he take the little sword from the hands of his learned master. He is already an officer—an important person in our geographic realm. He is close to adulthood and look how his heart is beating now. (Timkovskii 1874, 24)

Timkovsky came from impoverished Ukrainian nobility and received his initial education at the Kiev Church Academy together with socially inferior students. Having graduated from Moscow University, he embarked on a spectacular career in the Senate, yet until late in his life, he nurtured mild envy for his peers, who were lucky to enter the military. Wearing the uniform of an officer, especially from a Guards regiment, constituted the main attribute of noble status; young noble males continued to detest civil service in spite of all efforts of the state to make it attractive to them. In order to break the imaginary connection between the noble status and the military career, one needed a completely different set of moral values, as well as behavioral and emotional patterns.

The Alternative Project

Unlike St. Petersburg schools, Moscow University was initially designed not so much to fashion pupils morally, but to develop more specialized fields of knowledge. However, the specific atmosphere of Moscow University and its schools was shaped by the powerful influence of Freemasons and particularly by the Rosicrucian circle.

Moscow Rosicrucians were no less dissatisfied with the current moral practices and inner lives of the Russian nobility than Catherine and Betskoi, but they regarded the court and high St. Petersburg society as prone to Voltairianism, hedonism, and disbelief, and therefore as no less, if not more, corrupt, degraded, and ignorant than the rank-and-file nobility. They also shunned military service as alien to true Christian values. Ivan Lopukhin, one of the leading thinkers of the movement, renounced a promising position in the army to become a judge and to engage in philanthropic activities. His example was followed by other prominent Moscow Rosicrucians, such as Ivan

Turgenev, who chose a career in education, and Aleksei Kutuzov who left the military service to go to Germany in search of true esoteric wisdom.

As we saw in the previous chapter, Freemasons aspired to Europeanize the behavioral, intellectual, and emotional makeup of the Russian nobility by fostering education through the import of Western, especially Protestant and Pietist, moralistic literature and by bringing up younger generations in the spirit of rigorous moral discipline. The takeover of the Moscow University and Noble Boarding School was one of their most powerful and successful enterprises.

In 1778 the Mason Mikhail Kheraskov became one of the curators of Moscow University. A year thereafter he leased the university press to Nikolai Novikov, the intellectual and organizational leader of Russian Freemasonry, and invited the prominent Freemason Ivan Schwartz to lecture at the university. A well-informed memoirist writes that the creation of the Noble Boarding School was also Kheraskov's idea (Sushkov 1858, 3). Freemasons' interest in education received a significant boost after Schwartz's successful trip to the Wiesbaden Masonic congress in 1782, where he managed to negotiate for the Russian brethren the status of independent province, which allowed organization of Masonic activities on the basis of the statutes of the Rosicrucian order.

Schwartz also brought to Russia thirteen works on education for translation and dissemination. He started giving open university lectures on philosophy and founded a translation seminary to prepare cadres necessary to spread Masonic teachings across Russia (Schwartz 2008, 141). Like Betskoi and Catherine, Freemasons were interested in educating children from their most tender age. In 1785, after Schwartz's death, the university press began to publish the first Russian children's magazine, *Detskoe chtenie dlia serdtsa i razuma* (*A Child's Readings for the Heart and Reason*), edited by Novikov's disciples Aleksandr Petrov and the young Karamzin (before he became a prominent writer). *Detskoe chtenie* was immensely popular and remained in print until 1820. Referring to his childhood in a remote province, Sergei Aksakov, writer, memoirist, and father of the major Slavophile thinkers Ivan and Sergei Aksakov, wrote that the gift of an incomplete set of *Child's Readings* became a life-changing event for him (Aksakov 1984, 245).

Of course, this successful magazine did not consist of solemnly religious and mystic materials, and neither were the curricula of the university, the gymnasium or the Noble Boarding School dedicated to the dissemination of the teaching of the Rosicrucian order. Knowledge in the order was subject to a regime of strict secrecy. Masonic discipline was strictly hierarchical, and every step up the ladder implied greater access to knowledge. Ivan Lopukhin started his description of the "interior church" with the outer part of the mystical temple. People located there "think about the search for truth and begin to see the vanity of this world," but are still prone to "fall into worshipping the idols" (Lopukhin 1913, 15). The pupils and students of the Moscow educational establishments were not even at that stage in their development, but nevertheless needed moral and spiritual guidance to embark on the right path toward the temple. Dmitrii Sverbeev recollected discovering that his father belonged to a Masonic lodge only after his death, but declared that he could easily see the connection between his membership in this circle and the "moral side of his life" (Sverbeev 1899, 27). Obviously, the elder Sverbeev, himself a pupil of Schwartz, regarded his fourteen-year-old son as too young to be admitted to secret knowledge, but tried to set him on the necessary moral and intellectual path.

Moscow Rosicrucians continued their efforts to guide the educational process in the university even after their community was banned and the leaders arrested and exiled. Government persecution did not prevent them from believing that in the long term education would transform Russian society and bring about its moral and spiritual regeneration. Fedor Lubianovsky wrote in his memoirs that during his university years, he was nearly starving because his parents were not able to support him in Moscow. Having heard about this, Lopukhin, who had barely escaped exile himself, came to his apartment and took him to see the university rector, Professor Chebotarev, also a Freemason, who provided him with free room and board so that he could continue his studies. Regarding Lubianovsky as a promising young man and prospective Freemason, Lopukhin kept an eye on his progress and took care that a future member of the brethren would not be lost to the search of higher wisdom. As a student at the historico-philological faculty, Lubianovsky attended courses in chemistry and anatomy, hoping to understand the "ways in which substance is transformed into a better one" and "the miraculous organization of the human body for its temporal and transitory life on earth" (Lubianovskii 1872, 32). His chemical and biological interests show that he was already involved in esoteric studies. Freemasons searched for the philosophical stone that could transform all metals into gold, as well as for a panacea—a medicine against all illnesses. Classes in natural sciences guided by Lopukhin were meant to prepare Lubianovsky for his further esoteric studies.

Another prominent Moscow Rosicrucian committed to education was Ivan Turgenev, Lopukhin's closest friend. He translated John Mason's manual *On Self-knowledge*, a treatise that taught young people to scrutinize their thoughts and behavior in order to correct them and achieve moral perfection. He attached to the third edition of this treatise a special *Epistle to My Children*, in which he urged his sons to follow the instructions given in the book. As part of their education, Turgenev's children were assigned translations of moralistic books. His eldest son, Andrei, translated *A Biblical Moral Book for Adult Children Taken from the Books of Solomon*, a standard didactic guide for teenagers written by the Danish priest Jacob Friederich Feddersen, as well as fragments from *Autobiography*, by Benjamin Franklin. As encouragement for his efforts, Turgenev's translations were later published in Moscow. When he turned eighteen, his father gave him *Analogies between Bodily and Spiritual Births*, by Heinrich Ziegmunt Oswald, a short introduction into higher wisdom, also consisting mostly of purely didactic meditations, but based on the teachings of the founders of German mysticism, Jacob Boehme and Johann Georg Giechtel. Arguably, Ivan Turgenev decided that his son was prepared for the next step in his spiritual development and could be admitted at least to the courtyard of the temple (Zorin 2016c, 271).

The results of this moral fashioning hardly conformed to elder Turgenev's expectations. Initially he educated his sons on the family country estate, to which he was exiled for Masonic activities. Having been pardoned in 1796 after Catherine's death, Turgenev returned to Moscow and was appointed director of Moscow University. Not surprisingly, his children were admitted to the Moscow Noble Boarding School. Following the guidance given to them, all his sons kept diaries full of intensive introspection and soul-searching. However, none of them tried to climb the hierarchy of esoteric knowledge. The eldest son, Andrei, became the organizer and the leader of the Friendly Literary Society, a circle of young poets and devotees of Schiller and Goethe. His brother Aleksandr studied at the University of Göttingen, became a prominent statesman, but then abruptly resigned and spent most of his life abroad pursuing various literary activities and amassing a large if unsystematic collection of historical documents. Although he joined one of the Masonic lodges, the third brother, Nikolai, is much more widely known as a liberal thinker who was active in Decembrist circles and became a political émigré (Schönle 2016b). The Turgenev brothers absorbed the Masonic ideal of self-improvement through intensive reading, learning, and diary writing; however, their lives show a decisive break with the generation of their fathers and mentors. Contemporary European literature and liberal political ideas were much more attractive to them than the moral and pietistic upbringing they received both at the university and in their family.

Home Education

Gradually the elite began to recognize the value of a solid education, for girls as much as for boys, if only as a ticket to speedy social promotion and advantageous marriage, but also as a means to prepare them to become better servants of the state. Rapidly changing patterns of education created or amplified social disparities, to the extent, in some instances, of causing communication problems between generations or in-laws. Parents were generally involved in the education of their offspring in one way or another, especially in the early years. The recollections of Aleksandr Vorontsov illustrate that it was usual for fathers to participate in their children's education:

> Twice a week there were French comedies at the Court Theater, and our father took us there to the box he obtained. I mention this circumstance as it contributed greatly to giving us, from our tender childhood, a pronounced liking for reading and literature. My father subscribed from Holland to a quite well assembled library, in which there were the best French authors and poets, as well as historical books, so that at the age of twelve, I was already familiar with the works of Voltaire, Racine, Corneille, Boileau, and other French writers. (*Arkhiv Kniazia Vorontsova* 1872, 5:12–2)

The upper strata of the nobility had the means and possibilities to give their children a robust education. As children grew older, wealthy families hired home tutors from abroad, sometimes several, for different subjects. These were in high demand and not easy to recruit. No efforts were spared to identify appropriate candidates. For example, to find a suitable tutor for the young Ivan Bariatinsky, it was no less than Kant who was consulted. In 1779, the Königsberg philosopher received a letter from Hieronymus Wielkes, who had been professor in the Berlin Corps of Cadets and then became personal tutor to the Volkonsky family in St. Petersburg. Wielkes's letter to Kant gives us a sense of the expectations families placed on foreign tutors:

Princess Bariatinsky, born princess von Holstein Beck, seeks for her young prince, aged between 9 and 11, an able home tutor, who is as conversant with French as with German, and furthermore possesses the other necessary sciences and knowledge, is not a novice in polite demeanor, and is therefore capable of giving a rounded education to a young man of such birth for all future circumstances of his life. (Kant 1922, 258)

The critical phrase here is "ganz zu bilden," which we translated as "giving a rounded education,"—that is, not simply to impart knowledge, but to mold the personality in a comprehensive and definitive manner so that the young prince should be equipped, by dint of his knowledge, skills, moral qualities, and social graces, to succeed in all walks of life. Likewise, Freemason Ivan Turgenev, whose standing on the social ladder was significantly inferior to Volkonsky's, tasked his young friend and pupil Nikolai Karamzin, the future prominent writer and historiographer, to engage Johann Caspar Lavater to find a tutor for his sons. Lavater duly agreed to cooperate and sent his distant relative Georg Christoph Tobler to assist his Russian correspondents.

These tutors were not necessarily given free rein, but were often expected to follow agreed educational plans designed in consultation with the family or by some external party, often a foreigner. One of those was Jacob von Staehlin, who had left his hometown of Memmingen in Upper Swabia at the age of twenty-six to make a career at the Russian Academy of Sciences and had been the personal tutor to the future Peter III for three years. He devised several private educational projects for the elite in the 1760s and 1770s—for example, the *Plan for the Education of a Knight* (1764) destined for the education of Nikolai Sheremetev. His and other plans emphasized not only the acquisition of useful skills and knowledge, but also the physical and moral development of the person, often, as in this case, with reference to Christian teachings. Ultimately, according to Staehlin, the aim of education was to fashion "a citizen of the world, and in particular of his own country"—in other words, a person in tune with European arts and sciences, but also knowledgeable about Russia (Staehlin 2001, 217).

Using the freedom of travel established by the 1762 manifesto, some members of the aristocracy preferred their children to study abroad, but even then they aspired to keep close control over their education. In her memoirs, Ekaterina Dashkova claimed that she accompanied her son for several years to Edinburgh and Dublin, and eventually on a European Grand Tour, as "the education of my son," she maintained, "was the object of my most tender care. I wanted to preserve his principles intact and to save him from the thousand seductions to which a young man is prey. The outcome of my thoughts on this subject was to take him to foreign countries" (Dachkova 1999, 144). Natalia Golitsyna blamed the poor educational progress of her sons in Strasbourg partly on their undisciplined and pliant tutors, and advised parents to send their sons to study abroad only if their fathers could accompany them (RGB OR, f. 64, k. 113, ed. 1, 32ob). She also denounced the attitude of the professors themselves, who were more concerned to retain their well-paying pupils as long as possible than to teach them anything useful. Despite initial positive impressions, Golitsyna concluded that her sons had been poorly taught in Strasbourg and needed to begin their education anew in Paris.

Prince Ivan Bariatinsky developed in 1815 a plan for the education of his son Aleksandr, born a year earlier. In a letter to an acquaintance, Bariatinsky explained that "my only aim is to educate my son for the benefit of the fatherland and for his own, and to make him into a genuine and therefore enlightened Russian, that is, not one full only of national prejudice" (RGB, F 19, op. 1, p. 154, l. 32). To achieve this form of "enlightened Russianness," a combination of national and cosmopolitan identity, Bariatinsky envisioned that his son should begin by studying Latin, Greek, Slavonic, and "especially" Russian, playing down French and German, although his orientation was slightly undermined by the fact that he wrote his plan in French. Then the emphasis was to be on practical disciplines such as mechanics and agronomy, which should lead to genuine agricultural experiments, the proceeds of which would be given to the poor. Once the boy mastered the use of hammer, plow, and other tools, he would be taught the history and geography of the fatherland, before embarking, at age sixteen, on a six-year long journey across Russia, followed by four or five years abroad. Traveling was key to this plan, instead of attendance at court and in society, as when on the road, "physical and intellectual qualities develop much faster, and with such impetus and energy, which young men educated in cities and academies cannot achieve" (Zisserman 1888, 7). Traveling would protect the child from the "illusions" taught in academies and teach him to despise vice.

The emphasis was very much placed on knowledge of Russia, its institutions, and its failings, although the young traveler would be accompanied by an international crew of tutors, including a German conversant with classical languages and a scholar of mechanics from England, Holland, or Switzerland, as well as a Russian teacher familiar with things Russian and a few other teachers of indifferent provenance. While traveling, young Aleksandr would keep a diary of his journey, written in Russian, which he would then translate into French, English, or another language, suggesting that the knowledge of foreign languages was taken for granted. Bariatinsky also indicated that his son should self-evidently be familiar with his religion. Ultimately, he implored his wife not to make their son into a military officer, a courtier, or a diplomat. Instead he should join the Ministry of Foreign Affairs (presumably as an in-house advisor) or the Ministry of Finances, where he would be in a position to contribute to the public good and serve the monarch, before retiring to his estates to oversee their improvement.

Bariatinsky's educational plans were abandoned following his death in 1825, and it is a matter of historical irony that his son Aleksandr became a renowned field marshal who subjugated the Northern Caucasus in the 1850s and captured Shamil, the fierce Dagestani imam and freedom fighter. Common to the educational practices of the elite is the notion that the purpose of education was ultimately to prepare for service to the country, but that the state of moral education in Russia was such that this goal required isolation from the pernicious influence of society and the court and from the failings of existing educational institutions. Hence the preference for home education by foreign tutors or education abroad. This was all the more so as education was also seen as a way to gain access to European knowledge, arts, and social networks—that is, to become at once cosmopolitan and Russian. The top echelon of the elite thus attempted to keep the education of its children under its control, observing a careful distance from state institutions and certain social practices, but without, of course, compromising its standing at court and in society.

Understandably, poorer nobles could not afford these strategies, even though the understanding of the necessity of education for the future career of a son was beginning to reach the lower rungs of the social ladder. In Little Russia, where due to Polish influence the clergy was better educated and enjoyed greater respect, it was common to send children to local parish priests (Timkovskii 1874; Lubianovskii 1872; Vinskii 1914, a.o.). However, in the inner governships of mainland Russia, the provincial gentry searched for foreign tutors with the same zeal as their superiors. The competence of these provincial tutors is difficult to evaluate, but it gave rise to sharply negative descriptions. The famous poet Gavrila Derzhavin, who in his childhood lived for a while in the remote province of Orenburg, wrote in his memoirs that in the absence of other teachers he was sent

> to study German with the German Josef Rose, who for some sort of crime had been sentenced to hard labor. He was also teaching the children, both male and female, of the best and noble families who held different positions in Orenburg. This teacher, apart from being cruel and of corrupt morals and torturing his pupils with most painful and even indecent punishments—it would be disgusting to talk about this—was completely ignorant. Children could only exercise by rehearsing words he gave to them and copying them from Rose's manuscript written in perfect handwriting. (Derzhavin, 1876, 9)

Derzhavin's mother was very poor and nearly illiterate; she probably could not understand what she was doing, but she was obviously trying to follow the general practice. The desire of the "best and noble families" of Orenburg to teach their children some foreign language was so great that they were ready to subject them to "indecent punishments." Clearly, they regarded learning rudiments of German as an affordable form of Europeanization that could lead to a future successful career or marriage—indeed, it is worth noting that girls were also participating in this educational enterprise along with boys. In his memoirs, Derzhavin portrayed himself as a self-made man and enjoyed exaggerating the misery and ignorance in which he grew up in order to contrast it to the fame and status he achieved both as a statesman and a poet. His description could be somewhat hyperbolic, especially as he himself confessed that he "managed to learn German to be able to read and speak beautifully." By the early nineteenth century, when he was writing his memoirs, the image of foreign tutors achieved its nadir in Russian culture.

In his comedy *The Minor*, which premiered in 1782, Fonvizin presented a savage satire of such a home tutor, Vral'man (Mr. Liar), a former coachman who found it more profitable to offer his services as tutor than as driver, despite his lack of any useful knowledge. Mitrofanushka, the stupid and lazy provincial ignoramus at the center of the plot, also had two Russian teachers, but even the worst of them, a former clergyman, cannot be compared in cynicism and incompetence to Vral'man. After Fonvizin, the view prevailed that foreign tutors were adventurists coming in pursuit of economic opportunity, but lacking in any pedagogical preparation and more likely to inculcate disdain of Russia than to raise the educational attainment of their wards. Both Fonvizin's Vral'man and Derzhavin's Rose were Germans, but special notoriety accrued to French tutors, who were often perceived as conscious agents of foreign influence.

It is difficult to ascertain the preponderance of spurious teachers, and it is likely that they were more successful in deceiving the provincial gentry than the upper nobility in the capitals. French tutors hailed from vastly diverse social, professional, and cultural origins, giving rise to diverging views about them (Mézin and Rjéoutski 2011, 105–121). In any case, the ideological rejection of foreign tutors grew together with the practice of hiring them (Chudinov 2004). The rapid spread of language proficiency among the elite beginning in the 1760s and the refined education many of them achieved in subsequent decades suggest that there were many serious educators among these home tutors, even beyond the famous figures who tutored the very top of the hierarchy, such as Staehlin, Frédéric-César de la Harpe, or Gilbert Romme.

No doubt under the influence of Rousseau, some tutors were themselves uneasy about the polished demeanor and social graces they were meant to inculcate to their wards. Gilbert Romme and Jacques Démichel, the tutors of Pavel and Grigorii Stroganov, emphasized the physical observation of nature, rather than knowledge derived from books, and steered their pupils away from French literature (Rjéoutski 2016, 127–129). And yet, some members of the elite harbored misgivings about the frivolous moral influence to which young men were exposed during their education by such home tutors. The poor nobleman Grigorii Vinsky, who himself later worked as a tutor in the family of rich landowners, devoted a whole paragraph of his memoirs to justifying why foreigners can be trusted to serve as tutors in Russian families. Seeing himself as a Little Russian (Ukrainian), he accused Great Russians, the "moskals" as he called them, of ignorant prejudice toward all things foreign (Vinskii 1914, 18–20, 28).

During the Napoleonic wars the prejudice against French teachers acquired the dimensions of a national obsession. "Everything that is our own becomes bad and despised in our eyes. The French teach us everything: how to walk, how to stand, how to bow, how to sing, how to speak, and even how to blow our noses," wrote Admiral Shishkov, one of the early ideologues of Russian cultural and political exceptionalism (Shiskov 1824, 2:14). Nationalizing

the educational process became one of the major goals of Russian statesmen. In early nineteenth century, the famous liberal and anglophile Nikolai
Mordvinov submitted to the emperor a memorandum called *Russian Tutors*—
its initial title was *On the Ways of Spreading Education by Compatriots in
Russia*—in which he claimed that "foreign teachers and mentors constitute
the main threat to Russia's future" (Mordvinov 1902, 5:42). Mordvinov called
on home education to be discharged by Russians, not foreigners. To this effect,
in order to entice Russian teachers to become involved in home education, he
proposed to award them ranks and career progression equivalent to those of
teachers in official institutions. He believed that native private tutors would
in general be more useful than university professors, who "produce little, do
not invent anything, and are lazy in teaching their pupils" (45). Despite being
a statesman, he shared the elite mindset of diffidence of state-sponsored institutional education, while seeking to address an increasingly widespread fear
about the pernicious influence foreign tutors could have on the moral development of the offspring of the elite.

The Struggle for a National System of Education

In the late eighteenth and early nineteenth centuries the number of educational
institutions in Russia significantly increased, which was due to the successful
school reform of the 1780s based on a model earlier implemented in the Austrian empire (Black 1979; de Madariaga 1981) and to the opening in 1804 of
new universities in St. Petersburg, Kazan, Vilno (currently Vilnius, Lithua-
nia), Derpt (currently Tartu, Estonia), and Kharkov (currently Ukraine). The
desire of provincial nobility to provide regular education to their children was
also growing—they kept demanding more schools and volunteering to fund
them (Lappo-Danilevskii 1904).

Still, the wishes of government officials and the demands of the nobility did
not completely match. The history of the inauguration of Kharkov University
is especially revealing. Vasilii Karazin, a local noble, had convinced Alexander
I that Kharkov's noble community was ready to fund the university. The
emperor was very pleased and gave his consent, but even with the imperial
decree in his hands, Karazin had to use all his eloquence to convince his peers,
who were in reality collecting money for a military school, to contribute sufficient funding to the university, which was both significantly more expen-
sive and less attractive to them. Finally the pressured nobles agreed to pledge

400,000 rubles, out of the million that was promised initially, but even the diminished sum was never collected in full (Abramov 1891).

To enhance the status of civil service and university education, one needed extraordinary measures. It was left to the son of a village priest, Mikhail Speransky, to propose a comprehensive program of reforms. Speransky's astonishing career ascension was due both to his exceptional capabilities and his skills in navigating the patronage network (Raeff 1957). Between 1807 and his fall from grace in 1812, Speransky was the second most powerful man in Russia after the emperor Alexander. One of the first papers he submitted to the monarch was the memorandum *On the Improvement in General Education* (1808). In it Speransky complained about the lack of "moral feeling of the necessity of education" among the nobility. Speransky believed that home schooling was deficient both because of the well-known drawbacks of foreign tutors and because "the government is left without ways to control the spirit of education and to lead the younger generation toward uniform public rules" (Speranskii 1907, 730). He blamed the "small number of people studying in all universities and gymnasia" on the system of ranks established by Peter the Great, which constituted the backbone of civil service in Russia and impeded meritocratic principles of promotion.

Like many other major Russian statesmen, Speransky was a mystic and a visionary. Bringing together the utopias of Betskoi and Novikov, he planned to resolve the problems inherited from Peter's reforms by adopting an inter-connected set of measures that dealt with both education and civil service. As it was impractical to abolish ranks completely, Speransky suggested that only university graduates should be conferred a rank that granted inheritable nobility. For those who were already in service, the university degree could be substituted by an examination. In 1809, these ideas were authorized in the imperial decree *On Examinations in Sciences for Promotion of Collegiate Assessors and Civil Councilors*, which raised the prestige of university degrees, but attracted Speransky the wrath of nobles.

To capitalize on this initial success, Speransky launched in 1810 a uni-versal Masonic lodge, where thousands of young Russians would receive the moral, religious, and intellectual preparation indispensable for entering the civil service (Zorin 2014, 210–217). In addition, the top positions in the civil service were to be filled by the graduates of the Lyceum at Tsarskoe Selo, an elite school that opened in 1811. Speransky was the mastermind behind the Lyceum and personally designed the curriculum. A central place in it was reserved for the law, taught by the prominent liberal thinker Aleksandr Kunitsyn (Berest 2011). The statutes of the Lyceum were written by his closest associate Ivan Martynov, who earlier prepared the decree *On Examinations* and was an ardent Anglophile.

The upstarts Speransky and Martynov were planning to create a Russian version of British aristocracy. Like the Cadet Corps and Smolny Institute, the Lyceum combined isolation with political centrality. It was situated outside St. Petersburg, but in immediate proximity to the imperial palace. In the summer, the pupils playing in the garden could see the emperor walking around with members of his cabinet. The Lyceum was also the first Russian educational establishment where the pupils were free from corporal punishment—they were supposed to acquire the moral independence and personal dignity necessary for their future high destiny. While earlier Russian elite schools were meant to produce officers and ladies-in-waiting feeling themselves in personal service to the imperial family, the Lyceum aimed to forge a corporate identity of belonging to the upper echelons of power with a natural right to participate in decision making. In a way, it was designed to resemble more Eton College than Russian schools of the eighteenth century. These effects were greatly reinforced by the unfolding of major political events: the opening of the Lyceum nearly coincided with Napoleon's invasion of Russia and the subsequent march of the Russian army to Paris. The boys suddenly found themselves at the center not only of Russian but of world politics.

While the Masonic lodge initiated by Speransky never took root and was soon closed by the emperor, the Lyceum survived Speransky's downfall in 1812 and became a legendary site of Russian culture, a reputation mostly due to Alexander Pushkin, who spent his adolescence there and immortalized the spirit of idyllic brotherhood in his poetry. However, this mythology, which spread in the nineteenth century, extolled not ministers and governors but poets and rebels, as several graduates from the first intake of the Lyceum became members of the Decembrist conspiracy.

Shortly after the Decembrist rebellion, the new emperor, Nicholas I, summoned Pushkin from exile to St. Petersburg. The emperor wanted to enlist the most famous Russian poet to contribute to his ideological system, which was just taking shape, and at the same time to provide a sound account of the causes of the rebellion. The first commission Pushkin received was to write a memorandum on public education. Nicholas knew that many conspirators came from the elite educational institutions and desired to figure out what had so dramatically gone wrong.

Like most educational reformers before him, Pushkin believed that education, "or rather the lack of education" was the root of evil. In his letter Pushkin explicitly attacked Speransky for his landmark reform—the introduction of the examinations for civil service—yet his analysis is conspicuously close to Speransky's memorandum, which he could not have possibly read. Pushkin blamed the Table of Ranks for the lack of interest of young people and their parents in real education, but agreed that it would not be practical to abolish this system. He strongly condemned private education and advised Nicholas to "suppress" it. He proposed to confer higher ranks upon the young people educated in state institutions. Even his sharp criticism of the examinations was based on assumptions he shared with his opponent: Pushkin thought that the introduction of these exams reinforced the preference of nobles for military service, instead of counteracting it.

Nicholas was deeply dissatisfied with Pushkin's memorandum. In a response to Pushkin drafted after a conversation with the emperor, the chief of the secret police, Count Benkendorf, wrote:

> His Majesty has deigned to note that the idea you cherish, that enlightenment and personal genius are the sole foundations of perfection, is dangerous for general tranquility. This premise has led you yourself to the brink of the abyss and precipitated many young people into it. Morality, zealous service, and dedication should be preferred to inexperienced, immoral, and useless enlightenment. (Pushkin 1962–1965, 7:660–661)

The emperor was clearly disappointed at the results of the major educational projects of his predecessors. While the proportion of nobles involved in the conspiracies could be seen as negligibly small, the alumni of the elite schools, including the Cadet Corps, the Noble Boarding School, and the Lyceum, and the scions of the most distinguished noble families were significantly overrepresented among their ranks. While the new race of human beings envisaged by both Betskoi and the Rosicrucians may have failed to materialize, the social type of a Europeanized Russian—well-educated, self-confident, patriotic, yet morally and intellectually independent from the court—which the state had been striving to create for a century, had finally come into existence, and the emperor was expressing his explicit dissatisfaction with it. He was critical of the educational formula that produced a poet who succeeded in transposing European literature from Voltaire to Byron into an emerging national literature, an educational regime that also prepared the young Russian officers who stunned Paris with their ancien régime French, who felt at home in Parisian theaters and at the Académie française, and whose conspiratorial societies developed from Masonic lodges. The state was not happy with the results of its efforts. The elite educational institutions themselves were to survive and prosper, but the utopian vision of their founders was thrown aside and forgotten.

6

. . . .

THE RISE OF LITERATURE AND THE
EMERGENCE OF A SECULAR CULT

In 1843 the prominent Russian literary critic Vissarion Belinsky opened his cycle of articles on the works of Pushkin, the first comprehensive popular history of Russian literature, with a provocative statement:

> Russian literature is not an endemic but an imported plant. . . . Its history consists of the perpetual attempt to get rid of the results of artificial transplantation, to grow roots in the new soil and to draw strength from its nutritious juices. The notion of poetry was ordered by post from Europe and shipped to Russia, where it emerged as an overseas innovation. (Belinskii 1955, 107)

Since that time, generations of scholars have struggled to prove Belinsky wrong and to demonstrate the native origins and indigenous character of Russian literature. However, the observations of the founder of Russian literary criticism remain as pertinent as ever. Modern literature was a Petrine innovation imported alongside such products as tobacco and coffee, from "civilized" Europe. As Belinsky seemed to believe, these different imports pursued a similar goal: literature was necessary to embellish and enhance court ceremonies. It also had a more elevated aim: the autocracy needed a language and rhetorical means to communicate with the educated minority. For interaction with the illiterate peasant majority, it was the church that traditionally functioned as the mouthpiece of the throne. August manifestos, which everyone in the country was supposed to be acquainted with—for example those dealing with the coronation of a new monarch, the beginning and end of war, or the draft—were announced in churches during Sunday services. However, mobilizing the elite required more sophisticated rhetorical strategies, which only a literary culture could supply.

In keeping with the top-down emergence of Russian literature in the eighteenth century, in this chapter we will give particular attention to the ways in which the court established the basic elements of a literary culture and, in particular, defined the role of the writer in society. Subsequently we will trace how writers sought to emancipate themselves from subservience to the throne and how they began to articulate new functions for literary discourse, in particular as a vector to express the emotions and the interests of the upper nobility, its primary audience. Finally, we will explore how writers addressed the outcome of Europeanization, in particular the critique that it was no more than superficial gloss or that it led to a loss of national identity.

Literature as Service

The first step to establish a literary culture was to demarcate it from the writings of the church. Peter enforced this basic distinction by introducing a new alphabet to be used for the publication of government documents and for books on secular matters, while the church had to continue to print in the old Cyrillic alphabet. Peter commissioned Dutch and Russian printers to develop new typefaces, and by 1710 he had settled on a simplified Russian alphabet, which he mandated by decree for all but church publications. In parallel, he also required the use of plain language, rather than convoluted Old Church Slavonic, thus making print production available to a broader readership (Cracraft 2003, 99–103). He ordered the translation of a raft of technical and scientific literature, books on arithmetic, astronomy, navigation, military strategy, architecture, history, and others, as well as etiquette books and some classical literature. The offshoot of this brisk import of translated literature was a rapid expansion of the Russian language by way of neologisms, mostly in the form of loan words from Western European languages. It has been estimated that during Peter's reign the Russian language was enriched by about 4,500 words (Cracraft 2003, 104).

This does not mean that "civil" literary culture became secular overnight. In order to transform the worldview of his subjects, Peter needed to produce a regular stream of texts explaining and justifying his reforms. To this effect, he appointed an erudite monk and professor from the Spiritual Academy in Kiev, Feofan Prokopovich, to become his main apologist. Prokopovich had studied at the Kievan Academy and temporarily converted to Catholicism to receive schooling from Jesuits in Rome. He was as versed in classical literature as in Orthodox writings and was attuned to intellectual developments in early modern Europe. He wrote poetry, including satirical spoofs on the church. He professed a rationalized form of Orthodox piety and was more interested in the wording of the scriptures than in church traditions, which showed Protestant influences (he had also studied in German universities). He was keen to move away from the convoluted baroque idiom of church homiletics and expressed himself in a more approachable, less rhetorical form of Old Church Slavonic. For Peter he wrote treatises, laws and regulations, and, most importantly, a series of panegyrical sermons, which were pronounced in public and disseminated in print. In one of these sermons, he carefully laid out what amounts to an absolutist theory of power, drawing on German natural law. Peter was presented as a ruler anointed by God to create a new Russia. Prokopovich was thus instrumental in forging the mythology of Peter the Great as a reformer who singlehandedly dragged Russia from benighted ignorance into a glorious enlightened future, thus creating a new dawn for the country. In so doing he combined Orthodox messianism with Enlightenment rationalism (Zhivov 2002a, 446). Traditional churchmen were deeply offended by Prokopovich's reforms to Orthodox piety and his resolve to diminish and constrict the influence of the church, but without access to the printing press, which was entirely under the control of the court, their resistance was ineffectual.

The Petrine reforms brought about a type of Russian writer who was a salaried clerk performing literary translations or writing court poetry for special occasions. Poets such as Gottlob Friedrich Wilhelm Juncker and Jacob von Stäehlin were initially invited from Germany to compose inscriptions for court illuminations and fireworks, to celebrate the achievements of the Academy of Sciences, and later to write odes on festive days (Pumpianskii 1937, Alekseeva 2005). Thus the main function of literature during Petrine times was to support court ceremonies and celebrations and to articulate "scenarios of power"—that is, to provide tropes and images that legitimized and mythologized the ruler (Wortman 1995).

There were rare exceptions to the state-managed panegyrical literature, notably the writings of Prince Antioch Kantemir (1708–1744), the son of the ruler of Moldavia and author of the first literary satires in Russian (who spoke Italian in his family). In his Russian-language poetry he imitated Horace and Boileau, and from one of his satires we know that he also composed popular love songs. However, Kantemir spent most of his adult life as an ambassador in London and Paris, from where he would send a succession of monarchs futile pleas to allow the publication of his satires. His first posthumous editions appeared initially in French and German translations, and the first Russian collection came out only in 1762, after the accession of Catherine the Great to the throne. In the first half of the eighteenth century, Russia was not yet ready to support and condone the poetic muse of a dilettante aristocrat.

Translators like Vasilii Trediakovsky (1703–1769), who provided Russian versions of the poems of his German peers, were usually recruited from the ranks of the clergy. It was from social inferiors that the Russian elite was to learn the contemporary political mythology, the imagery of state ceremonies, and the rules of polite behavior, as taught by the monarchy. And it was educated commoners who were to produce the necessary texts for the nobility's consumption.

Trediakovsky's literary career illustrates the precarious standing of the independent-minded writer in this period. The son of a priest from the southern provincial city of Astrakhan on the shores of the Caspian sea, he studied at the Slavic-Greek-Latin Academy in Moscow, then traveled abroad and stayed first in the Hague and then for three years in Paris, where he attended the Sorbonne and Port-Royal. Upon his return, he published a translation of Paul Tallemant's *Voyage to the Isle of Love* (1730)—an allegorical seventeenth-century novel in prose and verse meant to serve as a primer for the gallant courtship practiced in aristocratic salons. This type of aristocratic culture did not yet exist in Russia, and Trediakovsky aimed to supply the necessary behavioral and emotional codes for polite society, which was also a way to secure a place for himself in the emerging high society on the basis of his education, personal capabilities, and literary achievements. His translation was supplemented by a collection of poetry in three languages—Russian, French, and Latin (Lotman 1997, Zhivov 2002b).

These plans were, however, totally frustrated. Aristocratic salons failed to materialize in his lifetime, while the Russian monarchy was not ready to recognize the rights of a self-proclaimed member of the republic of letters. He found work at the St. Petersburg Academy of Sciences as a translator and slowly rose to the rank of professor, but his profile as a learned scholar did not help him in society. In 1740, Trediakovsky was commissioned to write a poem for the parodic wedding ceremony of court jesters. He was, in effect, asked to act as a buffoon. After trying to reject the order, he was locked up and beaten until he consented to the assignment. This beating constituted one of the accusations against cabinet minister Artemii Volynsky, whose fall from imperial grace followed several months later, and so Trediakovsky was granted compensation for his ruined health and very public loss of face. Nevertheless, this episode illustrates the low status of the writer in the eyes of the court. After being pushed out of the Academy in 1759, Trediakovsky spent the last ten years of his life as a recluse working in near destitution, a victim of the low status of the writer in society.

Another commoner, Mikhail Lomonosov (1711–1765), the son of a prosperous fisherman from the Arkhangelsk region on the White Sea coast, was more successful as he managed to secure the patronage of Ivan Shuvalov, Empress Elizabeth's favorite. Lomonosov was also a student of the Slavic-Greek-Latin Academy and later studied abroad in German universities, from where he sent his *Letter on the Rules of Russian Versification* and the *Ode on the Conquest of Khotin*, two texts that to this day have been considered to have laid the foundations of Russian poetry. Upon his return, Lomonosov secured an affiliation with the St. Petersburg Academy of Sciences. While, unlike Trediakovsky, he saw himself as a natural scientist, his official duty was to write laudatory speeches and odes for official occasions and to help Voltaire collect materials for his *History of Peter the Great*, which the court of Empress Elizabeth considered as a major propagandistic endeavor to establish Russia's credentials as a European power.

Lomonosov's authorial success depended on his skillful ways of playing along with the conventions of patronage, which by mid-century became literature's main institutional setting and public role. To compensate for his lack of social status, he had at once to affirm his exceptional literary and scientific skills and to lower himself by singing the praise of his patrons (Zhivov 2002b, 597). He wrote twenty panegyrical odes and established the importance of the ode in the Russian literary system. These long poems, written on the occasion of some august celebration, were not commissioned, but presented by the poet to the ruler as a way to draw attention to his person and poetic skills. They also included a healthy dose of self-promotion and self-interested advocacy, including, for example, barefaced praise for the support of science (Zhivov 2002b, 603–608). The ode became a forum in which writers tried to negotiate their dependency from their patrons, mixing their praise with self-assertion.

After her accession to the throne, Catherine attempted to follow the same model. She had little sympathy for Lomonosov, who was the poet of Elizabeth's reign par excellence, and after his death she invited one more seminary student, Vasilii Petrov, to serve as her personal librarian and reader, and by default as the official court poet. In her *Antidote* (1770), which she wrote to refute Chappe d'Auteroche's *Voyage en Sibérie*, Catherine dedicated a special section to the successes of Russian literature and covered Petrov with lavish praise. In so doing, however, she provoked the dismay and outrage of noble writers, who were satirizing and parodying the parvenu (Gukovskii 2001). This reaction was a symptom of the major change in the status of literature that occurred in the 1750s–1760s with the influx of the first generation of educated noble writers, who easily gained dominant positions in the literary world, which they preserved for at least a century. While elite landowners still commissioned works of art such as paintings, sculptures, or music from their serfs, professionals coming from lower social layers, or foreigners, they largely reserved literary pursuits for themselves. Nobles started to experiment with literature as a way to affirm their prerogatives as a social estate and articulate their vision of the world, their system of values and emotions.

Literature as "Useful Entertainment" for the Elite

In the 1830s, in his *A Journey from Moscow to Saint Petersburg*, Pushkin highlighted with considerable pride this autonomous aristocratic character of Russian literature:

> Patronage is until the present day the practice in English literature.... In Russia writers could not solicit patronage from people they considered equal to themselves without abasing themselves deeply; relations among them did not have

the marks of servility which darken a great number of foreign literatures. What in England and France was considered as honor would go down here as debasement. A writer here cannot present his book to some count or general in the hope of receiving 500 rubles or a richly decorated ring. (Pushkin, 1962–1965, 7:286, 631)

How could high literature written by nobles reach such startling poise in Russia? The author who arguably contributed most to asserting the aristocratic self-confidence of Russian literature was Aleksandr Sumarokov (1718–1777), although he, too, tussled with the authorities to defend his authorial and social dignity. A graduate of the Cadet Corps, Sumarokov staged his tragedies at his alma mater, and later became the director of the first professional Russian theater. In 1759, he started publishing his private satirical magazine *The Industrious Bee*, which he dedicated to then Grand Duchess Catherine, whose position at the court of Empress Elizabeth was quite precarious. Contrary to Lomonosov, Sumarokov tried to build his literary career outside patronage relations, convinced as he was of his intrinsic social status as a nobleman.

The rise of independent journals was one symptom of the fact that literature was in the process of acquiring a new social standing and function. A close-knit group of Moscow writers started editing a private literary magazine called *Useful Entertainment* (1760–1762), later continued as *Free Hours* (1763). The articles and poems published in *Useful Entertainment* and *Free Hours* often speak of a circle of virtuous minds, who are subject to suspicions and slander by vile persons, a motif that is typical of Masonic apologetics and reveals the social self-awareness of the new literary aristocracy. It is still not completely clear to what extent these literary enterprises were connected with the emerging Masonic lodges. Like Sumarokov, the leading contributors to Moscow journals, Mikhail Kheraskov and Aleksei Rzhevsky, were Freemasons. These two later became members of the order of Rosicrucians, the most esoteric branch of Masonry. Freemasonry was instrumental in countenancing the moral independence of the emerging aristocratic literature.

Catherine initially attempted to secure the loyalty of these writers, lending them her support. During preparations for her accession to the throne, this group of writers actively participated in designing the masquerade *The Triumphant Minerva*, a spectacle meant to present the program of the new reign and the coming era of Astrea. Sumarokov, Kheraskov, and Ivan Betskoi (the future organizer of the new Russian educational system) were assigned the task of creating a vision both of the Dark Age the country was leaving behind and the Golden Age awaiting it. The masquerade was part of the coronation festivities planned for the wider audience of Moscow residents and visitors. For the first time, the monarchy did not use the educated graduates of the seminary or invite foreigners to create a ritual for distinguished society. Instead, a group of ambitious noblemen designed a program of public entertainment laced with a powerful ideological message. Lomonosov and Shuvalov were satirized during the performance, which made the case that along with all other important political, cultural, and ideological activities, literary pursuits belonged to the noble elite, and so the system of patronage was no longer appropriate (Pogosian 2010). Shortly afterward, Kheraskov replaced Shuvalov as curator of Moscow University.

However, the idyll between the new ruler and noble intellectuals proved to be short-lived, as Sumarokov's career illustrates vividly. For unknown reasons, a chorus written by Sumarokov for the accession masquerade, its most overtly political segment, was omitted from the program and replaced by another one. In the new chorus, the author confessed that he did not dare to attack vices. Instead he substituted political criticism with repeated exclamations of "hem, hem, hem," suggesting that his voice had been suppressed (Gukovskii 1936, 186, 188–200; see also Pogosian 2010, 124). Dismissed from the theater in 1761, Sumarokov gradually lost his credit at court, before finally moving to Moscow, a city full of disgruntled nobles, where he tried in vain to establish his authority over the local theater. His heroic attempts to establish some sort of copyright for his own tragedies proved completely futile. With the support of the empress, the city commander, Count Petr Saltykov, ordered his tragedy *Sinav and Truvor* to be performed, notwithstanding the vociferous objections of the author, who believed that the actors were not ready for it. Driven to total despondency and misery, Sumarokov went so far as to threaten Catherine with a warning that in this situation he would have to revert to writing novels, then a more popular genre, which he believed could be commercially successful. Tellingly, the author saw this outcome as an utter disgrace not only for himself as the founder of Russian theater, but also for Russia in general, and he hoped he could convince the empress to prevent such an outrage.

Literature became highly important for noble writers, as it conveyed a sense of the moral superiority of their desired way of life. The educated nobles were unable and unwilling to challenge the leading role of the court in establishing official cultural policy, especially in the theater. Instead, they regarded their literary pursuits as activities through which they could assert their partial independence from the court. To some extent, this role could exist within the structures of the empire and was compatible with their status as a landowning and service estate. Unlike the representatives of lower social layers co-opted by the court as professionals, noble writers developed a culture of leisure writing. Appeals to the Horatian ideal celebrating the pursuit of tranquility as a reaction against court life were usual in Russian literature since Kantemir's satires and were common in *Monthly Publications*, published by the Academy of Sciences in the 1750s. Since the 1760s, with the appearance of the first literary magazines in Moscow, they stopped being an exercise in conventional pastoralism and became a glorification of the pleasures of life on the noble rural estate.

The titles of the first journals, *Useful Entertainment* and *Free Hours*, clearly pointed to this understanding of literary activity as an expression of noble leisure and independence, and so did the titles of subsequent periodicals, such as *The Evenings*, *Leisure Time Beneficially Used*, or *Pleasant and Useful Passing of Time*. From its inception in the early 1760s, noble literature promoted the ideal of an economically and culturally independent moralist developing his personality outside the tribulations of the court and enjoying sweet and permissible pleasures in the lap of nature. This general tenor of noble literature significantly facilitated the characteristic merger of the Horatian neo-stoic ideal with the cult of sensibility that emerged and spread through Europe at roughly the same time, including in such radical manifestations as Rousseauism.

This type of response to Rousseau was not unique to Russia. The French aristocracy also indulged in the cult of natural simplicity and tender feelings, attempting to give moral legitimacy to its social status (Darnton 1985, Maza 1997). However, in Russia, where the overwhelming majority of Russian nobles could not afford such a lifestyle and had to enroll in state service, with all the obligations and hardship that came with it, as well as the special ethos it mandated, this idealization became especially powerful as a compensatory, if unreachable, ideal. For many nobles, the mythology of the family country estate merged with nostalgia for their childhood years—the only time in their lives they could really reside there—and with the cherished ideal of blissful living in proximity to nature.

Between Recreation and Accommodation

The adaptation and assimilation of European preromantic literature corroborated the self-perception of educated nobles. In particular, the Rousseau-inspired cultivation of nature supplied a rationale for the idealization of the country estate and thus fulfilled the emotional and cultural needs of the nobility as a landowning corporation. However, European literature did not provide adequate patterns to shape and express the service identity of the nobility, with the notable exception of battlefield patriotism and its topos of heroic readiness to die for the fatherland. The patterns and norms that underpinned other aspects of the service duties of the nobility included unconditional loyalty to their superiors, assent to and familiarity with the system of patronage, and self-assessment based upon the rank one had managed to achieve. These values, which the Russian elite had also interiorized (Marasinova 1999; Schönle and Zorin 2016), stood in clear contradiction to the pastoral ideal of private life. The reconciliation of these contradictory ethical and emotional paradigms was not an easy endeavor, and an educated noble had to navigate between the specific demands of disparate behavioral codes.

The social career of the poet Gavrila Derzhavin (1743–1816) illustrates these tensions neatly. In 1783, Catherine was deeply impressed by an ode, which the poet, at that time an obscure provincial nobleman, had dedicated to her. She wanted to promote him, but in this instance, given Derzhavin's gentry background, a courtly sinecure would have been inappropriate. Although Derzhavin actually came from a poorer background than Lomonosov and Petrov, as a nobleman, he could only be promoted through state service. The empress appointed him as a governor, then moved him to another province, and only after he failed miserably at both positions did she appoint him as personal cabinet secretary, a job he took significantly more seriously than she had intended. Derzhavin wanted to be known not only and not mainly as a poet, but also as a statesman, and he struggled to reconcile the two roles. In retirement, he found himself unable to construct a single narrative about his career and dictated two different autobiographies: a conventional one relating his service to the monarch and the fatherland, and a second one in the form of a commentary on his poems (Fomenko 1983). His official and authorial identities could not be reconciled in his own mind.

In a similar way, in the 1780s, the young poet Mikhail Murav'ev (1757–1807), a disciple of Kheraskov, was dreaming about combining the roles of an *homme de société* and a poet. In order to achieve this goal he aspired to domesticate the French tradition of *poésie fugitive* connected with high aristocratic culture. Murav'ev bemoaned his failure at both tasks: in polite society, as he put it, he remained "the pupil who did not learn his ABC" and, in poetry, a bard who "forgot the art of singing"—that is, who never acquired the skills to write proper poetry. While France successfully produced several generations of gallant poets, from Voltaire to Dorat (Masson 2002), Russian nobles aiming to "favor the dawn of Russian poetry with their accomplishments" faced significant adversity. Murav'ev complained that it was not possible to follow Marquis de Boufflers in Russia's "heavy and grey air" (Murav'ev 1957, 218–220).

And yet Murav'ev's dream that Russia would produce her own de Boufflers, that is a successful aristocratic dilettante writer, came true. In 1797, Nikolai Karamzin issued three volumes of a poetical almanac called *Aonides*, where he collected the works of several established poets and dozens of dilettantes dabbling in the composition of songs and other genres of sentimental poetry. The contributors included both unknown names from remote parts of the country and princes or eminent courtiers, including Senator Iurii Neledinsky-Meletsky, who became an author of popular songs. Aristocrats and high-ranking servicemen competed in poetry glorifying idyllic rural bliss. One of the authors of the almanac was Murav'ev, who had not published anything for a long time, as he was instead serving as tutor to Catherine's grandsons, Grand Dukes Alexander and Konstantin. In this role, trying to reconcile his different selves, he wrote sentimental stories as didactic material for his august pupils.

Yet harmonizing authorial and service identities remained problematic. In the same year, 1797, Murav'ev attended the coronation of Paul I and lobbied to obtain a promotion in rank, carefully describing his efforts in letters he regularly sent to his wife. At the same time, he kept a travel diary for his wife and sons in which he endeavored to convince them that he despised ranks and riches and longed only for family bliss. When he was bypassed in favors, he sent home rapturous letters denouncing his futile endeavors and expressing his aspiration to create a future Arcadia in his "natural environment." At the same time, he was submitting desperate pleas to his superiors asking them to bring him out of the profound humiliation to which he was brought by his failure to obtain promotion to the rank of general. There is no reason to suspect the writer of hypocrisy—in either case he felt and behaved as was appropriate for a serving noble on one side and for a sentimental writer on the other. Eventually, his efforts succeeded and he became a general. Later, when Alexander became emperor, Murav'ev was appointed vice-minister of national education and a supervisor of Moscow University, yet despite his meteoric social ascent, he never abandoned his sentimental ideals and aspirations (Zorin 2016a, 187–197).

Theater as a Moral Compass

Catherine continued to sponsor poets such as Petrov and Derzhavin, but in general, poetry was significantly less important to her than theater. She completely disqualified Sumarokov as the leader of Russian theater because she wanted neither to share the laurels with him nor to lose control over this institution. She believed that theater was to play the main role in her civilizational project. She followed the famous discussion on theater between D'Alembert and Rousseau and rallied to the side of D'Alembert, who wrote that theater "educates the taste of the citizens and provides them with a refinement of manners and delicacy of feelings that is very difficult to acquire otherwise" (D'Alembert 1821, 417). After her accession to the throne, she invited the philosopher to St. Petersburg, offering him the position of tutor to the heir to the throne, Grand Duke Paul (Kobeko 1884). D'Alembert rejected the offer, but from the memoirs of the grand duke's actual tutor, Semen Poroshin, we know that theatrical impressions played an enormous role in Paul's upbringing (Poroshin 2015). Later on, Catherine happily reported to Friedrich Melchior von Grimm that her beloved grandson Grand Duke Alexander memorized at the tender age of eight all the plays performed in the Hermitage theater (Ekaterina II 1878, 329).

The logic of Catherine's approach is not difficult to grasp. Theater is uniquely capable of delivering to the public a socially approved emotional repertoire, which is embodied in expressive gestures and, at the same time, fully purged of the casual empirics of everyday life. The audience thus forges a sort of emotional community, where members have an opportunity to compare their own reaction with that of their peers and to check the "correctness" of their feelings right in the moment of experiencing them. Theater thus contributed to the interiorization of a politically suitable emotional regime, ultimately shaping the identities of Catherine's aristocratic subjects.

Court theater, with its attendant practices, was uniquely conducive to discharging these functions. The ritualization of courtly life undermined the barrier between the stage and the hall, especially as the candles were not extinguished during the performance (Johnson 1995, 11–13). The popularity of amateur performances in the aristocratic milieu to some extent allowed the actors and the spectators to switch places. The shaping of the emotional world of the audience took place in parallel with acquiring basic social skills before the attentive eye of the monarch. Of course, court theater could influence the souls and manners only of a limited audience, but as the court was supposed to serve as an object for imitation, its practices and cultural norms acquired universal importance.

Catherine did not limit herself to such traditional forms of theatrical patronage practiced by other monarchs as providing generous funding, appointing the highest courtiers as directors, or attending performances regularly. She took everyday theater management into her own hands, wrote comedies and comic operas and supervised their production, influenced the choice of plays to be staged and the distribution of roles, defined the complicated rules of public access to different performances, and monitored the behavior of the audience.

The personal presence of the monarch constituted the semiotic focus of the spectacle. Catherine was at the same time producer, spectator, and main participant of the performance, and she knew how to play all these roles skillfully. She had two personal loges in the Winter Palace opera theater at her disposal, and she sometimes changed between them in the midst of a performance. One was located at the end of the hall and opposite the stage; this represented her status and gave her an ideal point for observation. The other lodge was near the stage, to emphasize her direct connection with the play and to allow the audience to see her reactions and adjust their perception accordingly (Evstratov 2016a, 198–204).

Theater played an important role in the educational process. Both the Cadet Corps and, later, the Institute for Noble Girls (or, as it was called, the Smolny Institute) had their amateur theaters. The life of the pupils of these institutions was tightly controlled, including strict censorship of their reading lists. The girls in Smolny were allowed to read only books of historical and didactic content. The goal of this regulation was to protect them from reading novels usually full of amorous adventures (Cherepnin 1915, 1:121). Still, they were regularly involved in theater performances. Rehearsals went on throughout the year and occupied a lot of time, and the expenses for the costumes and decorations were quite substantial (Vsevolodskii-Gerngross 1913, 383).

Mirroring the theater repertoire of the period, most of the plays staged at the Institute had plots dealing with love and marriage.

Catherine modeled Smolny on Saint-Cyr, the school founded by Louis XIV, where the students were also involved in performances. However, Madame Maintenon, the patron of Saint-Cyr, specially commissioned Racine to write plays on religious topics (Piéjus 2000, 94–104, 127–137). Catherine initially planned a less radical solution along the same lines—she wrote to Voltaire explaining that the guardians of the institute tried to avoid plays that have too much passion, but failed to find adequate works. So she asked her correspondent to provide her with a list of less offensive plays and to purge overly risky passages from existing ones to make them suitable for the girls, who, in her own view, performed their roles better than local actors. Voltaire promised to oblige, but never delivered. Catherine and her associates nevertheless thought it necessary to encourage theater, believing that benefits from it outweigh the dangers (Vsevolodskii-Gerngross 1913, 374–379).

Performances in the Smolny started in the early 1770s with Voltaire's *Zaire*, followed as a token sign of patriotism by Sumarokov's *Semira*, a play modeled on Voltaire's tragedies. Thereafter, the repertoire performed by the demoiselles was nearly entirely comic and entirely francophone. Along with the court theater dominated by a French troupe, the theatrical exercises at the closed educational establishment were part of the top-down Europeanization of the Russian elite undertaken by the empress. They also served to establish in the eyes of the public the image of the Russian empire and its court as one of the centers of European civilization. Catherine ordered her own comedies to be translated into French and German and had them sent to Voltaire and then, after his death, to Grimm and Zimmerman. Her close involvement with theater doomed from the very beginning Sumarokov's efforts to spearhead the development of Russian theater.

The efforts of the empress to promote theater produced significant results: during the last quarter of the eighteenth century the nobility became more and more involved both in amateur theatrical productions (Lotman 1994) and in organizing serf theaters on their country estates. Various records name between seventy-five and ninety manorial serf theaters in the provinces (Stites 2005, 224). Sometimes it is impossible to distinguish between an amateur noble theater and a serf one, as masters, family members, and their friends participated in the performances alongside their peasants. Of course, only the richest part of the nobility could afford to remove a significant number of serfs from agricultural work. It was more or less the same section of the elite that was able to benefit from the Manifesto on the Freedom of the Nobility and forgo income from state service in favor of the refined pleasures afforded by life on their estates. By definition, it was also the most educated and Europeanized part of the nobility.

For generations of writers such as Alexander Griboedov, Alexander Herzen and Nikolai Leskov, serf theater functioned as one of the most powerful symbols of social evil. Yet the nobles who organized serf theaters regarded their lifestyle as highly enlightened. In introducing the highest achievements of European culture on their estates and in provincial towns, they were following the example set by the empress. The richest landowners often brought to their performances royal splendor and melodramatic effects worthy of the performed repertoire.

Arguably, the most famous serf theater belonged to count Nikolai Sheremetev, the scion and only heir of the richest Russian aristocratic family. The theaters in his palaces on the outskirts of Moscow competed with court theater in lavish stage effects and in the quality of staging and performance. Appropriately for the master, Sheremetev developed an affair with the leading actress and singer of his troupe, Praskov'ia (Parasha) Kovaleva (her stage name Zhemchugova came from the Russian word *zhemchug*—a pearl). In the households of wealthy Russian nobles, such relations were trivial, but in this instance, the affair gradually evolved into passionate love and finally led to a marriage that constituted the most spectacular misalliance in Russian history since 1721, when Peter the Great married Martha Skavronsky, the daughter of Latvian peasants, who later became the empress Catherine I. In order to legitimize his marriage, Sheremetev hired genealogists, who provided him with forged papers testifying that his lover came from a family of Polish nobles. The Polish nobility was extremely numerous and mostly poor, but despite this, the forgery was blatant, as were the motives for it—Sheremetev needed to make his choice more respectable and to legitimize his son, the heir to his immense fortune. As Douglas Smith perceptively noted, the story of a nobleman who falls in love with a woman of common origins and goes through deep inner conflict between love and honor, only to discover that his beloved is a hidden noble, constituted a traditional plot of comic operas. Parasha herself had played in such comedies, and in the end, she herself became the character of such a play, even if her fortunate transformation took place not long before her death in childbirth (Smith 2008, 206–216). The real life story mimicked the traditional plot of the French comic opera, showing to what extent the theatrical patterns were interiorized by the Russian aristocracy.

The Quest for Shaping a Broader Public

As theater could reach only the upper stratum of the nobility, the broader group of provincial gentry was lacking the means of cultural Europeanization. Publishing had wider reach. In 1769 Catherine launched the satiric magazine *Vsiakaia vsiachina* (*All Sorts of Things*), encouraging the import of British-style moralistic journalism. In it, she wielded an anonymous pen to castigate various moral foibles and social pathologies. A plethora of similar short-lived publications followed suit. Nikolai Novikov, the editor of the magazine *The Bee*, took advantage of the pretended anonymity of *All Sorts of Things* to engage the empress in a discussion about the uses and abuses of satire, but despite this, Catherine chose to continue to support his publishing enterprises. Novikov's second magazine, *The Painter*, started in 1772, earning the lavish praise of *O Times*, the first comedy written by the empress, which was staged and published anonymously.

Novikov was by far the most renowned and successful of Russian eighteenth-century publishers (Jones 1984, Marker 1985). He started his career in 1768 as a member of the Society for the Translation of Foreign Books, a body founded and generously endowed by Catherine and chaired by her personal cabinet-secretary Grigorii Kozitsky. Novikov helped with organizing the venture, but in spite of its august support, the society stopped its activities in 1774 due to the absence of an efficient book distribution system. After engaging in several other publishing enterprises also commissioned by the empress, Novikov moved to Moscow in 1779, leased the press of Moscow University, and embarked on a publishing venture that finally brought a qualitative change to the national book culture. While previously literature was available mostly to only the narrow circles of St. Petersburg and Moscow literati, Novikov paid special attention to developing the book trade in provincial cities and towns, where the hunger for books was acute. The overwhelming majority of the books he published were translations. For the university press, he commissioned the publication of a significant amount of contemporary European fiction, including Lessing, Sterne, Swift, and Beaumarchais.

In 1783, trying to satisfy the growing demand for books, Catherine issued a decree that allowed the establishment of free presses. As usual, she wanted both to promote publishing and to control it. Prior to her decree, the license to publish books was awarded only to special state institutions: the Senate, the Holy Synod, the Academy of Sciences, and Moscow University. In 1802, in his article *On Book Trade and Love for Reading in Russia*, published in the influential magazine *The Messenger of Europe*, Nikolai Karamzin stated that the distribution of books increased more than tenfold in the final quarter of the century. The author attributed this momentous change to the activities of Novikov, who, according to Karamzin, "multiplied the mechanical means of book publishing, commissioned the translation of books, established book-shops in provincial towns, and tried hard to instill the love of reading among the public" (Karamzin 1964, 2:176).

It is difficult to obtain hard data about sales figures and assess the actual dimensions of the book market. However, the number of subscribers to the most successful magazines gradually increased from several hundred in the late eighteenth century to thousands in the early nineteenth (Marker 1985, Samarin 2000). Karamzin, who was arguably the first Russian professional man of letters, was offered the hefty sum of six thousand rubles annually for publishing *The Messenger of Europe*, which was nearly four times larger than his revenue from his estates, suggesting that the market for magazines had matured (Korchmina and Zorin 2018). Books became not only numerous, but affordable—Karamzin wrote in his article that even nobles with the mea-ger annual income of five hundred rubles were collecting libraries. He gave special mention to the increasing reading habits of women and children—at country fairs provincial noblewomen were ordering "not only caps, but books as well."

Karamzin had firsthand information about Novikov's role in the history of book production in Russia, because he was part of the project nearly from its inception. Understandably, in his article he was more reserved about his own role, which in many ways was no less decisive than that of his mentor. As a junior member of the Moscow Rosicrucian brotherhood led by Novikov, Karamzin became the main translator for *Children's Reading*, in which he also published his first original works. In one of them, titled *The Walk*, he described the time he spent in the countryside around Moscow with *The Seasons* by James Thomson in his pocket. The book allowed him to verify the way he responded to the beauty of nature and served as a tuning fork to adjust the pitch of his heart, a mode of literary reception typical of the times, as we explained in chapter 1.

A print text lacks the ability to represent socially approved models of feeling expressed in bodily form, which was so important in the theater. However, it allows a constant replay and refining of feelings when readers measure their responses against the emotions expressed by the author. It also enables the individual consumption of cultural, behavioral, and emotional patterns across national borders. Unlike a theatrical performance, a book is easily portable. Later, the cultured provincial landowner Andrei Bolotov praised Karamzin for publishing his books "in a small format, which could serve as pocket book and be used as pleasant reading during walks" (Guberti 1887, 24).

The proliferation of printing presses following the liberalization of publishing prompted the need to create a separate structure for censorship. Prior to the liberalization of book printing in 1783, the function of censors was performed by specially nominated clerks of the organizations allowed to operate a press. In the initial period after the liberalization of the press, Catherine believed that the role of censor could be performed by local authorities, but they evidently lacked the necessary qualifications. As early as the mid-1780s, the empress grew disturbed by the booming enterprise of Novikov and the Friendly Learned Society he established in Moscow, as they overstepped the sphere she had delineated for them. In 1793 she also closed down an independent press in St. Petersburg and temporarily arrested the publishers. The censorship regime was made more restrictive under Paul I, who also banned the import of books and even musical scores. However, it was only in the early nineteenth century that censorship as a separate institution with specific functions was introduced in Russia.

Literature and the Birth of the "Nation"

The incompetence of local government in questions of censorship became spectacular in 1790, when with the permission of the St. Petersburg police chief, Nikita Ryleev, Alexander Radishchev published *A Journey from Saint-Petersburg to Moscow* on his own private press. This publication became the most outrageous violation of the political and cultural order Catherine was striving to establish and arguably, the most seditious work issued legally in Russia until the appearance seven decades later of Chernyshevsky's *What Is to Be Done*. For more than two centuries, scholars have been arguing whether this book represented a revolutionary proclamation or a plea to authorities to implement major reforms, including the abolition of serfdom and censorship—Radishchev provided enough ammunition for both points of view.

Most likely, the author of this strange text written in a bombastic style was himself wavering between the desire to scare the government with a threat of peasant rebellion and the hope that such a rebellion would do away with a political and social system he hated. Catherine was infuriated. She accused the author of "disseminating the French infection" and being at once "a Martinist" (her usual name for Moscow Rosicrucians) and "a rebel worse than Pugachev" (Khrapovitskii 1874, 340), thus characterizing him both as a Western-style mystic and revolutionary, and as a peer of the instigator of a Cossack rebellion that took place in the 1770s. Radishchev was imprisoned, subjected to a mock trial, and condemned to capital punishment, before Catherine commuted his sentence to ten years of exile in Siberia. Radishchev's condemnation marks the nadir of relations between literature and the throne.

Radishchev was arguably one of the most European of eighteenth-century Russian Europeans. Having studied at the University of Leipzig in his youth, he brought back not only a deeply held attachment to Enlightenment ideals, notably the conviction, inspired by Helvetius, that the texture of national life could be changed through legislative means, but also a passionate republicanism and religious worship of personal freedom. He did not believe in representative government, considering human rights to be inalienable and not transferrable to any sort of elected body. Tyrannicide constituted to him a more dignified way of protecting human rights than any system of checks and balances. As early as 1790, Radishchev denounced the Parisian Convent for violating individual liberties, accusing it of "not going far enough from the casemates of the Bastille" (Radishchev 1958, 186).

This way of thinking was radical even by the standards of the French revolution, at least in its early years, and totally incompatible with such realities of Russian life as serfdom, absolutist monarchy, censorship, and lack of respect for personal dignity. It was precisely the extent of the contrast between ideals and social reality that made such radicalization possible. Radishchev could not imagine any means to achieve his goals and had to believe in the civic virtues dormant in the Russian peasant, who, in a hundred years' time, would establish a republican order by breaking Russia up into hundreds of Swiss-type cantons based on direct participatory democracy. However, during the interrogations, as he faced the accusation of inciting a peasant rebellion, Radishchev pleaded not guilty, asserting that Russian peasants do not read books. He had not been thinking about actual serfs living on the estates owned by his relatives, peers, and himself, but about creating an idealized image, which joined together the Roman worship of liberty, forgotten among the upper classes of society, and the Herderian vision of the national soul, as reflected in folk songs and music.

Radishchev's vision was an extreme case of a general quest for national identity, which acquired pan-European dimensions by the end of the century. The growing Europeanization of the Russian elite made this challenge ever more acute. Rousseau, who was immensely popular in Russia, wrote in *Du contrat social* that Peter's "first wish was to make Germans or Englishmen when he ought to be making Russians." As Paris set universal norms in fashion, customs, and habits, its cultural domination supported and promoted by the francophony of the cosmopolitan European nobility, this new national awareness inevitably acquired anti-French dimensions. Rousseau compared Peter to a French preceptor who teaches "a pupil to be an infant prodigy and for the rest of his life to be nothing whatsoever" (Rousseau 1971, 198–199).

Accusations about the imitative and superficial character of Russian Europeanization became a challenge the Russian elite and its literary apologists had to deal with. When Peter enshrined European appearance, manners, and lifestyles in law, he took it for granted that he was promoting the only way civilized human beings can look and act. This attitude could easily coexist with patriotic attachment to one's own country and pride in its military and cultural successes. With the spread of the idea of national character and national traditions, these assumptions became significantly more problematic.

Like many other major cultural trends, the search for the ancient roots of the country was instigated and sponsored by Catherine. Starting in the 1770s, she edited collections of quasi–folk proverbs, played Russian games, and arranged folk dancing at court. She also subsidized Novikov's publications of old chronicles, sent ethnographic expeditions to the provinces, and wrote plays dedicated to the earliest chapters of Russian history. Catherine enthusiastically approved Denis Fonvizin's attack on Gallomania in his comedy *The Brigadier* (1769), which became a canonical satire on the slavish imitation of things foreign. The play was modeled on *Jean de France* by the Danish playwright Ludwig Holberg. Even patriotic feelings needed some sort of European model.

Following Holberg, Fonvizin (1745–1792) mocks the excessive use of borrowings from French instead of using simple Russian words. It is difficult to say whether this manner of speech was characteristic of some part of the Russian or Danish nobility, or whether it was invented by the authors to achieve the required comic effect. In any case, by the turn of the century, the language question became a rallying cry for the proponents of Russian national identity. The pamphlet *On Old and New Style*, by admiral Aleksandr Shishkov (1754–1841), published in 1804 during the reign of Alexander I, constituted an attack on "Gallicisms," French borrowings in Russian, which the author saw as a sign of political disloyalty to the Russian throne. Shishkov proposed a whole set of words of his own invention to replace borrowings that were already in use in the language. His Herderian conception of language as an embodiment of the national soul was most likely inspired by *Wörterbuch für Verbesserung und Verdeutschung der deutschen Sprache*, compiled by the German linguist Joachim Campe. The German idea of national unity based on shared language and culture appealed to the Russian educated elite notwithstanding the fact that Russia, unlike Germany, was not divided into dozens of mini-states, but was a powerful multinational and multiconfessional empire.

Shishkov's book itself was not free from Gallicisms (Zhivov 2009), as the new Russian nobility already could not do without them and had to oscillate between full-scale francophony and using a highly Gallicized Russian replete with lexical and grammatical borrowings from French. General Petr Kikin, a future hero of the war of 1812, called Shishkov's *Discourse on the Old and the New Style*, which urged Russians to stop using French, "Mon Evangile"! In the last years before the war, Alexander I's sister Grand Duchess Ekaterina Pavlovna, who was the main hope of the patriotic party, grew highly popular among the elite. The grand duchess herself saw it as her duty to lead the nation in the approaching battle against Napoleon, and in order to make herself ready for such a task, she asked Karamzin to give her lessons in Russian, as she could barely speak the language.

The militant monarchist and conservative Shishkov accused the educated stratum of Russian society of betraying the cultural legacy of its ancestors, which is paradoxically not unlike the remonstrations by the radical Radishchev. Shishkov even dared, albeit in a very cautious manner, to criticize Peter the Great for importing into Russia unnecessary foreign customs, together with useful innovations. But the main blame for spoiling the language and thus for introducing ways of thinking alien to Russian traditions was, according to Shishkov, imputable to Karamzin, whom he never mentioned by name but made it easy to recognize between the lines. The ensuing debate between the followers of the two writers became one of the most defining polemics of literary life in the first decades of the nineteenth century.

These accusations had nothing to do with the actual linguistic, political, and social views of Karamzin, who at the time had developed a way
of thinking not unlike his opponent's. In his travelogue, he had described
Europe as a system of national monades, each endowed with distinctive
cultural characteristics. This perspective inevitably led him to address the
question of Russia's place in this system, its character, and its originality.
After his return to Russia, Karamzin progressively gravitated toward historical topics and, after 1804, spent the twenty-two remaining years of his
life working on his magnum opus—*The History of the Russian State*. Partly
published in 1818, it made Russian pre-Petrine history accessible for the
first time to the general readership in the same manner as his *Letters of a
Russian Traveller* had packaged contemporary European culture for general
use. While one can discern different shades between Shishkov's linguistic
nationalism and Karamzin's political and historic one, the larger point is that
they all inherited Rousseau's idea that sovereignty inhered in the body of the
nation, which they sought in different ways to reconstruct, converging on
the need to (re)discover the sources of national identity. Paying homage to
Karamzin after his death, Pushkin said that he "discovered Ancient Russia
as Columbus did America" (Pushkin 1962–1965, 8:67) In order to do so, in
the same Columbus-like manner, Karamzin had, as it were, to travel abroad:
the whole idea of national history as defined by the national character had
distinctly European origins.

In exactly the same manner, individual Europeanized nobles were constantly trying to construct their self-perception from imported material and
to search for a place at the crossroads between European culture and the leg-
acies of their own country. The twenty-one-year old Andrei Turgenev wrote
in his diary in 1803:

> For a person the road must be their *Selbstheit* [original selfhood]. They must
> always be themselves and retain it everywhere, even though Rousseau and
> Fénelon might be their mentor. Wieland said this, even when talking about
> Christ. It is not me (a person) who must enter into Rousseau, but Rousseau must
> enter into me and make me myself. (IRLI OR, f. 309, ed. khr. 272, l. 55ob-56)

Turgenev wrote this several months before he decided to end his life because
he believed he had failed to live up to the standards he had set for himself.
He searched for his own individuality, which he wanted to preserve under all

circumstances, but needed Wieland to teach him this wisdom and Rousseau to show him an example of this unwavering originality.

The main literary legacy of Andrei Turgenev is his diary, full of intense introspection, self-accusations, and attempts to assess his actions, thoughts, and feelings in comparison with the characters of European preromantic and sentimentalist literature. He planned to bind his copy of *The Sorrows of Young Werther* together with white sheets of papers and write his diary inside his favorite book. His untimely death had very strong similarities with Werther's suicide. His tragic life story illustrates the tensions that arose at the beginning of the nineteenth century between the comprehensive Europeanization of the elite and its urgent quest for national and individual distinctiveness.

Informing his friend Aleksandr Bulgakov about the sudden death of Andrei Turgenev in 1803, Grigorii Gagarin, an exquisite courtier and admirer of French gallant poetry, copied into his letter the poem *Sons of the Fatherland Give an Oath* written by the deceased. The fervent patriotic feelings and the desire to die for the fatherland expressed in the poem made Gagarin proud and prompted him to exclaim that nobody deserved to live more than his late friend. His letter, however, was written in French, and Gagarin himself spent most of his life outside Russia (Zorin 2016c, 424–428, 470; Zhivov 2008). The new pursuit of national identity deepened the gulf between the court, which remained too cosmopolitan for comfort, and the sentimentalist aspirations of the new generation of nobles, who in search for the Russian soul became uneasy with their own Europeanization, while being thoroughly permeated with European modes of feelings and thought.

The moment of retrospective analysis for the majority of Russian nobles arrived in 1813–1814, when thousands of officers made a European campaign through German states all the way to Paris. The Parisian public, expecting an invasion by hordes of unshaven warriors, was surprised to meet sophisticated Europeans speaking exquisite ancien régime French and frequenting the Académie française and Parisian theaters. The lessons taught by the St. Petersburg court theater and by *The Letters of a Russian Traveller* had been fully assimilated and implemented. The project of artificially creating an educated Europeanized elite worked brilliantly. However, this success laid bare the cracks in the foundation of the experiment.

Nowhere can the emerging problems better be seen than in the life stories of the children and pupils of Mikhail Murav'ev. As discussed above, Murav'ev faced contradictions between his status as a high-ranking statesman and a sentimentalist writer, contradictions requiring various adjustments and negotiations. However, he still managed to navigate them without too much damage and trouble. For his sons Nikita and Aleksandr, an irreconcilable gulf opened up between the values they were taught and the duties of service, a gulf that eventually led them to participate in the Decembrist conspiracy. Their opposition to serfdom and absolutist rule contradicted the oath of loyalty to the emperor, which they tended to reinterpret as loyalty to the nation. On the other side of the political spectrum, Murav'ev's august pupil Emperor Alexander I remained, until the end of his life, torn between the sentimental republicanism taught by his mentors and his role as the absolute monarch of a huge, traditional empire. These were, of course, extreme cases—the majority of nobles did not have to face such stark existential choices, but they highlight the challenges many of the members of the elite had to deal with.

According to Belinsky, the historic task of Russian literature during the first centuries of its development was to "nationalize" itself in order to take root in the native soil. This gigantic task was, as the critic believed, finally achieved in Pushkin's *Evgenii Onegin,* a novel in verse in which each of the main characters was shaped by different strands of Western literature: Tat'iana by the novels of Richardson, Rousseau, and de Stael; Onegin by Byron and contemporary French prose writers such as Constant and Chateaubriand; and Lensky by Schiller and Goethe. These different backgrounds cause significant and often fatal misunderstandings between the characters, but all of them realize that they belong to the same cultural entity, an entity clearly and strictly differentiated not only from lower estates, but also from the part of the nobility that had not yet digested the newest achievements of European culture. Tellingly, neither of the two male protagonists ever served the state or had the slightest inclination to do so in the future. Belinsky argued that precisely these characters were the sublime expression of the national spirit and that Pushkin himself viewed his French-speaking female heroine as the embodiment of the Russian soul. Be it as it may, this novel, which marked Russian literature's accession to full maturity and originality, represented at the same time a parting with the culture of the cosmopolitan Europeanized nobility. The subsequent conflict between the Slavophiles and Westernizers, which began in the immediate aftermath of Pushkin's death, transformed the contradiction between different attachments and behavioral codes from a question of subtle navigation and reconciliation into the necessity of making an existential and ideological choice.

7

. . . .

THE EUROPEANIZED SELF
COLONIZING THE PROVINCES

At the time Catherine II acceded to the throne, the vast provinces of the Russian empire were an under-administered, poorly understood, yet economically critical territory. The empire was managed by unofficial agents—landowners, merchants, and Cossacks—who collected taxes on behalf of the government, supported only by a few officials in district chancelleries, namely a *voevoda* and two or three other officials. These people discharged all manner of executive, fiscal, judicial, and police functions, a conflation of responsibilities that created backlogs and conflicts of interest. Administering the provinces was comparatively cheap, but wholly inefficient. There was little investment to speak of, notably in infrastructure or education, and few channels of communication to provide the government with an understanding of the state of the empire. It is characteristic of its administrative failings that in the early 1760s, the government was unable to establish

with full certainty how many district chancelleries it possessed altogether
(Jones 1984, 82).

Provincial towns were in a particular sorry state, featuring few amenities
and little architectural coherence. These were low-density agglomerations, in
which vacant lands separated individual houses. Narrow streets, mostly without pavement or at best covered by tree logs, followed crooked, random trajectories. And deplorable sanitary conditions fostered the spread of illnesses
(Chechulin 2010, 70–74). Only churches and monasteries were built of bricks
or, more rarely, stone, other buildings being made of wood, generally in the
log-construction manner of Russian *izbas*. Apart from the few officials in the
chancelleries, towns were inhabited by merchants, traders, or peasants and
largely ignored by the nobility.

In this chapter we will briefly delineate official attempts to understand and
transform the provinces, before considering the elite's response to the role it
was given to assist in improving the empire economically, administratively,
and aesthetically by assuming a role in local administration. We will seek
to evaluate the extent to which the elite began to identify with their provincial abodes and, if so, to determine what particular sites commanded their
attachment. We will try to ascertain how local ties, and the responsibilities
that came with them, affected their subjective world and outlook, if at all, and
how Europeanization played itself out in the minds of the provincial elite.
And we will suggest that the colonization of the provinces resulted not in the
blanket Europeanization of the inhabitants of the provinces, but in the creation of scattered, discrete sites of Europeanized sociability. These sites were
often fashioned after the elite's lifestyle in the capitals, thus canceling out any
regional distinctiveness and identity.

Getting to Know the Provinces

The government's first imperative, prior to launching any development program, was to gain knowledge of the conditions and resources of the empire,
a need made all the more acute by its size and diversity. In 1768 Catherine
mandated the Academy of Sciences to organize several expeditions to take
stock of "what can contribute to the prosperity of the empire" (Pallas 1788, 1:
iii). She was particularly interested in the physical and economic geography
of her dominions, that is in everything concerning natural resources, agro-
nomic practices, and industry, but the remit given to scientists also included

consideration "of the mores, customs, religions, cults, languages, traditions, monuments, and antiquities" of the surveyed populations (1: v). These expeditions were to establish an exhaustive inventory of the natural and human resources of the empire, providing comprehensive knowledge of the diversity of its physical and human geography.

One of these expeditions was headed by Peter Simon Pallas, originally a zoologist from Berlin, who was invited to join the St. Petersburg Academy of Sciences in 1767. The expedition proceeded for six years through central Russia, the Urals, Western Siberia all the way to Lake Baikal, then to the Altai Mountains and eventually to the Caspian Sea. Pallas sent regular dispatches back to St. Petersburg, which were subsequently collected in a three-volume edition first published in German and then translated into various languages. His audience, in other words, was the empress, but also the pan-European scholarly community and educated reader.

Pallas approached the empire very much in the manner of a scientist of his times, deploying a classificatory method that inventoried and organized all the species of natural history he encountered on his way. He operated within an Enlightenment-inspired axiology, disparaging some of what he saw as "yet in infancy"—that is, at an earlier stage of civilizational development (Pallas 1788, 1:27). The journey through the Russian empire was hence a journey back in time, through various periods of human evolution. Nevertheless, his relation to the past was generally respectful, despite the occasional snide comment, and he took care to identify architectural structures and ruins that merited preservation. As he visited a burial vault, he blamed "the curiosity of our century" for disturbing the remains (1:43). Pallas's attitude toward the empire's ethnic diversity was not unique. A few decades later Johann Georgi would still claim that the Russian empire contained "all the stages of transformation from the ancient, simple World very close to its natural condition to the present World, refined and enriched by needs" (quoted by Slezkine 1994, 187).

While predominantly inventorying what was common, known, and therefore recognizable, Pallas also sought to come to terms with what was singular and extraordinary—in excess, as it were, of the classificatory web he cast on the data he collected. When his typologies proved unequal to the task, he resorted to descriptions *a contrario*, defining a phenomenon by what it is not. He also took particular note of local designations, which he related to common terms, suggesting an incipient awareness that language is an important marker of identity.

Pallas was nowhere more challenged than when he dealt with human populations. Here, too, he proved alert to what was distinctive in the customs, beliefs, and dress of an ethnic group (the published volumes contain detailed illustrations of ethnic costume). Yet, on occasion, the limited knowledge of his informants threatened his ambition to provide an exhaustive sum of knowledge. When he interrogated the Mordvins about their original pagan beliefs (knowing all well that they had been forcibly converted to Christianity), he was frustrated by their ignorance and became abruptly dismissive: "This is all I could extract from these stupid people," he noted in one instance (Pallas 1788, 1:109). A similar situation arose with respect to the Chuvash, whom he called "idiotic," noting that more research would yield much of interest (1:138). It was not only that the ignorance of locals disrupted the integrality of his scientific project, but also that the discrepancy between their current beliefs and what he imagined as their original culture undermined Pallas's historical universalist masterplot, as local ethnicities failed to coincide with their anthropological role as "primitives," holdovers from more ancient times.

Nevertheless, overall, his travel account provided a graphic and detailed view of the provinces, highlighting much that was worthy of scientific interest, economically promising, or aesthetically rewarding. With regard to agricultural and industrial practice, his evaluation was at once laudatory and redolent of European superiority. He generally praised the work ethic of local populations. The town of Arzamas, for example, "owes its prosperity to the industriousness of its inhabitants and makes visible on a small scale the advantages that factories and manufacture can bring to the state at large" (1:69). The empire was thus full of prospects, surely music to Catherine's ears. Yet Pallas also repeatedly underscored the rudimentary techniques used by locals and evinced great frustration when his suggestions for improvement fell on deaf ears, as happened when he criticized a distillery in Simbirsk. His conclusion here, perhaps a cautionary tale for Catherine, was that "the most severe ordinances are sometimes helpless to root out customary methods, however bad they are" (1:131). The empire thus provided a mixed picture, full of potential and promise, but also capable of resistance and inertia.

Ivan Lepekhin, a physician and adjunct at the Academy of Sciences, was another scientist dispatched on an expedition at the same time, even following partially the same route. Compared to Pallas, he paid greater attention to popular beliefs while on Russian territory and developed some awareness of the relativity of knowledge. In Vladimir, he met an old woman who practiced folk medicine and used the herb aconitum soongaricum (*tsar-trava*), which he considered highly poisonous. After scolding her for her recklessness, he came to regret his high-handedness, as the folk healer stopped supplying him with information. But he was also led to reconsider the superiority of his knowledge when he realized that the old woman would not enjoy popular respect had she dispatched several of her patients to the netherworld. He conceded, "Everyone who does not have preconceived ideas about poisonous bodies would agree that what we consider poison can in the hands of a sensible person be a divine medicine" (Lepekhin 1771, 16–18). The provinces, in Lepekhin's eyes, were the realm of much benighted belief, but also the place where one could glimpse a fleeting vista into the insufficiency of one's own knowledge. In this strange, sometimes even grotesque universe of the Russian provinces, scientific dispassionateness turns against itself, poking holes into the self-assured superiority of Enlightened knowledge, suggesting a rise of reflexivity and relativity (Slezkine 1994, 177–178).

Contrary to Pallas, Lepekhin also tackled questions of political economy. He was not shy to draw attention to serious tensions between serf communities and local authorities (57). On his way, he condemned various practices in the Russian village, such as the proximity of barns and living quarters, a fire hazard (59); the clear-cutting of forests for new fields, which destroys valuable timber suitable for ship-building (62); and the use of bast shoes (a wasteful use of linden) (65). He disparaged the low craftsmanship in Russian towns, which he linked to the fact that serfs undercut artisans by selling their own handcrafted objects (91–92). In summary, despite token scientific objectivity, his overall view of the provinces was of a benighted, dysfunctional, and slightly uncomfortable realm, where one's enlightened superiority could begin to crack under the onslaught of the vast forms of difference in evidence in the provinces. It is telling that to pursue his aims, he deemed it necessary to conceal his professional identity as a doctor. Taken together, these expeditions demonstrated the enticing potential of the provinces, but also the huge complexities of the "civilizational" task at hand.

To gain knowledge of the provinces, Catherine not only dispatched scientific expeditions, but also undertook to travel herself. In 1767, she embarked on a trip along the Volga to Kazan, where she apprised herself of the state of Muslim Tatars. The purpose of her journeys was not simply to survey the achievements of her government, but also to establish communication with local populations, obtain useful information about their lives, improve their education, influence their views of the state, and, most importantly, elicit consent to her policies. While displaying interest in the history of Tatars in Kazan, she also ordered the governor to organize theatrical representations (Ibneeva 2009, 276), no doubt to inculcate her notions of civility to the local public. While traveling down the Volga, she wrote a "History of the Volga Bulgars" and also supervised a collective translation with officials in her suite of Marmontel's *Belisarius*, a novel that advocated religious tolerance. G. V. Ibneeva concluded that "at that time the ethnic heterogeneity of the empire was not simply a fact of consciousness, but something that was to be studied and something Great-Russians were to be proud of" (321). She might have added, perhaps, that this openness was driven by the administrative weakness of the empire, which did not have the resources to enforce homogeneity in the immediate term. Securing the allegiance of local elites was a pragmatic necessity, regardless of their confessional and ethnic background. The historian V. O. Kliuchevsky reported that Catherine considered Muslim polygamy useful in order to increase the population of the empire. Hence she was in no hurry to force the conversion of her Muslim subjects (Kliuchevskii 1989, 5:301).

Scientific and imperial journeys thus marked the beginning of a serious engagement with the provinces, based on the implementation of scientific classification and incipient historical research, all within the premises of an overarching notion of state utility, but also with a certain degree of respect for vernacular particularities. This endeavor formed part of what Willard Sunderland called the "territorial consciousness" arising in the eighteenth century, a way of thinking of the nation in terms of its territorial expanse, which was approached through the rationalizing lens of abstract geometric markers that could be "populated" by an inventory of their content, all of it in the interests of better management (Sunderland 2007, 49). The cameralist mindset at the heart of this enterprise required an efficient and precise administrative structure, which prompted Catherine to initiate in 1765 a cadastral land survey that aimed once for all to define the boundaries of estates and resolve disputes among landowners, an undertaking that had eluded her predecessors.

Transforming the Provinces

The provincial reforms announced in the Fundamental Law on the Administration of the Provinces of the Russian Empire, which was promulgated on

November 7, 1775 (PSZ 1830, vol. 20, no. 14.392, p. 229–304) pursued rationalizing aims. This law reorganized the administrative structure of the empire into a two-tier system consisting of provinces (*gubernia*) and districts (*uezd*). Provinces were equalized in size and vested with substantial administrative responsibilities; indeed, many functions were devolved from the center. They were headed by a governor-general, in charge of two provinces, who represented the monarch locally and was assisted by one governor for each province. Districts became units of twenty to thirty thousand inhabitants and were endowed with judicial and police functions (Jones 1973, 222–255).

These reforms required a drastic rise in the number of officials at both province and district levels (Jones 1984, 92–93). These positions were mainly staffed through elections among the main social estates (nobility, merchants, and peasants), thus allowing some degree of self-government (Jones 1973, 232). They resulted in the creation of numerous district towns, as each district was run from a small urban center. In fact, Catherine boasted of founding 216 towns (PSZ 1830, vol. 22, no. 16187, 358–359). As a result of these reforms, the provinces were now spanned by a much tighter network of towns that were developing into centers of administration, commerce, and entertainment. Nikolai Karamzin captured the intentions, if not necessarily the reality, of the reforms when he stated in his "Historical Encomium to Catherine the Great" that the reforms "opened up a new sphere of activity for [provincial] nobles, brought them out of their enforced (*proizvol'noe*) confinement, united them into society, and acquainted them with one another." He also touched on the Europeanizing agenda of the reforms, adding that "previously, some sort of coarse oriental magnificence distinguished wealthy nobles in the provinces, but now a common taste in life brings [various] conditions together and adorns ordinariness without luxury, giving even penury the appearance of contentment." Most importantly, in each province, the nobles now could find a "flourishing capital ... which beckoned them to the entertainments of the best European cities and ... showed that extensive steppes and forests in Russia do not obstruct the success of polite mundanity" (Karamzin 1802, 111–112).

The provincial reforms presented the nobility with places and institutions where they could come together and begin to develop a sense of corporate identity, a degree of self-consciousness as a unified social estate. The balloting to elect representatives often turned into protracted celebrations over two to three weeks. Describing life in the town of Penza in the 1790s, Ivan

Dolgorukov highlighted that provincial towns had become centers of sociability (and much backstabbing) for noble town-dwellers and landlords from the surrounding countryside. The reforms brought about a relocation of a segment of the elite from St. Petersburg and Moscow to the provinces. Chechulin calculated that after implementation of the reforms about 15 families of the "more educated estate" lived in district towns and about 100 in provincial towns (Chechulin 2010, 502). In Riazan, for example, the number of nobles residing in the city rose from 15 to 544 between 1750 and 1795. The number of nobles rose dramatically in absolute terms, and slowly in proportion to other estates (Mironov 1990, 82–83). Army regiments were often quartered in towns, in which case officers would contribute to social life. Provincial towns were given the right to owning a printing press, which allowed the emergence of provincial newspapers (Smith-Peter 2008). Some were also equipped with a theater (Kupriianov 2007, 118–152; Kuptsova 2012, 585). Thus, provincial towns progressively turned into centers for sociability and some cultural entertainment.

What administrative model lay behind the reforms? In its preamble, the law on provincial administration argued that reforms were required as a response to the spread of Enlightenment and the increase in population, which created a need for a more stringent order and greater care on behalf of the state. The law thus rested on the sense that modern times had superseded traditional ways of being, demanding greater formalization of procedures. It argued that "in ordaining the responsibilities and rules of each position . . . it [the law] guaranteed general peace and security." Meant as a response to the Pugachev rebellion, when a peasant jacquerie nearly toppled the government, the law also articulated a vision of the state's role in fostering private initiative (Jones 1984, 18–23). In so doing, it empowered officials with considerable responsibilities, but despite envisioning some separation of powers, it lacked the checks that would make a self-regulating system possible. Instead the law invoked God "to instill in the heart of those employed in this matter zeal toward the precise and earnest execution of their functions and aversion against idle luxury and all other vices . . . so that negligence in their responsibilities and disregard of the common good entrusted to them be considered a major abuse" (PSZ 1830, vol. 20, no. 14.392, p. 231). Thus, on the one side, the law envisioned the establishment of the cameralist principles of a well-ordered system, in which officials are bound by duty to the state, but on the other, it offered no mechanism to guarantee the civic devotion of state representatives other than a prayer to God. Not surprisingly, these reforms resulted in widespread corruption at the local level. A similar tension inhered in the fact that on the one hand the reforms aimed to establish a legally underpinned order, but on the other, the law presented the reforms as a manifestation of the motherly care of the monarch, thus tapping at once into systemic and personalistic models of government, into legalist and absolutist political theories. The reforms deployed a syncretic amalgam between various European philosophies: liberal ideas about self-interest as the engine of progress were adopted from Anne-Robert-Jacques Turgot and Adam Smith (Nisbet 1980, 180–191) and combined with German cameralist ideas about the well-ordered state and the subjects' duties to it (Jones 1984, 11–12, 18–23), all of it within the overall framework of absolutist power vested in the monarch.

The rationalist ordering impulse at the heart of the law was also in evidence in the (re)development of towns. In 1785, the Charter on the Rights and Interests of Towns in the Russian Empire stipulated in its first article that all towns had to be developed following regular plans approved personally by the empress (PSZ 1830, vol. 22, no. 16187, p. 359). Inspired by the construction of St. Petersburg, the plans conceived of towns as unified wholes organized rationally. This entailed removing objects obstructing the radial or grid plans that were superimposed upon the existing geography, spanning the town and its nearby settlements. Towns were organized around a central axis, with a square in the middle surrounded by official buildings (Jones 1984, 95). Streets were broadened and straightened, facades designed in the same spare neoclassical style that also dominated the construction of country estate mansions. As Jones suggested, the uniformity that resulted from this template-based construction reflected the civilizing notion that by regulating the external environment, one could change the moral character of townsmen and "enlighten" their hearts (97).

One of Catherine's pet projects was the city of Tver, whose center had burned down in 1763. Following a plan developed by I. I. Betskoi and with input from the empress, it was reconstructed mostly in stone and brick, with, in the center, a regular grid of thoughtfully proportioned streets and stylistically unified facades. The project rested on careful management of panoramic vistas, signaling a regime of rational visibility, and placed visual emphasis on the official buildings at the center of its composition, the embodiment of state power (Shkvarikov 1939, 112–126). The remodeling seemed indeed to affect the mentality of its resident nobles, who raised money for a statue to Catherine and showed other signs of public-spiritedness. In 1782, governor-general Iakov Bruce described it as "a masterpiece of order, obedience, and exactitude" (Jones 1984, 131). The same principles continued to be implemented throughout the reigns of Alexander I and Nicholas I. The Englishman William Hastie and the Italian Luisi Rusca prepared an album of standardized facades for private town houses. Hastie, "the standard-bearer of conformity," became the empire's master planner until his death in 1832 (Cross 1997, 307–308).

Provincial and Local Consciousness

This rationalist approach to the management of space and the rhetoric of public good complicated the emergence of provincial consciousness and identification. Nevertheless, among local officials, some awareness emerged that historical accidents had produced a degree of local or regional distinctiveness. Statistical surveys of various regions were meant to be an inventory of the "wealth of the nation," as it were, but they progressively went beyond their brief. To take but one example, the *Topographical Description of the Kharkov Province*, published anonymously in 1788 but attributed to the director of the Kharkov gymnasium I. A. Pereverzev, started with an extensive survey of Eurasian history, with reference to works by Abul al-Ghazi Bahadu, Prince Mikhail Shcherbatov, Gottfried Achenwall, and Samuel Pufendorf, a remarkably eclectic array of sources. The author assumed the preexistence of Russia, from which the Kievan principality was severed in the thirteenth century as a result of the Tatar occupation, and he tracked the resulting emergence of a distinct "south-Russian" identity. As Kiev fell under the influence of the Polish kings for the next three hundred years, "this fateful separation of South Russia from North or Great Russia forever transformed its inhabitants to the extent that a different tribe or nation arose from it; from there also comes the Little Russian, Ukrainian dialect, which became a constituent (*udel'nyi*) language of the Slavonic tribe" (*Topograficheskoe opisanie* 1788, 13–14). Although he regretted this fall from a presumed original unity of the "Russian" people, the author clearly considered this breakup to be irreversible, and it is remarkable for the times that he granted Ukrainian the status of a separate language. He argued that "the dominating clan exerts extensive influence on the way of life of the dominated peoples, forming a whole nation. A particular kind of economy, changes in thought and language, and overall character ... come from that." As a result of this top-down nation building, the local "South Russian" population internalized borrowed forms of daily life, while retaining certain facets of their original identity, which gave rise to a "varied mixture" in evidence to his day (14–15). While initially this progressive adaptation did not seem "burdensome," the situation changed as a result of conflicts between Russia and Poland, so that many residents migrated eastward back to Russia, settling on vacant lands and laying the foundations of what eventually became the Kharkov province in 1780, yet continuing to represent a distinctive national formation.

In the course of his statistical survey, Pereverzev mentioned certain Ukrainian national traits (referring now to Sloboda Ukraine—that is, the Kharkov province rather than the wider "South Russia") to explain the prevailing poverty, notably the phlegmatic character and propensity toward petty despotism of Ukrainians, which together led to a lack of industry and to family fragmentation (80–82). He called on the government to exercise "sustained control" of this situation, writing primarily from a statist perspective. Along with such unflattering comments, he also made positive observations—for example, that in their pride, Ukrainians "obey the voice of the government without servility" (90), or that there is balance, harmony, diversity, and pleasantness in the coexistence between the three main social estates (91). He also favorably compared Ukrainians to Russians, as, for example, he contrasted the condition of two villages, one Ukrainian and one Russian, or when he praised Ukrainians for consuming alcohol for the sake of friendly sociability, rather than to become inebriated (93). Indeed, he commended Ukrainians for their "European civility, devoid of Asian savagery," presumably the result of being preserved from Tatar influences. All in all, the author approached Ukrainians with some degree of sympathy, and while making the economic interests of the state paramount in his evaluation of their moral character, he also interjected some awareness of cultural distinctiveness and, indeed, relativity in his appreciation.

The writings of this local official suggest that while state policies imposed structural homogeneity and some abstract uniformity, they also tolerated a degree of local particularism. The *Description* (*opisanie*), including its historical survey, was incorporated into the sixth volume of L. M. Maksimovich's *Novyi i polnyi geograficheskii slovar' Rossiiskogo gosudarstva* (New and Complete Geographical Dictionary of the Russian State), which suggests official approval (Maksimovich 1789). Pereverzev saw himself at once as an agent of the state and as a mouthpiece of a more regional identity. Does that mean, as Sunderland maintained, that we can speak of the local elite's "identifica-tion with the province" and its "provincial patriotism" (Sunderland 2007, 47)? How did the elite respond to the top-down, state-driven rationalization and Europeanization of its way of life, and to what extent did it grow local roots? We can trace the elite's subjective investment in the provinces by looking at the place with which it identified most strongly, the country estate.

The Country Estate as Display of the Europeanized Self

The aristocratic country estate represented a key site of Europeanization in the provinces. By boosting the role of provincial and district towns as centers for trade, sociability, and cultural entertainment, the provincial reforms reduced the isolation of country estates and improved security across the provinces. Enhanced conditions allowed the elite to enjoy life on country estates even beyond the vicinity of the two capitals. In many cases, the lands granted to the upper nobility over the course of the century, or inherited from their fore-bears, had included little more than peasant villages and at best featured an unassuming mansion, requiring extensive development. The end of the eigh-teenth century and the first decades of the next therefore witnessed a con-struction boom, when many of the lavish countryseats of the Russian elite came into existence, often pushing families into considerable debt.

As they built their residences, the aristocracy chose an architectural idiom not fundamentally distinct from that espoused in the capitals. Building styles imported from the West radiated into the provinces from the capitals. The same architects, often foreign or foreign-trained ones, were recruited for both city and country pads. A generic neoclassical style became wide-spread, sometimes inflected with Palladian proportions (Roosevelt 1995, 34–73). In some instances, villas were modeled after buildings in the cap-itals. Ivan Bariatinsky's palace in Mar'ino, for example, imitated Pashkov House in Moscow. F. A. Tolstoi's mansion at Ivanovskoe was a replica of his Moscow residence (53). Architectural detail, indeed whole structures, could be prompted by the latest fashion landowners had seen on their jour-neys through Europe or in paintings and engravings. Sometimes garden fixtures evoked cherished memories from childhood or foreign travel, as in Pavlovsk, the residence of Paul I and Maria Fedorovna. Designed as a memorial garden, Pavlovsk encoded the grand duchess's childhood memo-ries of Montbéliard and of her family's summer residence of Etupes, along with the couple's souvenirs of their common European Grand Tour in 1781–1782 (Nesin and Sautkina 1996, 35–37). Several structures in the garden, and indeed its very layout, were partially designed after Chantilly, north of Paris, in memory of the warm reception the couple was given there (Hayden 2005, 110, 120). As the elite competed to recruit architects and landscape designers from a relatively narrow pool, and as they thought to emulate famous European country seats, a certain degree of imitativeness, or at least consistency in the architectural language, cannot be ignored. Stateliness was more important than originality.

Along with mansions, the elite developed extensive gardens, often in an eclectic style combining a regular layout in the immediate surroundings of the mansion with a landscape garden extending beyond. The taste for the English style of gardening had received sanction from the highest authority; in 1772 Catherine boasted of her "anglomania" to Voltaire and ordered the construction of an English garden at Tsarskoe Selo, partially modeled after Stowe in England. She used English paintings and engravings to serve as design models (Cross 1997, 269). But her English garden was built next to the French one, rather than in its place, a stylistic juxtaposition that became more or less the norm for many estate gardens. Eclecticism was in any case intrinsic to the style, as gardens also featured Chinese pavilions, Turkish mosques or baths, classical ruins, Swiss chalets, Italian bridges, and other imitative features such as a Mount Zion or a Parnassus. These too, of course, derived from Western examples—the mosque and Chinese temple at Kew gardens became influential models, for example. Current scholarly literature in Russia justifies this eclecticism as a way to recreate a version of paradise by embracing within the garden the totality of the universe (Dmitrieva and Kuptsova 2003, 22–24), yet few among the elite took this sort of naïve symbolism at face value. Rather, they arranged such display of foreign-inspired structures and landscapes to affirm their distinction, which, as they saw it, inhered in their Europeanized and cosmopolitan outlook and education.

Stylistically derivative as they were, country estates were hardly literal replicas of European models. They had several distinguishing features. The obligatory presence of a church or chapel in proximity to the mansion reflected the religious practices of the elite, who attended church along with their serfs. The presence of farm buildings and factories as well as peasant villages in the immediate surroundings betrayed the fact that estates also functioned as working farms. The use of fences to protect against roaming cattle and the

occasional brigand destroyed the garden's seamless transition into the surrounding landscape, which landscape design in England took as an axiom of
faith, enabled by the use of the ha-ha (Coxe 1803, 71). And the fields beyond
the grounds were not enclosed with hedges.

Upon traveling through Russia in 1813–1814, J. C. Loudon included
a description of Russian gardens in his *Encyclopedia of Gardening*, which
provides an insight into what a British garden expert found unusual about
Russian landscape gardens. He noted that "clipped trees ... are partially continued," that carriage roads have been laid through the grounds, "which make
the gardens rather unpleasant to walk in," that the practice of introducing
"manufactories as garden buildings" is widespread, and that some mansions
are "disfigured by the contiguity of a number of somber wooden and brick
houses, which, however, is quite à la mode Russe; for close to almost every
nobleman's dwelling in the country is found a village of peasants." As a result,
he continued, rustic buildings are not popular, as they are "too near to the
common hovels of the peasantry." In general, not without some sense of cultural superiority, he noted that "extent, exotics, and magnificent artificial decorations are more the objects of the modern style in Russia, than scenes merely
of picturesque beauty," which he attributed to a "want of refinement of taste"
and an "inaptitude for the natural style," as Russian nobles were primarily
interested in "surpassing [European nobles] in the display of wealth" (Loudon
1835, 246–255). He seemed to decry both the eclectic garishness of Russian
gardens and their functional polyvalence, as places that articulated more the
social ambitions of landlords than their longing for pastoral delights. Yet if he
implied that the Russian elite did not fully get the point of imitating nature, he
could not deny their energetic efforts to de-Russianize the landscape. Indeed,
he noted admiringly that more pineapples were grown in the vicinity of St.
Petersburg than anywhere else on the continent, and that the imperial botanic
garden freely distributed seeds and saplings of exotic plants to private individuals (244, 261). Thus, as seen from the point of view of a British garden
expert, the Europeanization of the landscape had been distorted by Russian
ostentatiousness and unrefined extravagance, which is not to deny that elite
landowners aspired to demonstrate their European credentials.

Everyday life on the country estate was likewise strongly subject to processes of Europeanization. As we saw in the first chapter, the material culture
of the elite was permeated by European styles of furnishings, with artifacts
directly imported from France, Italy, England, and elsewhere and subsequently

produced by local craftsmen in the same style. Replicas of classical sculpture were shipped from Italy. Perhaps encouraged by the copy gracing the gardens of Peterhof, Bariatinsky purchased a Venus of Medici in 1818, which he sent back to Odessa, along with what is listed in the register of his purchases as the "corpse of Pitt" and a marble bust of "His majesty Emperor Alexander" (apparently made in Italy, since the entry is in Italian) (RGB OR, f. 19, op. 1, d. 204, l. 12, 16). Perhaps surprisingly, the portraits adorning the walls of country mansions were not limited to family forebears, but also included historical figures, notably officials of Catherine's time along with foreign historical personalities—for example, the Aztec emperor Montezuma or other figures from the Americas, Africa, or Asia (Chechulin 2010, 401). (Chekhov captured this penchant for exoticism when he placed a map of Africa on the walls of the country mansion in *Uncle Vanya*.) Chinese tapestries were also in vogue, as were trompe l'oeils, which depicted classical and pastoral landscapes. Many elite landowners assembled extensive collections of art and artifacts from around the world. They also collected eclectic libraries, with titles in all major European languages. To give an example, the list of books (purchased for 3,333 francs) Bariatinsky shipped back to his estate in 1819 contained numerous titles on agronomy, morality, and religion, but also a four-volume *History of Women*, Schiller in French, *Selected Works* of Fénelon, a volume on tactics in legislative assemblies, and a ten-volume edition of Machiavelli's works in the original (RGB OR, f. 19, op. 1, d. 204, l. 3).

Country estates were sites of sociability more than pastoral retreat, and entertainments largely mirrored metropolitan forms of pastime. In his ode to country living "Evgeniiu: Zhizn' Zvanskaia," the poet Gavrila Derzhavin wrote: "When this rural amusement bores us/ Inside the house we enjoy the entertainments of the capital" (Derzhavin 2002, 388). Wealthy landowners erected theaters, trained a cast of serf actors, and put on the same repertoire as in the capitals (Kuptsova 2012). E. N. Korovina identified eighteen estate theaters in the countryside around Moscow (Korovina 2005). Some estate owners kept an orchestra;—for example Bariatinsky, who used serf musicians, some of whom had been trained in St. Petersburg. A. B. Kurakin, in contrast, hired foreign musicians on wages, an even more consequential way of Europeanizing the delivery of aesthetic enjoyment on the estate (Dolgorukov 2004, 1:288). The cost of maintaining such an ensemble was considerable. Despite being a committed amateur composer, Bariatinsky advised his son in his will to disband his orchestra, "a ridiculous luxury" and "fashion" he felt guilty about. "One can make better use of men than to turn them into bad musicians," he added (RGB OR, f. 19, op. 5, d. 72, 21ob). The elite also threw lavish balls on their estates, as well as garden parties enhanced with illuminations and fireworks, all in direct emulation of the celebrations held by Catherine in her imperial gardens.

Nevertheless, sociability in the provinces differed in two respects from celebrations in the capital. First, it was customary—and necessary, in light of the sparse density of estates—to mingle with noble neighbors of all ranks. Conversely, the local gentry could freely pay courtesy visits to their elite neighbors when they were in residence. Hospitality was a widely shared norm, and it could assume a coercive force as visitors were often expected to stay on for several days, while they were plied to lavish offerings of food and alcohol (Rasskazova 2014, 166). As a result, the elite interacted with a more disparate range of nobles in the provinces than in the capitals. Kurakin, who loved to parade his riches in front of his guests, subjected them to strict regulations, which were stipulated on a kind of statute displayed prominently, which organized the behavior of his guests at various times of the day and protected his privacy (Schönle 2007, 174–177). Second, the coexistence with serfs living in the estate villages also affected the nature of sociability: occasionally, on religious holidays, landowners hosted parties for their serfs, a way, on the one side, to express their patriarchal duty of care, but also, on the other, to turn serfs into spectators of their distinguished munificence. Wealthy landowners needed the local gentry and the serf population to act as a sort of public for their performance of distinction and wealth.

Even the enjoyment of nature, the main distinguishing feature of countryside living, was a constructed attitude mediated through Western models. The notion of pastoral retreat was first made popular through eclogues and idylls, classical genres of poetry revived in the eighteenth-century in the context of a Rousseau-inspired infatuation with nature and a critique of social artificiality and conformity. The topos of Horatian retreat, redolent of stoic and epicurean notions of tranquility, clearly influenced the elite, although these ideas also generated resistance from civic-minded members of the polity (Kahn 2002–2003, 669–688; Newlin 2001, 17–98). Kurakin argued specifically that in retiring to his estate, he was embarking not on a pursuit of individual happiness but on a path of self-improvement modeled after Roman antiquity, which should make him more useful to the state: "Remember how they lived in ancient Rome," he wrote to his brother Aleksei, "never in demeaning idleness, always either in active service to the fatherland or in remote and complete isolation, to tend to oneself and equip the spirit with new strengths and the mind with new knowledge and new abilities; that is the way they still live in many European countries" (quoted in Schönle 2007, 168). Pastoral retreat was a ticket to the European way of life.

Priscilla Roosevelt called aristocratic estates a "Western oasis" and "enclave" (Roosevelt 1995, 33). Indeed, as we have seen, the elite either directly emulated Western styles of living, or, to the extent possible, strove to reproduce their urban lifestyle, itself, of course, being thoroughly inflected by European conventions. They demonstrated little interest in cultivating a regional identity, and their commitment to local self-government proved shallow. By and large they attempted to transplant Western styles of living onto the countryside.

The Country Estate as a Performance of Economic Thought

Economic behavior was an important dimension of the elite's Europeanization. The pursuit of economic profit created tensions if not contradictions with more or less deeply held moral views. Wealthy landlords established distilleries on their estates and entertained extensive trade relations with tax farmers, who served as middlemen. According to Dolgorukov, when he settled on his estate of Nadezhdino, Kurakin made a quick fortune from bootlegging, handsomely climbing out of the debts he had contracted as a courtier (Dolgorukov 2004, 1:288). To staff his distillery, he put his serfs back on corvée and used them as free labor (308). In a letter to his brother Aleksei, Kurakin commiserated that despite thinking of his serfs as his brethren, "from my uncontrollable desire to treble my income, I am the sole cause of the suffering and great hardships of my neighbor, whose fate is in my hands. In the depth of my heart, I wish my serfs bliss, but in reality, against my will, I distance them from it" (quoted in Kogan 1960, 125).

The elite clearly engaged with the economy of their country estates. In addition to the *Works of the Free Economic Society*, there were at least four other periodicals (at different times) devoted to agricultural matters, for which the elite represented about a third of subscribers (Samarin 2000, 126). Michael Confino described in great detail the agronomical experiments undertaken by landowners until the emancipation of serfs in 1861. He concluded that despite close familiarity with Western agronomical thought, nobles remained profoundly conservative in their economic behavior, as they feared that the entire fabric of their agricultural economy would unravel if they introduced even modest reforms (Confino 1969). This discrepancy between theoretical awareness and actual behavior points to the ambiguities of the elite's self-Europeanization.

Confino's conclusions aptly capture the nobility's behavior on average, yet there were quite a few members of the elite who experimented with modern agricultural methods to enhance the productivity of the land and at the same time act on their concern for the well-being of their serfs. Bariatinsky, for example, styled himself as an agronomist and imported the best tools and seeds from Europe to improve the yield of his lands and lighten the burden of his serfs (Schönle 2016a). He also experimented with diverse field rotations and won an award from the Moscow Agricultural Society for his method of drainage. The Sheremetevs devolved much independence to their serfs, giving them actual title to their lands (Dennison 2011), secured by contract, despite the fact that such documents had, officially, no legal force. In the 1810s, Dmitrii Poltoratsky built a successful English farm and horse-breeding stables using hired labor, in particular serfs temporarily removed from their lands and paid daily wages (RGB OR, f. 233, op. 5, d. 45). And A. T. Bolotov was indefatigable in translating Western theories as well as trialing his own ideas, disseminating the results through the Free Economic Society, but also in journals he founded himself to this end.

What is of greater interest to us, however, beyond the actual innovations introduced by one or another of the nobles, who remain clearly a statistical minority, are the changes in mentality that arose from the reception of Western agronomical literature. The Free Economic Society, founded in 1765, and other agricultural societies that followed suit in the nineteenth century, provided a forum for the discussion and dissemination of ideas and techniques. While their overall effect on agricultural practices and social relations on the estate remained limited, they debated ideas that substantially affected the identities of the elite. Most importantly, the Free Economic Society advocated the principle that one ought to apply science and the practice of experimentation to daily life; in other words, it taught a reason-based and intellectually alert mode of living, rather than blind obedience to traditional ways. And it suggested that supporting the spread of knowledge required importing the best theories from European countries, which could serve as examples to imitate (*Trudy* 1: i).

In the same vein, the Society fostered the notion that there was a need for debate, and therefore promoted fora that would facilitate the exchange of ideas. These included the assemblies of the Free Economic Society, as well as the journal itself, which invited contributions from all members near and afar. The elite perceived the need for additional settings, and Bariatinsky, for example, developed a project for a debating club and library while staying in Paris and Geneva during the French revolution (RGB f. 19, op. 2, p. 253, d. 1, l. 5ob). The Free Economic Society inculcated a certain idea of citizenry, whereby patriotic service was redefined as service to society and community, including the local commune of serfs, rather than simply allegiance and service to the monarch. Of course, this rhetoric of public utility, advocated explicitly in the first volume of the Society's *Works* (*Trudy* 1: v), was meant primarily as a pledge that members of the Society acted in pursuance of the common good, rather than their private interest, and it did not envision the possibility of a contradiction between service to the ruler and service to society. Nevertheless, civic language permeated the proceedings and publications of the Society.

The Society fostered an interest in Western political economy, an emergent body of thought. For instance, A. Ia. Polenov, who had studied in Strasbourg, prepared an essay for the Society on the occasion of a competition announced in 1766 debating the proposition whether peasants should be granted the right to own their land; Polenov argued the liberal case that property fosters self-interest, which in turn encourages industry, so that giving peasants hereditary property of their lands would improve their living conditions and thereby also the wealth of the state. While this essay won a prize from the Society, the award committee required Polenov to rewrite his submission and substantially weaken its content, and Polenov duly obliged. In spite of this, the society prohibited its publication (Beliavskii 1960, 396–402). By and large, despite the considerable overall timidity of the Society, the response of its members to the submitted essays shows that the elite tended to be more inclined to support some form of serf emancipation than lower-ranking nobles (Leckey 2011, 74). The Society also drew attention to the importance of education as a way to bring about the moral transformation of serfs and hence foster their diligence and industry. In suggesting that freeing the rational mind would produce concrete social and economic improvements in rural Russia, the Society instilled the ideology of progress and faith in the future. In the preface to the translation of *The Rustic Socrates*, by Hans Caspar Hirzel, an honorary member of the Society, Vasilii Novikov developed a physiocratic argument about the centrality of agriculture to the prosperity of the state, while the conclusion of this piece of popularized economics stated that "we live in a century in which one can expect the most fruitful changes. The freedom to think has shattered all fetters, and reason dares to shed light on all objects; even faith and government cannot be excluded from it" (Girtsel 1789, 2:324).

There was some degree of pluralism in the views expressed in the *Works* of the Society. Roman Vorontsov, a member of the aristocratic elite, published an article in which he condemned the abusive behavior of estate stewards and bailiffs, who needed to be held in check to prevent them from taking advantage of their power and damaging social relations on the estate. To achieve this, he proposed to establish peasant courts, staffed with the best serfs, which would themselves discipline wayward peasants. Stewards would be kept at arms' length and would mainly ensure that the interests of the landlord were not disregarded in the daily self-management of the peasant commune. A set of incentives would encourage serfs to exert themselves and ensure a fair distribution of duties and taxes. By proposing to set up a kind of self-regulating mechanism, Vorontsov hoped to lessen the role of stewards and mitigate the impact of their despotic behavior (*Trudy* 5:1–12).

In contrast, the middle-ranked Bolotov argued that nothing but severe and demonstrative punishment could discipline serfs and ensure that they worked diligently. He thus envisioned an economy ruled by a steward endowed with a set of shining (and wholly unrealistic) virtues, who would preside over the estate as a selfless despot and exact complete obedience from serfs, resorting to strict punishment at their smallest offence, "as there is no other way to inculcate hard work and good economy in them" (*Trudy* 16:69–230, quotation on 188).

Timotheus von Klingstädt, a Pomeranian who was ennobled and took on various official positions in the Russian government and edited the *Works* for the Society, proposed yet other means—for example, ensuring that stewards were well trained in progressive agronomical practices. He suggested that young men could be sent for a few years to Livonia and Estonia, where land economy was more advanced, to be apprised of the art of supervising agriculture (5:60–69). Furthermore, he argued against punishing serfs, as "such strict techniques, which often turn into actual barbarity, resemble very little the mildness of manners and thought, which is now spreading among the whole Russian people in our flourishing times" (16:238). Instead, to him the problem lay in the petty wants of Russian serfs, who, due to their "savage" condition, did not desire the finer amenities of life. Yet by teaching them to desire new things, one could spur their industry and thereby lead to greater prosperity. In this sort of argument from consumption, luxury is "not only necessary, but even useful" (16:245).

For Petr Rychkov, a middle-rank landowner and official from Ekaterinburg who wrote about agriculture and economy, the principal culprit was the lack of education, and he acknowledged that in this respect Russians lagged not only behind European countries but also behind Muslims settled in Russia. The children of the best serfs should be taught literacy, he argued, and thus also learn the habits of work and discipline, rather than idleness; but he cautioned against teaching too many serfs to write, as this could encourage the production of fake passports (16:13–68).

In summary, a genuine, if limited debate unfolded on the pages of the Society's journal about issues that were at once practical and philosophical, such as the desirable ratio of punishment and inducement in managing serfs, the importance and extent of education, the role of stewards, and the limits of their power. This debate rested on various presuppositions about the moral character of Russian serfs. For some, this character was fixed, unalterable, and unredeemable, an anthropological constant, as it were, while for others it was liable to transformation through the right set of structures and incentives. Indeed, the malleability of human nature in response to changing conditions was one of the more significant "discoveries" of the time, as this notion undermined the religious idea of an established order of things, warranted by God and providence, which justified the social hierarchy.

Most of the premises used in these debates derived directly or indirectly from Western sources. The notion of human perfectibility through education goes back to John Locke's famous essay "Some Thoughts Concerning Education" (1693), which influenced a string of eighteenth-century philosophers, from Condillac and Rousseau to Helvetius. Driven to its ultimate conclusion, this idea is fundamentally secular, as it denies, or at least downplays, the doctrine of original sin. Vorontsov's mechanism to limit the power of stewards rests on ideas about the separation of powers in the polity, which in one form or the other originate from Calvin and Montesquieu, if not from the Roman Republic. And even Bolotov's model of a well-ordered estate society relentlessly controlled by a selfless and ideal despot has Western credentials. It closely resembles the German cameralist ideas that influenced Peter the

Great's vision of the state. By and large, the members of the Free Economic
Society were universalists, in the sense that they assumed one could trans-
pose ideas and techniques from the West and successfully implement them in
Russia without much adjustment.

The strongest reaction against the universalist premise came from Fedor
Rostopchin, who in 1801 hired a Scottish farmer to supervise the transformation of his estate of Voronovo into an English farm, but who subsequently, in
1806, wrote a withering pamphlet after his experiments failed. In it, he listed
a series of circumstances that make the English model of farming unsuitable
to Russia. Among his main arguments were the harsh climate and short season, the absence of a dynamic market for grains and meat, the abundance
of land, which makes fertilizing unnecessary, and the national character of
Russians. To him, the introduction of English farming techniques was a fad
not unlike other amusements imported from England, such as "horn music,
English gardens, racing horses, colonnades with porticos, hound hunting, and
serf theaters," as there is no benefit from English farming other than to prettify
the landscape (Rostopchin 1806, 45). Instead, he argued for the wisdom of
the Russian tradition, "not out of obstinacy and ignorance," but because he
was "used from childhood to love and respect the ancient Russian way" (44).
Rostopchin's arguments are not unreasonable, but in arguing for a kind of
climatic determinism (which had been anathema to Catherine, as it seemed
to condemn Russia to the backwaters of European progress) and in resorting
to an invented notion of Russian tradition, he surreptitiously deployed equally
Western ideas, notably Montesquieu's ideas on the relation between climate
and political system and Herder's ideas of national identity. Nevertheless,
Rostopchin was, if not the first, then one of the most vocal proponents of
relativism, the notion that any project of development should start from the
distinctiveness of Russia's climatic, economic, and moral conditions.

These debates show that the state of rural Russia had become a hot topic
in the minds of a select segment of the elite, and that in thinking about ways
to enhance life in the provinces economically, socially, and morally, nobles
advanced ideas directly or indirectly borrowed from Western Europe. This
Europeanization of the mentality and ideology of landowners was, however, anything but straightforward imitation. Even those who argued for the
transplantation of specific political ideas made allowances for the reality of
serfdom, and only a few questioned its right to exist. Indeed, for most members of the elite, the serfs were almost a separate species, an anthropological
"other." Conversely, even those who praised the distinctive features of Russian

agricultural practice did in fact fall back on ideas derived from the European Enlightenment. Europeanization was not a one-directional, teleological affair.

What emerged as a result of these discussions was a set of disjunctions in the provincial life of the elite. While these heady intellectual debates unfolded over the pages of the Society's journal and in other venues, the elite continued to enjoy the fruits of serfdom and the support of the state, which translated into the ability to enact an aestheticized "performance" of Europeanization on their estates, notably by adopting a lifestyle characterized by urban forms of entertainment, as we saw above. At the same time, the elite were under pressure from the government to participate in the running of provincial affairs, which they did only halfheartedly. While they developed ties with their country estates, they nurtured scant attachment to the geographical province or region where it was situated. Even those who participated in provincial administration showed little enthusiasm for the local town. Serving in Penza, Dolgorukov asked himself rhetorically why he put on amateur performances of Sumarokov's "silly" comedies, rather than something more edifying, given that in a provincial town, theater had the obligation to educate young people. His answer was blunt: "Because I was not a Penza patriot, but a Muscovite emigrant, and therefore I did not consider it my duty to educate the young" (Dolgorukov 2004, 1:344). All that mattered to him was to devise some form of entertainment in order not to capitulate to "boredom and philosophical meditation" (337). To a large extent, the axiological poles of the elite's existence were the capitals and the estate, two sites where they deployed performances of their Europeanized selves that were in fact more similar than distinctive to place. The provincial towns were more resistant to European refashioning, and the government's ideas about their modernization consisted primarily of their rational standardization. It is therefore not entirely surprising that the elite showed weaker allegiance to them. As Susan Smith-Peter has argued, in conjunction with the government, the elite denied the provinces any historical meaning and erased their local distinctiveness (Smith-Peter 2015).

Patriotic Responses to Provincial Deficiencies: Two Case Studies

We can derive further evidence of the increasing complexities of the Europeanization agenda in the provinces from a brief look at Dolgorukov's account of his journey to Odessa and Kiev and from Aleksandr Bakunin's views on landscape design and estate management (Bakunin was the father of the anarchist Mikhail Bakunin). The dismal state of the provinces threatened to disrupt patriotic pride, and Dolgorukov's journey illustrates the intellectual contortions required to sustain his self-esteem as a Russian subject despite his Western outlook and the shabbiness he discovers in the provinces. In his *Slavny bubny za gorami*, an account of a journey taken in 1810, Dolgorukov made no bones about his ultimate allegiance: if he had been able to afford it, it is to Paris that he would have traveled (Dolgorukov 1870, 1). He looked at the world through a Westernizing lens, comparing Vladimir to Switzerland (87) and the ruins of a fortress in Serpukhov to a Roman portico as seen in *vedute* engravings. Yet he bemoaned the fact that only few people seem aware of the aesthetic prospects of this place: "There is a strange prejudice," he wrote, "one's own is always abhorrent" (4): despite his European frame of reference, he wrote from a patriotic Russian perspective. He was clearly an urban dweller and called Moscow his "motherland" and "paradise" (1). So part of his undertaking in traveling across the province was to highlight its European credentials. In Tula, he praised the construction of an embankment to create a promenade, an idea modeled on Moscow, itself emulating St. Petersburg. In many places he praised the infrastructure created by the government, evincing particular fondness for sites associated with Catherine II. Yet time and again he lamented the poor state of things in Russia, the lack of amenities for travelers, the absence of picturesque landscape, the paucity of theatrical culture, the scruffiness of institutions, the inept teaching in schools, and the venality of stationmasters, to mention but a few of the shortcomings he described, which, however, in no way undercut his patriotic feelings.

While privileging trade, consumption, and investment in public amenities, Dolgorukov was scathing about "anglophiles" who disparage Russia's achievements. In Tula he waxed ecstatic about iron and steel craftsmanship, but complained that "our anglophiles would not even want to have a look at it," so convinced are they that things are better in London (11). When he visited the estate of an unnamed grandee, he noted with disdain that "an Englishman runs the estate in the English manner, and the serfs go hand in cap the Russian way: that's what they call estate management" (24). Similarly, he was dismissive of the English style of landscape design (58), and his general view of nature was that it requires human improvements. Overall, he frowned upon sentimentalist aesthetics that celebrate a kind of Rousseauistic nature in the raw.

In short, complexities begin to emerge in Dolgorukov's worldview. While he took pride in the European credentials of certain provincial sites, he also drew a dismal portrait of the general backwardness of the provinces. His pride in Russia made him all the more ashamed of its blemishes, yet least of all could he stand those who dismiss everything in Russia out of hand. He had a particular axe to grind with anglophiles, evidently much preferring French culture. But the point is not simply that Dolgorukov differentiated between French and English models of culture and development. It is also that his idea of Russia was ambiguous. On the one side, he strongly identified with a statist view: it is the government that drives forward the Europeanization of the country through its investment, a policy which he associated in particular with Catherine and which underpinned his love of Russia. Yet on the other side, he also displayed a primeval, spontaneous bond with Russia, regardless of its amenities.

Once he entered Ukraine, or Little Russia, as he put it, he became deeply skeptical of the Russian imperial strategy to Europeanize the borderlands. In Poltava, which he saw as being in a foreign country and strongly disliked, despite its importance to state mythology as the site of Peter the Great's victory over Charles XII of Sweden, he introduced the distinction between two kinds of patriotism: one inspired by *rodina* (motherland), the other by *otechestvo* (fatherland). Only the Russian language, he contended, has a word like *rodina*, which betokens an instinctual, unquestioned love for the country, implying that only Russians experience such elemental feelings for the nation (64). In context, this distinction implied that while he experienced an emotional bond with Russia and its territory, he was less sanguine about the Russian empire's expansion beyond its ethnic boundaries, even when it pursued Europeanizing aims. Thus, while he praised the regular street layout in Tula (7), he was scornful of attempts to make Poltava look like St. Petersburg, because "all such attempts are not appropriate to this site, [which is] poor, lowly, and, as the French say, *mesquin*" (67). The use of a French put-down to disparage efforts to modernize a provincial Ukrainian town is symptomatic of his sense of cultural superiority. Overall, he presented Little Russia as a country with a barren landscape, little sociability, no public entertainments, and a deeply backward people.

The disjunction between Dolgorukov's treatment of the Russian provinces and the imperial borderland is revealing. In Russia, his spontaneous love for the country redeemed all its shortcomings, while similar failings in Ukraine only drew his scorn. Likewise, if the government's Europeanizing efforts in Russia were fodder to his identity and pride as a subject of the Russian empire, similar policies in the borderland were deemed pointless. We witness a mutually reinforcing overlayering of nativist and statist patriotism, of essentialism and constructivism, where Russia stands both for a nation unified by instinctive and unconditional bonds and a nation that deserves allegiance precisely because the state is in the process of engineering its Europeanization. In contrast, due to its natural situation, he deemed Ukraine unsuitable to such civilizing transformation, as if the borderland served as a foil to consolidate his Russian patriotic pride despite the Russian provinces' obvious and visible failings.

Being no less patriotically inclined, Bakunin took a different stance with regard to the provinces. As he retired from diplomatic service abroad to put his family affairs in order, he settled on the estate of his mother at Priamukhino and largely attempted to disassociate himself from the lifestyle of the elite. He avoided polite society, shunned patronage—to the extent possible— and refrained from ostentatious consumption. He was scathing about the Europeanized landscapes of his peers, calling French and English gardens the "graveyard of taste and nature" and "an accumulation of every local and foreign flaw, along with the exclusion of all pleasant aspects of nature" (Bakunin 2002, 51–52). He specifically decried the contradiction between manicured gardens and decrepit peasant villages in their vicinity. In his view, a properly Russian garden would start with improvement to the villages, so as to integrate all of the physical landscape—villages, woods, fields, meadows, and gardens—into an aesthetically seamless environment (53). The idea that gardens should echo the surrounding environment is one he might have found in Rousseau's *Nouvelle Héloïse* (Schönle 2013).

While rejecting—at least in theory—the practice of creating Europeanized enclaves, Bakunin also enhanced the patriotic meaning of his estate by creating sites of historical memory in it—for example, a summerhouse dedicated to Field Marshal Mikhail Kutuzov. Bakunin took exception with the dismissive ways the Free Economic Society described Russian serfs (Bakunin 2002, 62), advancing the liberal argument that with the correct set of economic incentives, notably the right to own the property they till, peasants would become free, autonomous, self-sufficient, and moral citizens (GARF, f. 825, op. 1, d. 259, l. 50–54; Agamalian 1999, 65). Although his rhetoric does not conceal the sense that serfs in their present condition are less than fully "human," he at least envisioned the possibility of their future moral transformation. The same applies to his vision of nature: recognizing the unpicturesque drabness of the Russian landscape, he asserted that nature and climate are under human control (Bakunin 2002, 60), so that in time the application of human agency would bring about their beneficial transformation, just as it did in various European countries. His way of accommodating himself to Russian realities operated not through a complicated bricolage of various forms of nationalist discourse, as Dolgorukov did, but through a leap of faith into Russia's future prospects, accompanied by the resolve to hasten their arrival through his own industry. The promise of the future injected meaning into the present, despite its dispiriting failings.

Dolgorukov and Bakunin both sought for ways to carve out a sense of national identity despite the deficient conditions of the provinces. Dolgorukov combined trust in the Europeanizing policies of the state with an instinctual love for his country, which helped him buttress his identity as a subject of the ruler while allowing his patriotic pride and Westernizing convictions to mesh. Bakunin took a more resolute stance, rejecting much in the polity of his days and retiring to his estate to foster the transformation of nature and the moral improvement of his serfs on a small scale. Either way, both accommodated themselves with the present only by subscribing to a transformational project, the state-led Europeanization of ethnic Russia on the one side, and the natural and moral improvement of the provinces and their residents on the other. It would take a few more decades for this dynamic to be given its most radical literary expression, namely in the works of Gogol, who gave a famous literary treatment of this disjunction between sober assessment of the present and improbable hopes for a transformed future. The ending of *Dead Souls* describes precisely how an ignominious reality, the escape of a crafty imposter from a provincial town where he had been exposed, could turn into a glorious vision of Russia's headlong advance into a marvelous future.

What gets lost in this antinomy are the historical and cultural particularities of actual provinces. Thus, by and large, even when the elite did not contribute to the administration of the provinces directly, they participated in the effacement of vernacular differences through their aesthetic and economic behavior on their estates. They did so even when they fancied that in seeking refuge from court and society in their country pads, they would fashion an autonomous, self-determining identity. One way or the other, wittingly or not, they acted as agents of Europeanization in the provinces. They Europeanized themselves at the same time as, and by way of, trying to Europeanize the "subaltern" people in their care.

How transformational was the impact of the elite on the provinces? The geography of the provinces changed as they were now dotted with "enclaves"

of Europeanization—country estates and some district towns with centers built along rationalist classicist models. The communications network
between these islands of Westernization continued to draw everybody's
complaints. The economic and cultural gap between the elite on one side and
the local gentry, the merchants, and the serf population on the other only
grew wider. The mindset of the gentry remained unchanged. Bariatinsky, to
return to one of our characters, was incensed that his attempts to open the
local river to navigation was blocked by his neighbors, and he continued to
despise their unreformed, wasteful, and idle ways. There is little evidence that
the example he intended to set had any impact on the lower nobility in his
vicinity. Nor is there much evidence that the living conditions of the serfs
improved significantly under the stewardship of the elite, with a few exceptions. Agricultural yields on sown grain decreased in the second half of the
century, and an increase in output was solely due to the expansion of cultivated land, thus requiring more labor. Rising output did not improve nutri-
tion levels, and indeed, the biological status (height) of all classes deteriorated
over the eighteenth century, except for the nobility and clergy (Mironov 2012,
94–108). Bakunin's ideas about fostering self-interest and thereby productivity were discussed in various fora, but found little implementation in practice.
The edict on free agriculturalists of 1803, which, under certain agreed conditions, allowed nobles to emancipate their serfs and endow them with a plot of
land, had a limited, if not irrelevant, impact: according to V. I. Semevsky, only
160 landowners took advantage of it, with the result that 47,153 serfs were
emancipated (Semevskii 1888, 1:252–281). The colonization of the provinces
resulted not in the Europeanization of the whole of Russian society in its various strata, but in the development of scattered sites of Europeanized amenity
and sociability, which contrasted sharply with their unreformed surroundings. To the extent that it took life in the capitals as a model to emulate, this
sort of Europeanization also contributed to effacing any regional affiliation
and identification. For the elite involved in this process, their custodianship
over the provinces meant first and foremost that they had to confront the dismal reality of provincial underdevelopment and to adjust their patriotic pride
accordingly. We saw how Dolgorukov resorted to a combination of nativist
and statist patriotism to come to terms with this dilemma. Europeanization
occurred more in the mind of the elite than in the daily grind of the people.

CONCLUSION

In the previous chapters we have analyzed the manifold ways in which members of the elite embraced the European way of life. Through their travel, purchases, reading habits, and cultural consumption, from the recruitment of foreign specialists (such as tutors for their children and gardeners for its estates) to participation in imported forms of sociability and spirituality, the members of the elite were in regular commerce with European values and ways of thinking. At court they learned to live in the limelight, including in performance designed to impress foreigners. Through an intensive course of education delivered mostly by foreigners, whether in state institutions or at home, and by way of exposure to Western forms of spirituality, they assimilated the languages, skills, knowledge, values, and emotional repertoire that befitted European nobility. And the emergent domestic literature increasingly served to articulate their self-understanding as a community of Europeanized Russians. They even sought to design the places of their existence in accordance with European models, sometimes having to settle for fairly rudimentary or conventional tokens of Europeanization in architecture, interior design, or landscaping.

The discrepancy between intentionally designed islands of Westernized living and the surrounding physical, moral, and political landscape could not but weigh on the elite mind. In protest at this fragmentation of physical space, Aleksandr Bakunin refrained from installing an English garden on his estate until his serf village was spruced up and turned into pleasing views for the eyes. "I don't want," he stated, "my beautiful garden to exacerbate the ugliness of my village, but I want my village to be an attractive preface to my garden" (Bakunin 2002, 55). And indeed, in response, perhaps, to these disjunctions, we saw that the elite developed a propensity to live in the mind, travel in an armchair, and use visual contraptions to behold "Europe" at will. In light of the deficient reality on the ground, Europeanization thus also involved a willingness to live in the imagination, suspend one's disbelief, live off one's memories, and cultivate one's inner self through meditation, reverie, and reading—what Nikolai Karamzin called "enjoying the Chinese shadows of the imagination" at the end of his *Letters of a Russian Traveller*.

The practice of living in imaginary worlds was, of course, supported by the development of communities sustained by imaginary contact. In the last decades of the eighteenth century, the elite began to engage in prolific personal correspondence with addressees within Russia and beyond. Letter writing helped overcome geographical distance as these nobles displayed increasing physical mobility and dispersed across Russia and Europe, be it residing on their country estates, traveling on military dislocation, journeying or studying abroad, or simply moving between Moscow and St. Petersburg. These intense and regular exchanges of letters between husbands and wives; family members; friends; patrons, clients or fellow members of a patronage clan; members of a Masonic lodge; or with foreigners abroad—these exchanges not only sustained relationships across time and space, but also constructed a space of subjective interiority, where emotional, moral, and ideological affinities could be nurtured.

Family archives extant today show the extraordinary volume and intensity of these letter exchanges and suggest that personal correspondence was tightly woven within the fabric of everyday life. Writing letters was often a daily practice that took up considerable amounts of time and grew into a habit of conducting imaginary inner dialogues with addressees. As he traveled through Europe in 1817, for example, I. I. Bariatinsky led an extensive correspondence with his wife, writing sometimes two or three letters a day, a practice that punctuated what he experienced at the time with extended reflective interludes, during which he both conjured up his memories of previous visits to Europe and pictured in his mind the conjugal bliss he had experienced with his wife (RGB OR, f. 19, op. 2, ed. 17). This habit of regular writing served to enhance and validate the inner life of the writing nobility, to articulate, and also intensify, their emotions, and often to compensate for a surrounding reality felt to be emotionally wanting or dysfunctional.

Writing was sometimes surrounded by rituals. Aleksandr Kurakin, for example, erected a special temple in his garden, where he would betake himself to write his correspondence and organize his letter archive, and to which he invited his guests, to contemplate what we could call his performance of interiority. Literature of the time is replete with small ritualized scenes of interiority, such as, in Karamzin's "Poor Liza," the narrator's repeated walks to the ruins of the Simonov monastery on the outskirts of Moscow, where he would reminisce about Liza's sad fate.

Communities sustained by imaginary contact also extended beyond such networks of familiar bonds and became genuinely imaginary communities. The elite romanticized an emotional bond with the serfs they owned. Patriarchal ties, with their intimations of moral responsibility, became an opportunity to imagine a psychological identification and affiliation with the peasant village, laying the ground for the subsequent rise of nationalism. Nobles often fancied themselves as benefactors to their serfs, and expected deep gratitude for any acts of generosity they displayed, even if they hardly knew their serfs. The same Kurakin announced an officially approved will in 1807, in which he ordained the emancipation of his serfs upon his death, albeit with a set of stringent obligations lasting for the subsequent forty years. When his serfs tried to negotiate the conditions of their release, he annulled his will, disappointed by their "ingratitude" (Schönle 2007, 207–217). If nobles lived on the estate, they threw parties for their serfs as a way to exhibit their munificence. Landscape painting of the time often depicted work in the fields as an idyllic, blissful activity discharged by healthy, cleanly dressed serfs. Yet this idealization of agricultural labor did not prevent some nobles from trying to squeeze as much work from their serfs as possible, nor to complain bitterly in personal correspondence and elsewhere about their slovenly and deceitful ways. We have seen in the chapter on the provinces that Kurakin "wished his serfs bliss" from the depth of his heart, yet could not help increase their hardship by forcing them to work longer in his distilleries. In the nineteenth century, a clear disjunction opened up between the mythologization of the country estate as a site of communion with serfs and the harsh realities of noble-serf relations.

This imaginary "superstructure" of the elite's everyday life came in all shapes and sizes. In the case of an officer enlisted in an army regiment and stationed somewhere in the empire or abroad, marital life would for significant stretches of time amount to little more than an epistolary bond, a situation that could prevail for the greatest part of his existence, despite shared commitments to family and property. In this instance, even marital and family life took on an abstract, distanced quality, sustained by whatever emotions (and information) words could convey on the page, despite the post's considerable slowness (and risks of perlustration for those at the top of the pyramid). The maintenance of phatic contact was the first and most important requirement, as we see from the habitual, fastidious recording in letters of when missives had been sent and received. Thus, in light of the stringent requirements of service, even family life could presuppose a significant degree of vicarious shared living.

Letter writing served various other purposes. Rosicrucian Freemasons availed themselves extensively of epistolary exchanges in their attempt to fundamentally re-shape identity and sustain one another in their spiritual quest (Zorin 2016b). Managing estates while living in the capitals or elsewhere required regular exchanges of letters with intendants, stewards, or other intermediaries. Living on the country estate also inspired and necessitated considerable letter writing, as retired nobles wanted to stay abreast of court politics and continued to nurture patronage and friendship ties. For the elite, retirement to the country could be a provisional condition, as they often returned to service when called upon to a new post or by a new monarch. It hardly meant cutting ties with courtly affairs. Thus, the elite participated in multiple imaginary worlds at once, spending considerable amounts of time wielding their quills to cultivate various bonds that would sustain their identities.

The upshot of this practice of living in imaginary worlds and imaginary communities is the availability of choice on a personal level. The basic premise of living life in a purposeful, meaningful manner, which underpins the self-fashioning of the elite, requires the exercise of agency, that is of making choices among the range of behavior modes, values, styles, and communities available. There were various ways one could serve one's monarch and country, various ways one could design one's estate, and various social groups one could join. For the elite, these were partly personal decisions—for example, whether they lived in St. Petersburg, Moscow, on the estate, in a provincial town, or abroad; whether their sons were educated in Russia or abroad (girls did not have the privilege of a foreign education unless their parents lived abroad); whether they enlisted in the guard regiments, served in civil service, or at court; and whether they joined the Freemasons, spent time in the English clubs in St. Petersburg or Moscow, or attended one or the other salons or literary societies.

The freedom of choice was, of course, not absolute. Although free in theory, these choices subjected members of the elite to a (sometimes considerable) degree of social pressure, as well as to some administrative hurdles (for example, to obtain a foreign passport for travel abroad, which required paying off one's debts). And of course, they also incurred pressure from the monarch, who could quite specifically request subjects to serve in one capacity, office, or place rather than another, a request it was difficult, albeit not impossible, to turn down—all senior appointments and other personnel matters were subject to approval by the ruler (Raeff 1983, 99–100). Furthermore, the availability of a position depended on the good will of a patron, so that choice could be limited by the extent of one's patronage network. And of course, the lower one stood in the social hierarchy the less choice one had, with the exception of the basic alternative between service and retirement, to the extent that the latter was affordable.

It is very clear from the diaries of members of the elite that they nevertheless operated with the premise that freedom of choice was inherent to their elite status. More importantly, this freedom of choice exercised itself not only in existential decisions relating to education and career, but also in the multiplication of subject positions, forms of identification, and networks of sociability, a multiplication facilitated precisely by the notional, imaginary dimension of the worlds the elite inhabited and communities they joined. Plainly, it was entirely possible to serve at court, fight in battles between patronage clans, attend a Masonic lodge, care for one's country estate, purchase art abroad, and display the bust of Rousseau on one's desk, while spending free time reading *La Nouvelle Héloïse*, all more or less concurrently. The elite, in short, inhabited the intersection between various reference groups, each coming with its own language and behavior style.

The multiplication of spheres of identification resulted in a dramatic rise in the role reflexivity assumed in the life of the elite, which manifested itself in particular in the keeping of diaries and certain kinds of correspondence, but also in the spread of some Zeitgeist sensibilities, such as ideas of pastoral retreat in nature, sentimentalist reading, or melancholia. Developing a space for reflexivity became particularly important in light of the fickleness of court life, where one's standing was always at the mercy of some well-placed, malicious piece of gossip. The only place where the various imaginary worlds of the elite held together, despite the intrinsic differences between them, and where some enduring stability could be found, was the reflective mind, where various subject positions could be deployed, assessed, called into question, or rejected, where the coherence of one's life (or lack thereof) came into view, and where attempts could be made to correlate the past, present, and future and to deal with a sense of loss, which was also one of the striking features of the age. Literature assumed particular importance in this respect, as it offered a repertoire of models of identity and an associated language, which the self could interiorize and emulate. The sentimental self peddled in Rousseau's *Rêveries du promeneur solitaire* and in his *Nouvelle Héloïse* was clearly a huge influence, but so were the Horatian notions of pastoral retreat, Richardson's archetypes of amorous behavior, and the Anacreontic language of epicurean living. Of course these were exemplary models of identity that were never adopted and assimilated fully, but they nevertheless channeled behavior and emotions in certain directions and helped the elite organize and articulate their identities, even if their rhetoric should not be understood too literally.

The corollary of the ability to choose is that paths not taken, identities not explored endure in consciousness as lost opportunities and continue to haunt the present. It is hence not entirely surprising that reflexivity often took the form of mourning over a past whose prospects can no longer be recaptured. Sentimentalist literature, which in Russia began to permeate cultural discourse in the last two decades of the eighteenth century, was centrally preoccupied with this consciousness of loss—loss of a connection with nature, loss of the historical past, loss of a sense of the national collective, all, of course, highly constructed ideas.

Life lost its self-evident plainness; it became a task to work through, a challenge to live up to. The availability of different lifestyles imposed the necessity to choose among them, or to find ways to harness them together. Even religion became a discretionary matter, as we see from the elite families who for one reason or the other converted to Catholicism. Some young nobles, like Nikolai Turgenev, who spent several years studying in Göttingen and found it morally painful to return to Russia despite his burning desire to serve his country, ended up being continuously rocked back and forth between the aspiration to contribute to Russia's progress and the longing to live abroad. At some point Turgenev applied to serve in the diplomatic career, hoping thereby to conjoin these two objectives, but was crushed to be turned down (Schönle 2016). On the other side of the political spectrum, the arch-conservative, monarchist F. V. Rostopchin, who wrote in French of his disdain for the French but retired in Paris, after serving as rabble-rousing governor of Moscow in 1812 (and most likely giving the order to set the city on fire), illustrates similar tensions between an ideological identification with Russia and Europeanized lifestyle and manners. Although his wife and daughters converted to Catholicism, his daughter Sofia becoming "la comtesse de Ségur," the famous French writer of children's literature, he eventually returned to die in Russia.

As we have seen in previous chapters, loyalty to Russia and the sense of being Russian were not in the least affected by the adoption of European values and practices. Quite the contrary: the sense of refined worldliness that resulted from exposure to Europe only strengthened pride in being a subject of the Russian empire. Geopolitical and social affiliation trumped cultural identity, which only emerged as an important marker of identity in the nineteenth century, in the context of the rise of nationalism. In his *Letters of a Russian Traveller*, Karamzin had set a model of this sort of patriotism: while fully conversant with the languages and conventions of European countries, the traveler proudly identified as a Russian nobleman, which is how he introduced himself to Kant. Being Russian meant to evince a degree of cosmopolitanism, and neither choice of language of expression, nor of place of residence, could in any way diminish one's abstract identification with Russia.

On a more concrete level, however, the bond between place and identity was tenuous. The elite's physical peregrinations across the Russian empire and European countries contributed to loosening its affiliation with, or rootedness in, specific places. If they were born on a distant country estate, members of the elite sometimes romanticized their place of birth, but they rarely returned to visit. And if they did, they were often taken aback by its plainness. St. Petersburg, where they likely spent most of their time, was still under construction, and in no way could embody family history. The estates they used for summer residence, those closer to the capitals, were in most cases of recent vintage. With the exception of the mansions on the "Peterhof road" in the immediate vicinity of St. Petersburg and a few estates near Moscow, the construction boom in the countryside by and large started only in the late 1770s, and prior to that period, estates featured relatively modest and simple architecture. Existing palaces in St. Petersburg built in the first half of the eighteenth century changed ownership frequently, reflecting the vagaries of elite status at court. Only Moscow could represent attachment to ancestral family history, and even there, apart from the poorly maintained Kremlin and a few seventeenth-century halls, the vernacular architecture consisted largely of unassuming wooden buildings, sparsely spread over the sprawling surface of the city. Catherine certainly thought the city was ripe for extensive reconstruction and update (Martin 2013). In short, by and large, the elite's quarters had not yet accrued the patina of time, nor much family memory.

There are historical reasons for this state of affairs. In pre-Petrine Russia, land ownership was divided between patrimonial estates (*votchina*) and land held "in service" (*pomest'e*), the latter representing estates distributed as compensation for service, but which returned to the crown upon its termination. The service obligations of the nobility, which Peter strengthened and lengthened, curtailed nobles' ability to enjoy their estates, and in Peter's times many nobles stopped residing on their lands. Until its formal abrogation in 1762, the obligation to serve conflicted with the need to manage estates and the aspiration to live on them. Furthermore, as we have seen, the nobility did not obtain secure title to their estates until 1785 and, even then, could lose their lands if stripped of the claim to nobility by court decision; meanwhile, such a noble family also remained vulnerable to a neighbor willing to bribe the courts to grab a bit of ground. The absence of primogeniture and the resulting fragmentation of estate holdings likewise contributed toward weakening the bond between land and owner. In short, the country ties of the nobility were historically and legally weak, and the Russian nobility's regional roots cannot compare with those acquired by aristocratic families in formerly feudal societies.

Furthermore, the malleability of places, the propensity to stylize them according to the latest fashionable idiom, in particular the spread of a semi-official neoclassical template in architecture and foreign styles in landscape design—the fact, in short, that places were experienced as eminently changeable—also generated a specific dynamic in identification patterns. It made space and place subject to social pressure, which generally worked toward homogenization. As we discussed in the chapter on the provinces, the estate was a theatrical stage, a place where landowners performed an ideal version of themselves and required neighbors, serfs, and house servants to validate their display. This performative nature of country living also fostered a sense of impermanence. While this trend should not be overstated, it nevertheless meant that places were less able to carry personal and family memory, as well as to represent a sense of uniqueness, and hence to encode the subjective selves of their owners than if they had been ancestral patrimonial domains. For the rank and file, the architecture of their living quarters, whether in the capitals or in the country, was less a memory site than a medium of representation and distinction.

Toward the end of the century, the elite became more concerned to cultivate family memory, and as a result built up the memorial function of their estates through various means, from commissioning portraits and busts of forebears to collecting archives. Some landowners found ways to embed their personalities in their surroundings, resorting to devices as simple as naming separate features of their garden after people dear to them (Kurakin, for example, named alleys after his lovers, friends, and family members); using statuary to evoke the writers that influenced them (something I. V. Lopukhin implemented extensively in his Savinskoe); or even modeling architecture after places they visited or inhabited in earlier times (which is what Maria Fedorovna introduced at Pavlovsk). But what happened was the proleptic creation of a memorial culture, rather than its lived, spontaneous expression. In Pierre Nora's terms, the elite started *performing* memory by transforming their estates into so many *lieux de mémoire*, a transformation that betrayed an initial distanciation from the estates (Nora 1996, 7, 15). Memory was not inherited; it was constructed, reflecting the elite's modern (rather than premodern) sense of time.

The loose bond between identity and place, or what could perhaps more precisely be called the socialization of this bond, led to the rise of a metropolitan identity, rather than a regional one. The notion that places served to inscribe the social identity of the owners, but not necessarily their individual or familial selves, attenuated the difference between urban and country existence. Even when aristocrats spent considerable amounts of time and resources developing their estates, they were quick to abandon them, sometimes quite literally, when called into new service opportunities in the capital or elsewhere. All of this suggests a kind of interchangeability of living places, itself testament to what could be called a deterritorialized lifestyle. Of course, deterritorialization is not used here in the same way in which the literature on globalization deploys this term, where it means participation in instantaneous communication across the globe and in virtual spaces, leading to a loss of boundedness in a concrete locality (Tomlinson 1999, 106–128; Held and McGrew 2007, 3–4). Here it means that, with its seasonal migratory patterns and interchangeable locales, the life of the elite was less subject to the defining power of place than in more regionally grounded societies. Only in the nineteenth century, especially after the abolition of serfdom in 1861, did the country estate turn into a site of intensive nostalgic investment on the part of the elite, which led to the elaboration of a mythology about the country estate as the site of some authentic Russianness, an invented tradition very much alive to this date (Schönle 2007, 305–357).

The strictures and impositions of court society compounded this deterritorialization, the result of living across multiple sites and in imaginary worlds. Although it was the main seat of imperial power, the court rarely inspired complete identification on the part of the elite. While it exerted a magnetic force on everyone moving in the higher reaches of the social hierarchy, the court also generated a great deal of frustration and fear, and increasingly so over time. The elite, which derived its own brilliance from the light emanating from the court, at the same time felt the need to develop its own, autonomous standing, a need made more acute by its vulnerability to changes of monarchical favor. All rulers in the eighteenth century (and beyond) were in the habit of relying on favorites, who could be, and eventually were, abruptly dismissed. But beyond this intrinsic instability, court life required forms of deference, even abjection, which could not but create feelings of ambivalence. The prime site of the elite's social world was thus one that created a confused mixture of feelings, from awe and vanity to acute dependency and fear. This ambivalence prevented outright identification, but also foreclosed complete distanciation, as in most instances, the "pull of power" tended to override even rebellious tempers. The court was certainly no "home" and, more broadly, one could say that the nobility did not quite have its own place, but continuously strove to create an abode it could call its own, whether in the capital or on the estate. Home was an aspiration more than a reality.

The court was of course not the only source of power in the polity. The bureaucracy exerted a force of its own, and so did the institutions in which the elite might have a stake—the army, the Masonic lodge, the Academy of Sciences or the Academy of Arts, clubs and societies—each coming with its own set of procedures and norms. Society exerted a pull somewhat independent from the court, acting in part through patronage clans, but also through the dissemination of fashions in dress, literary and artistic taste, and the like.

All of these sources of power exerted pressure on individual members of the elite and influenced the process of forming their identity. The various facets of identity the elite derived from its exposure to different places were not gathered in an organic, neutral, "horizontal," fashion. They needed to be integrated in some hierarchical order, organized into some coherent shape. Was one primarily a servant of the empress, an officer faithful to his regiment, a socialite dependent on his patron, a writer committed to his art, or a landowner obligated to her serfs? Tensions between these and similar concurrent roles were bound to occur, as corporate allegiances—for example, to the regiment or the patronage clan—were extremely powerful. And this is where a continuous, unresolvable "tug of war" obtained, subjecting the elite to a plurality of demands and pressures, which influenced, and indeed hindered, its ability to integrate various facets of its identity. Hybridity was not only intrinsic to this way of life, but also fundamentally unstable, never achieving any sort of structured shape and remaining in flux, which clearly compounded the deterritorialization of the elite as it loosened any stable attachments.

This process of deterritorialization becomes especially evident when we consider the emotional world of the Russian elite and the basic emotional patterns promoted in the process of the sentimental education of the Russian nobility. The necessity to shape the elite and instill specific values in it implied systematic efforts on the part of the court to foster certain emotional patterns, which the upper echelons of society could appropriate and spread throughout the empire. A pivotal role in these efforts was predictably played by theater, as both artistic artifact and social ritual. Theatrical performances produce symbolic models of feelings that are at once visible and bodily expressive, as well as being pure and free from the empirics of everyday life. As most of the plays performed on the imperial stage were in French, the theater could also serve as a powerful instrument of Europeanization.

Court monopoly on the production of emotional patterns for public dissemination and emulation was undermined by the Masonic lodges, where an alternative and no less ambitious project for the complete renovation of humankind was developed. Clearly, it was also a Europeanizing project. Russian Freemasons strongly condemned so-called Voltairianism but sought to imitate the practices and emotional patterns developed by Catholic quietism, Protestant pietism, and European mysticism in general. They were disappointed by the low spiritual level of the Orthodox Church and looked to Europe for guidance, not only reading and translating a huge amount of moral and didactic literature, but directly placing themselves under obedience to foreign masters of the lodges and confessing to them the inner workings of their hearts.

While the "courtly" strategy of moral improvement was directed from outside inward, the lodges trained their members to find the truth inside themselves. The regeneration of humankind had to start from the microcosm, and only then would the macrocosm be transformed accordingly. Thus, instead of attending theater, it was reading that became the main vehicle for self-refining. This reliance on literary models of emotions was reinforced by the adaptation of the sentimental literary canon domesticated by late eighteenth-century Russian writers and especially by Karamzin, himself a disciple of the Freemasons. His *Letters of a Russian Traveller* gave Russian readers a compendium of the treasures of contemporary European culture in a conveniently packaged form. Karamzin was interested not so much in European landscapes and monuments as in the way to experience them. He constructed his narrator as a vehicle for conveying emotional patterns—one might say as a container to import them to Russia. He absorbed models of feelings characteristic of contemporary European culture and presented them to the Russian reader. This narrative and didactic logic implied that this time the traveler and his reactions had to serve as a tuning fork for his audience. This endeavor successfully reoriented educated Russian readers from different social layers, from the highest aristocracy to provincial gentry, and by the same token powerfully increased their ability to see themselves as Europeans without renouncing their deeply felt Russianness.

The emotional and intellectual life of the Russian elite was thus characterized by a specific type of hybridity, produced by the various competing systems of allegiance and emotional patterns they interiorized. The subjective ways in which it experienced and resolved hybridity were different from the hybridity theorized by Homi Bhabha in his work on colonialism. For Bhabha, "Hybridity is the process by which the discourse of colonial authority attempts to translate the identity of the Other within a singular category, but then fails and produces something else. The interaction between the two cultures proceeds with the illusion of transferable forms and transparent knowledge, but leads increasingly into resistant, opaque and dissonant exchanges" (Papastergiadis 1997, 279). In this framework, hybridity is an accident that results from the hegemonic power's inability to effect the complete transformation of the subaltern culture. More than that, the imposition of colonial authority creates a "split screen of the self and its doubling, the hybrid" (Bhabha 1994, 114): on the one hand, power, in seeking to impose itself, creates an essentialist, unitary identity, an "excess," as it were, of itself (112). In carrying out its discriminatory strategies against the subaltern culture, it shores up—homogenizes, idealizes—its own identity. On the other hand, as it extends its reach into the colonies and seeks to reproduce itself through its effects on vernacular cultures, it faces the "strategies of subversion" of the discriminated, undergoes estrangement, deformation, and uncertainty, which creates forms of hybridity. What the colonial power sees then in this split mirror is both itself and a grotesquely deformed and threatening doubling of itself as the face of hybridity, two facets that remain irreconcilable.

In the case of the eighteenth-century Russian elite, hybridity was experienced from the outset as an unavoidable condition, in that it was the only way to harness together the identifications resulting from exposure to the various places of the elite's existence. There never was a unitary culture that sought to reproduce itself and underwent a doubling between an ideal, essentialist incarnation and a corrupted one. Furthermore, in light of the ongoing self-transformation of Russian society at the time, hybridity was also the only way to accrue new identities on top of existing ones, which, as we have seen, were not summarily displaced, or disavowed, in Bhabha's terminology. This produced complex, unstable, even volatile combinations, but combinations that at least had potential for some syncretic fusing, rather than leading to an irreconcilable splitting. Hence the elite's sometime extraordinary ability to navigate contradictory "pulls" and to experience the bricolage of cultures as a "natural" condition. Contrary to the discourse of colonial countries, which set forth their values as universal ones, this was social transformation without recourse to exclusive, universalist rhetoric and with a better sense of the relativistic or situational boundedness of culture. Different from postcolonial hybridity, this phenomenon of identity accretion does not bring about the loss of indigenous culture. At most, it offers the elite an opportunity to gain some mental distance from its own culture, without, however, compromising it completely. This, too, is part of deterritorialization, a loosening of attachments, while inherited values and ideas endure at least in a palimpsestic form. Orthodox piety, even some residues of pagan belief, attachment to the tsar, personalistic notions of power, the habits of patronage—such systems of belief and practices continued to affect the elite despite the import of secular ideas, Western legal culture, and literary emotional patterns. Social transformation was not only gradual, but also multilayered, never causing a clear rupture with the past.

While it has not radically and fundamentally transformed Russia, the deterritorialization of the elite has served as a powerful mechanism of social differentiation, allowing its members to demarcate themselves strongly from the much more territorially bounded and defined lower classes. The cross-border connectivity Catherine fostered pertained almost exclusively to the (mostly upper) nobility. Serfs, it goes without saying, were in any case attached to the land, while merchants and tradesmen were also registered in specific towns, and only merchants of the first guild were allowed to trade internationally. Members of the clergy might go on a pilgrimage abroad, but only if sanctioned by church authorities, not of their own volition, while soldiers could move with their regiment into foreign territory during a military campaign, but remained restricted in their forays into indigenous lands. Thus deterritorialization affected only a very narrow upper circle of society.

This deterritorialization does not amount to globalization in the contemporary sense. There are substantial differences in scope, intensity, and velocity of cross-border communication, as well as in the very modes of interconnectivity, which are now substantially based on digital protocols. Yet, what we describe is also different from the notions of "archaic" and "early modern" globalizations proposed, for example, by Christopher Bayly. To put it simply, "archaic" globalization describes a pattern of trade and travel in the Middle Ages and beyond prompted by the notions of universal kingship and cosmic religion. Rulers fancied themselves as universal rulers and hence surrounded themselves with goods and people coming from distant lands, who were gathered at court to lend it an exotic aura. This created a demand for goods appreciated precisely for their difference. In parallel, religion was thought of not in national terms but in cosmic ones, which prompted the desire to visit sites of pilgrimage such as Jerusalem and Rome. Thus archaic globalization fostered the development of trade for pricey, luxurious commodities as well as the practice of traveling across borders in pursuit of communion with the sacred (Bayly 2004, 43).

Early modern globalization, which emerged around the years 1760–1830, was characterized on the one side by increased agricultural productivity, achieved by the use of more settled forms of land exploitation, and on the other by the "industrious revolution," the rise of a household demand for marketed goods and a corresponding reallocation of labor away from subsistence production toward work for the market, resulting in more specialized labor (de Vries 1994, 257): family labor was used more efficiently by purchasing certain goods and services from outside the household, for example imported food staples for breakfast (coffee, sugar), which created a demand for imported foods, while freeing energy for more specialized domestic production (Bayly 2004, 51). In Bayly's account, this industrious revolution enhanced capitalist production and cross-border trade and ultimately led to the development of "classes of consumers who had a common interest in acquiring positional goods that homogenized their status." In short, it fostered uniform class formation (65).

In Russia, this economic logic does not apply in the same way. The elite's demand for foreign goods arose not from an economic rationale, but in pursuit of honorific status, and it did not free up specialized, more efficient labor. Nor did it primarily sustain itself through increased land productivity; instead it benefited from rises in the price of commodities (mainly grain), which resulted from Russia's integration into the European market, and by appropriating a greater share of the proceeds of serf labor: according to Boris Mironov, "The state's share of income from serfs gradually fell from 50 percent to 12.1 percent over the eighteenth century," with most of the difference ending in the pockets of the nobility (Mironov 2012, 113). It also financed the purchase of foreign goods through debt and other financial instruments new to Russia (such as promissory notes). Yet contrary to archaic modernization, the symbolic intent of acquiring exogenous goods was not to universalize power or prestige, but to Europeanize it. Trade proceeded not from a cosmic worldview, but from a geopolitical one. Finally, it nurtured a logic of distinction, which operated at all levels and comprised both imitation and differentiation, which hindered the development of estate solidarity and homogeneity. The process Bayly described ultimately led to the national integration of society, as national identification took the place of dynastic affiliation, a phenomenon that broke the boundaries between the nobles, burghers, and tradesmen (Bayly 2004, 67). In Russia the cultural gap between the noble elite and other urban groups was so wide that this integration proved much more limited and fragile. In fact this cultural gap reinforced the social divide between classes or estates, as differences in language, appearance, habits, and beliefs became nearly insurmountable.

It would be tempting to account for Russia's difference as simply a matter of its delayed modernity, whereby Russia in the second half of the eighteenth century would find itself somewhere between archaic and early modern globalization. Yet the fact that cross-border connectivity in Russia was driven by a demand that ultimately led not to social and national consolidation, as in Bayly's paradigm, but to social fragmentation, is highly significant and qualifies the notion of delayed modernity. As a technique of social differentiation, Europeanization placed the elite in a morally complex relationship with its serfs. While culturally distinct, serfs were still cut of the same Russian cloth as the nobility in core regions of the empire, which prevented, or at least complicated, their efficient and ruthless exploitation, in comparison with the treatment of slave labor in colonial empires. Furthermore, cross-border connectivity was prompted not by an economic logic—the specialization of labor—but by the multiplication of identity positions and the resulting dramatic rise in reflexivity, which also set into motion distinctive historical trajectories. Finally, administrative centralization and national consolidation were also hindered by Russia's very nature as a contiguous empire with extensive multiethnic and multireligious frontier territories, which also conditioned its subsequent development. Altogether, these factors generated a set of contradictions between state and society, elite and the lower classes, as well as Russian and non-Russian groups, which made national integration impossible (Kappeler 2001, 238–243).

It would be all but impossible to pin down a single characteristic, or even a set of specific features of Russian Europeanization, that could not be found in the history of other Westernizing countries located to the East of Paris from Prussia to Japan. Neither the distinctly top-down direction of a process that started from enforcing new standards of clothing and everyday behavior and continued with the demand to interiorize values seen as European, nor its unashamedly elitist character were unique to post-Petrine Russia. The defining role of the state, the transfer of technology and of social, educational, and cultural institutions, the massive imports of ideas, behavioral practices, and emotional patterns, as well as the pursuit of enhanced connectivity as we define it in this volume, were in different proportions typical for many peripheral empires striving to overcome a perceived developmental gap with more advanced countries.

The reforms of Peter the Great in Russia served as a model for the Ottoman Sultans during the Tanzimat period in the nineteenth century as well as during the Kemalist revolution in the twentieth. They also inspired the ideologues and propagandists of the Meiji Revolution in Japan. In all three cases, the need for creating a new elite and for overhauling state institutions derived from pressing military challenges in the wake of major military defeats. Westernization was a response to the need to catch up with European countries, perceived to be more advanced militarily, economically, technologically, and culturally (Esenbel 2011, 167–168). And this transformation was regarded and promoted by the authorities as a significant step toward enlightenment, interpreted mostly in universalist terms.

Unlike Russian nobles, however, the Turkish and Japanese elites did not aspire to become Europeans, but only to emulate them, which relieved them of many of the difficult problems that shaped the identity building of their Russian peers. In addition, the ultimate goals of both the Meiji restoration and the Kemalist revolution were to foster the mobilization of a broader stratum of society, which would follow the example set by the elites. For the Kemalist state, nation building was at the heart of its ambitions, as the partial Westernization of the upper elite had already been achieved in the nineteenth century. During the Russo-Japanese war in 1905, Turkish public opinion was powerfully lifted by the Japanese victories as they gave an incontestable proof that a properly educated non-European nation could beat the Europeans (Esenbel 2011, 148–153).

Selçuk Esenbel, the leading expert in Turkish and Japanese Europeanization, wrote that "the Ottoman Turks liked to keep the use of Western culture 'close to their chest,' never to discard it, but modified it in a symbiotic unity.... The Japanese, on the other hand, preferred to keep their Japanese and European selves formally in separate realms and shifted back and forth as the occasion required" (xxii). She illustrates this functional distribution with reference to the structure of the Japanese home, in which European influence determined the design of the parlor and dining room, while traditional Japanese culture prevailed in a formal room. Yet, crucially, the private inner rooms of the home were characterized by a spontaneous mixture of the two elements (180–181).

According to Esenbel, "Both the Japanese and the Turks felt most comfortable in the 'inner rooms' of their privacy when they could freely combine everything without a specific rational structure. It is that private sense of the hybrid mixture of the local and the Western global components that comes closest to the 'comfort zone' that helps the individual survive through the modern experience" (xxii). With all the differences and tensions inherent in the fraught process of Europeanization, it nevertheless allowed for a "comfort zone," as even the most radical Europeanization could not threaten the underlying Turkish or Japanese identities of the elite.

At the other end of the spectrum, the Prussian or Spanish nobles were keen to adopt French manners, fashion, and language, as they knew that the Parisian court provided the golden standard of high civilization, and they did so in full confidence that their own European identity would not thereby be undermined or challenged. Despite obvious political, linguistic, and cultural differences, they felt that they belonged to a common European realm, defined by the feudal system, Western Christianity, and numerous dynastic ties. All these factors defining their shared heritage were especially relevant for the self-perception of political, economic, and social elites.

The Russian elite found itself in a more precarious situation. Both its Russianness and its "Europeanness" had always been and remained contested issues, in need of being constantly redefined, reaffirmed, and reexperienced. The specific dynamics of Russian Europeanization, as it unfolded in the eighteenth and early nineteenth century, were shaped by a historically unique accumulation of factors we have tried to trace in this book. This constellation accounts for the unique prominence, complexity, and intensity of the processes of Europeanization in Russia.

From our point of view, Europeanization was first and foremost a subjective phenomenon. It implied the readiness of the members of the elite to acknowledge, willingly or reluctantly, that becoming European, however different the understanding of that concept could be, was their duty as loyal subjects of the emperor, as officers and statesmen, as landlords and serf owners, husbands, wives, and parents. They felt they owed it to their monarch, their country, their families, and sometimes even their peasants. By becoming European they aspired to be better Russians, and by the same token they hoped that their Russianness would entitle them to be if not better, than at least a different sort of Europeans.

This process was by no means an easy one, especially in a basically premodern country like Russia. It implied difficult adjustment, conscious and unconscious compromises, intensive self-fashioning, self-reflection, and self-refining. However, up to a certain point this navigation between different and often conflicting sets of values was seen by the majority of Russian nobles as productive and promising both for themselves and for the country as a whole. It started to show its limits in the 1820s–1830s, in the context of dramatic political and ideological polarization, when the internal hybridity of the elite became unbearable and unsustainable, creating a sense of malaise and alienation.

Under Nicholas I, the government required explicit and complete obedience from its elites, destroying the freer interiorized compact between the elite and the state that had been fostered by Catherine. Choosing between loyalty to the throne or, more broadly, to the country, people, or nation, between an orientation toward further Westernization or toward (often invented) national traditions, and between adherence to the traditional religion of ancestors or to the modern belief in Enlightenment and science, became less a problem of individual navigation than a question of adhering to a specific political and ideological group. The elite found itself forced to take a stance in its relations with the government in the context of increasingly ideological and partisan national debates. In this radically transformed composition of public life, the Europeanizing elite managed to retain its social status and economic privilege, but it was gradually displaced from its mainstream position in the intellectual life of the country by a newly emerging social group, which would later be defined as the Russian intelligentsia.

Abbreviations

GARF   Gosudarstvennyi arkhiv Rossiiskoi Federatsii (State Archive of the Russian Federation)

IRLI RO   Rukopisnyi otdel Instituta russkoi literatury (Pushkinskii dom) (Manuscript Division of the Institute of Russian Literature. Pushkin House)

PSZ 1830   Polnoe sobranie zakonov Rossiiskoi Imperii s 1649 goda. Pervoe sobranie. 45 vols. St. Petersburg.

RGB OR   Rossiiskaia gosudarstvennaia biblioteka. Otdel rukopisei (Manuscript Collection of the Russian State Library)

RGIA   Rossiiskii gosudarstvennyi istoricheskii arkhiv (Russian State Archive of History)

RNB OR   Rossiiskaia natsional'naia biblioteka. Rukopisnyi otdel (Manuscript Department of the Russian National Library)

Bibliography

Archival Sources

IRLI RO, f. 309 (Turgenevy), d. 272, sh. 92–99; d. 1240. Venskie zhurnaly Andreia Ivanovicha Turgeneva.

IRLI RO, f. 309, d. 272. Dnevnik Andreia Ivanovicha Turgeneva 1801–1803 gg.

RGIA, f. 759 (Kantseliariia po uchrezhdeniiam imperatritsy Marii), op. 10, d. 349. Pis'ma I. I. Betskogo Peterburgskomu Opekunskomu sovetu.

RGB OR, f. 18 (Barsukovy), k. 30, d. 6. Stikhotvoreniia A. M. Pavlovoi.

RGB OR, f 19 (Bariatinskie), op. 1, d. 204. Iz zagranichnogo puteshestviia, khoziaistvennye zapiski 1818–1819.

RGB OR, f. 19, op. 2, ed. 17. I. I. Bariatinskii. Pis'ma k zhene Marii Fedorovne Bariatinskoi, 1817.

RGB OR, f. 19, op. 2, papka 253, d. 1. Chernoviki, zapiski, zametki, rassuzhdeniia I. I. Bariatinskogo.

RGB OR, f. 19, op. 5, d. 72. Conseils à mon fils ainé.

RGB OR, f. 19, op. 5, d. 117. Kopii pisem, razlichnye vypiski i zametki I. I. Bariatinskogo.

RGB OR, f. 19, op. 5/2, d. 12. Bariatinskaia Ekaterina Petrovna, ur. Golshtein-Bek, Zapiski o puteshestvii po Evrope.

RGB OR, f. 64 (Viazemy), k. 100, ed. 57. Rumiantsev N. P. Pis'ma k Golitsynei, kn., Natal'e Petrovne, 1789–1791, Frankfurt.

RGB OR, f. 64, k. 113, ed. 1. Golitsyna, Natal'ia Petrovna. Remarques sur mes voyages, 1783–1790.

RGB OR F. 233 (Poltoratskie), op. 5, d. 45. Primernoe polozhenie dlia obraztsovoi fermy ili khoziaistva. 1818.

GARF, f. 825 (Bakuniny), op. 1, d. 259. Tetradi s zapisiami Bakunina. 1810 god.

RNB, F. 1278, op. 1, ed. khr. 346. Journal du voyage en contrées étrangères, du comte P.A. Stroganov (1785).

Published Sources

Abramov, Ia. V. 1891. *V. N. Karazin. (Osnovatel' khar'kovskgvo universiteta). Ego zhizn' i obshchestvennaia deiatel'nost'*. St. Petersburg.

Adamson, John. 1999. "The Making of the Ancien-régime Court 1500–1700." In *The Princely Courts of Europe: Ritual, Politics and Culture Under the Ancien Régime 1500–1750*, edited by John Adamson, 7–41. London: Weidenfeld and Nicolson.

Agamalian, L. G. 1999. "A.M. Bakunin i ego proekt 'Uslovie pomeshchika s krest'ianinom.'" *Pamiatniki kul'tury. Novye otkrytiia. Pis'mennost'. Iskusstvo. Arkheologiia. 1998*, 52–73. Moscow: Nauka.

Ageeva, O. G. 2006. *Evropeizatsiia russkogo dvora 1700–1796 gg.* Moscow: Ros. AN, Institut rossiiskoi istorii.

———. 2008. *Imperatorskii dvor Rossii, 1700–1796*. Moscow: Nauka.

Aksakov, S. T. 1984. *A Family Chronicle: Childhood Years of Bagrov Grandson*. Moscow: Raduga.

Alekseeva, N. Iu. 2005. *Russkaia oda: razvitie odicheskoi formy v XVII–XVIII vekakh*. St. Petersburg: Nauka.

Andriainen, Stanislav. 2016. "The Everyday Life of Russian Officers at the Beginning of the Nineteenth Century." In Schönle et al., 2016b, *The Europeanized Elite in Russia, 1762–1825*, 158–175.

Anisimov, Evgenii V. 1993. *The Reforms of Peter the Great: Progress through Coercion in Russia*. Armonk: M. E. Sharpe.

———. 1995. "'Shvedskaia model' s russkoi 'osobost'iu': Reforma vlasti i upravleniia pri Petre Velikom." *Zvezda* 1:133–150.

Arkhiv Kniazia Vorontsova. 1872. Edited by P. I. Bartenev. Vol. 5. Moscow: Tip. A. I. Mamontova.

Bakunin, A. M. 2002. "Pis'ma A. M. Bakunina k N. A. L'vovu," edited by L. G. Agamalian, 43–95. *Ezhegodnik rukopisnogo otdela Pushkinskogo doma na 1997 god*. St. Petersburg: Dmitrii Bulanin.

Bashilov, A. A. 1871. "Molodost' Bashilova (Zapiski o vremenakh Ekateriny II i Pavla I.)" *Zaria* (December): 193–223.

Bayly, Christopher. 2004. *The Birth of the Modern World 1780–1914: Global Connections and Comparisons*. Oxford: Blackwell.

Bekasova, Alexandra V. 2004. "Die Formierung eines kulturellen Milieus. Russische Studenten und ihre Reisen im späten 18. Jahrhundert." In *Die Welt erfahren. Reisen als kulturelle Begegnung von 1780 bis heute*, edited by Arnd Bauerkämper et al., 239–264. Frankfurt: Campus Verlag.

Beliavskii, M. T. 1960. "Novye dokumenty ob obsuzhdenii krest'ianskogo voprosa v 1766–1768 godakh." In *Arkheograficheskii ezhegodnik za 1958 god*, 387–430. Moscow: ANSSSR.

Belinskii, V. G. 1955. "Sochineniia Aleksandra Pushkina." In V. G. Belinskii, *Polnoe sobranie sochineniia*, 7:97–582. Moscow: Akademiia nauk.

Berelowitch, Wladimir. 1993. "La France dans le 'Grand Tour' des nobles russes au cours de la seconde moitié du 18e siècle." In *Noblesse, Etat et société en Russie*, edited by Wladimir Berelowitch, 193–209. *Cahiers du monde russe et soviétique*.

Berelowitch, Wladimir, and Olga Medvedkova. 1996. *Histoire de Saint-Pétersbourg*. Paris: Fayard.

Berest, Julia. 2011. *The Emergence of Russian Liberalism: Alexander Kunitsyn in Context, 1783–1840*. Basingstoke: Palgrave Macmillan.

Berkhgol'ts, F. V. 1857–1860. *Dnevnik kammer-iunkera Berkhgol'tsa*. 3 vols. Moscow.

Berlin, Isaiah. 2008. *Russian thinkers*. Edited by Henry Hardy and Aileen Kelly. London: Penguin.

Betskoi, I. I. 1774. *Uchrezhdeniia i ustavy, kasaiushchiesia do vospitaniia i obucheniia v Rossii iunoshestva oboego pola*. Vol. 1. St. Petersburg.

Bhabha, Homi K. 1994. *The Location of Culture*. London: Routledge.

Black, J. L. 1979. *Citizens for the Fatherland: Education, Educators, and Pedagogical Ideals in Eighteenth Century Russia*. Boulder: East European Quarterly.

Bolotov, A. T. 1870–1873. *Zhizn' i prikliucheniia Andreia Bolotova, opisannye samim im dlia svoikh potomkov, 1738–1793*. 4 vols. St. Petersburg.

———. 1993. *Pis'ma o krasotakh prirody*. In *Izbrannoe*, 137–203. Pskov: POIPKRO.

Bondil, Nathalie. 2006. "'Gluttony' in the Fine Arts: Did Catherine II Have Taste?." In *Catherine the Great: Art for Empire*, edited by Nathalie Bondil, 169–177. Montreal: Montreal Museum of Fine Arts.

Bulgakovy, A. Ia., and K. Ia. 2010. *Pis'ma*. 3 vols. Moscow: Zakharov.

Bushkovitch, Paul. 1992. *Religion and Society in Russia: The Sixteenth and Seventeenth Centuries*. New York: Oxford University Press.

Buturlin, M. D. 1901. "Zapiski grafa M. D. Buturlina." *Russkii Arkhiv* 39 (11): 384–421.

Chechulin, N. D. 2010. *Russkaia provintsiia vo vtoroi polovine XVIII veka*. St. Petersburg: Rossiiskaia natsional'naia biblioteka.

Cherepnin, N. P. 1915. *Imperatorskoe chelovekoliubivoe obshchestvo blagorodnykh devits. Istoricheskii ocherk*. St. Petersburg: Gosudarstvennaia tipografiia.

Cherniavsky, Michael. 1961. *Tsar and People: Studies in Russian Myths*. New Haven: Yale University Press.

Chudinov, A. V. 2004. "Frantsuzskie guvernery v Rossii kontsa XVIII v.: Stereotipy i real'nost." In *Evropeiskoe prosveshchenie i tsivilizatsiia Rossii*, edited by S. Ia Karp and S. A. Mezin, 330–340. Moscow: Nauka.

———. 2007. *Frantsuzskaia revoliutsiia: Istoriia i mify*. Moscow: Nauka.

Clarke, Samuel. 1728. *Traités de l'existence et des attributs de Dieu, des devoirs de la religion naturelle et de la vérité de la religion chrétienne*. 2 vols. Amsterdam.

———. 1998. *A demonstration of the being and attributes of God and other writings*. Edited by Vailati Ezio. Cambridge: Cambridge University Press.

Cobenzl, Ludwig, Count and Joseph II. 1901. *Joseph II. und graf Ludwig Cobenzl. Ihr Briefwechsel*. Vol. 1, *1780–1784. Oesterreichische Geschichts-Quellen*, vol. 53. Vienna: In Commission bei Carl Gerold's Sohn.

Collis, Robert, 2012. *The Petrine Instauration: Religion, Esotericism and Science at the Court of Peter the Great, 1689-1725*. Leiden: Brill.

Confino, Michael. 1969. *Systèmes agraires et progrès agricole. L'assolement triennal en Russie aux XVIIIe-XIXe siècles*. Paris: Mouton.

Corberon, Marie Daniel Bourrée, chevalier de. 1901. *Un Diplomate français à la cour de Catherine II: 1775-1780. Journal intime du chevalier de Corberon, chargé d'affaires de France en Russie*. 2 vols. Paris: Plon-Nourrit.

Coxe, William. 1803. *Travels in Poland, Russia, Sweden and Denmark*. 6th ed., vol. 2. London.

Cracraft, James. 2003. *The Revolution of Peter the Great*. Cambridge, MA: Harvard University Press.

Cross, Anthony. 1997. *By the Banks of the Neva*. Cambridge: Cambridge University Press.

Czartoryski, Adam. 1887. *Mémoires du prince Adam Czartoryski et correspondance avec l'empereur Alexandre Ier*. Vol. 1. Paris.

Dachkova, Ekaterina. 1999. *Mon Histoire. Mémoires d'une femme de lettres russe à l'époque des Lumières*. Paris: L'Harmattan.

D'Alembert, Jean. 1821. "Description abrégée du gouvernement de Genève." In *Œuvres de D'Alembert*, vol. 4. Paris.

Darnton, Robert. 1985. "Readers Respond to Rousseau: The Fabrication of Romantic Sensitivity." In *The Great Cat Massacre and Other Episodes in French Cultural History*, 215–256. New York: Vintage Books.

———. 1990. "First Steps Toward a History of Reading." In *The Kiss of Lamourette; Reflections in Cultural History*, 154–187. New York: W.W. Norton.

de Madariaga, Isabel. 1981. *Russia in the Age of Catherine the Great*. New Haven: Yale University Press.

———. 1994. "The Russian Nobility in the Seventeenth and Eighteenth Centuries." In *The European Nobilities in the Seventeenth and Eighteenth Centuries*, edited by H. M. Scott, 2:311–376. Houndmills: Palgrave Macmillan.

———. 1998. *Politics and Culture in Eighteenth-century Russia*. London: Longman.

Denby, David. 1994. *Sentimental Narrative and the Social Order in France, 1760-1820*. Cambridge: Cambridge University Press.

Dennison, Tracy. 2011. *The Institutional Framework of Russian Serfdom*. Cambridge: Cambridge University Press.

Deriabina, Yekaterina. 2000. "Artist and Patron." *Stroganoff: The Palace and Collections of a Russian Noble Family*, edited by Penelope Hunter-Stiebel, 145–155. New York: Harry N. Abrams.

Derzhavin, G. R. 1864. "Opisanie torzhestva v dome kniazia Potemkina po sluchaiu vziatia Izmaila." In *Sochineniia Derzhavina*, edited by Ia. Grot, 1:377–419. St. Petersburg.

———. 1876. "Zapiski iz izvestnykh vsem proisshestviev i podlinnykh del, zakliuchaiushchie v sebe zhizn' Gavrily Romanovicha Derzhavina." In *Sochineniia Derzhavina*, edited by Ia. Grot, 6:401–790. St. Petersburg.

———. 2002. *Sochineniia*. St. Petersburg: Akademicheskii proekt.

De Vries, Jan. 1994. "The Industrial Revolution and the Industrious Revolution." *Journal of Economic History* 54, no. 2 (June): 249–270.

Dixon, Simon. 1999 *The Modernisation of Russia 1676-1825*. Cambridge: Cambridge University Press.

——. 2009. *Catherine the Great*. London: Profile Books.

Dmitriev, M. A. 1998. *Glavy iz vospominanii moei zhizni*. Edited by K. G. Bolenko et al. Moscow: NLO.

Dmitrieva, E. E., and O. N. Kuptsova. 2003. *Zhizn' usadebnogo mifa: Utrachennyi i obretennyi rai*. Moscow: OGI.

Dolgorukov, I. M. 1849. *Sochineniia Dolgorukogo (Kniazia Ivana Mikhailovicha)*. Vol. 1. St. Petersburg.

——. 1870. *Slavny bubny za gorami, ili Puteshestvie moe koe-kuda 1810 goda*. Moscow.

——. 2004–2005. *Povest' o rozhdenii moem, proiskhozhdenii i vsei zhizni*, 2 vols. St. Petersburg: Nauka.

Duindam, Jeroen. 2003. *Vienna and Versailles: The Courts of Europe's Dynastic Rivals, 1550–1780*. Cambridge: Cambridge University Press.

Ekaterina II. 1878. *Pis'ma imperatritsy Ekateriny II k Grimmu (1774–1796)*. Sbornik imperatorskago russkogo istoricheskago obshchestva, vol. 23.

Elias, Norbert. 1983. *The Court Society*. Oxford: Basil Blackwell.

Engelsing, Rolf. 1974. *Der Bürger als Leser. Lesergeschichte in Deutschland 1500–1800*. Stuttgart: J. B. Metzlersche Verlagsbuchhandlung.

Esenbel, Selçuk. 2011. *Japan, Turkey and the World of Islam: The Writings of Selçuk Esenbel*. Vol. 3. Leiden: Brill.

Etkind, A. M. 1996. "'Umiraiushchii Sfinks.' Krug Golitsyna-Labzina i peterburgskii period russkoi misticheskoi traditsii." *Studia Slavica Finlandiesa*. Vol. 13. 17–46.

Evstratov, Alexeï. 2016a. *Les Spectacles francophones à la cour de Russie (1743–1796). L'invention d'une société*. Oxford: Voltaire Foundation.

——. 2016b. "Russian Prince vs. 'German Swine': Public Slap in the Face, Émigrés, and Local Elites in St. Petersburg at the Time of the French Revolution." In Schönle et al., 2016b, *The Europeanized Elite in Russia, 1762–1825*, 242–260.

Faggionato, Rafaella. 2005. *Rosicrucian Utopia in Eighteenth Century Russia: The Masonic Circle of N. I. Novikov*. Dordrecht: Springer.

Faivre, Antoine. 1969. *Eckartshausen et la théosophie chrétienne*. Paris: C. Klincksieck.

Faizova, I. V. 1999. *'Manifest o vol'nosti' i sluzhba dvorianstva v XVIII stoletii*. Moscow: Nauka.

Fedyukin, Igor. 2017a. *The Enterpriser: The Politics of School in Early Modern Russia*. Oxford: Oxford University Press. (In print).

——. 2017b. "Sex in the City That Peter Built: The Demimonde and Sociability in Mid-Eighteenth-Century St. Petersburg," *Slavic Review* 76. no. 4 (Winter), 907–930.

Filaret. 1812. *Slovo po osviashchenii khrama vo imia sviatoi zhivonachal'noi Troitsy, v dome kniazia Aleksandra Nikolaevicha Golitsyna, 1 oktiabria*. St. Petersburg.

——. 1906. "Iz vospomianii." *Russkii arkhiv* 44 (10): 214–223.

Fomenko, I. Iu. 1983. "Avtobiograficheskaia proza G. R. Derzhavina i problema professionalizatsii russkogo pisatelia." *XVIII vek* 14: 143–165.

Fonvizin, D. I. 1959. *Sobranie sochinenii*. 2 vols. Moscow: Gos. izdatel'stvo khudozhestvennoi literatury.

——. 1983. *Izbrannoe*. Moscow: Sovetskaia Rossiia.

Frank, Christoph. 2006. "The Art of Governing the Arts: The Roman Patronage of Catherine the Great." In *Catherine the Great: Art for Empire*, edited by Nathalie Bondil, 183–191. Montreal: Montreal Museum of Fine Arts.

Freeze, Gregory. 1977. *The Russian Levites: Parish Clergy in the Eighteenth Century*. Cambridge, MA: Harvard University Press.

Garnovskii, M. A. 1876. "Zapiski Mikhaila Garnovskogo." *Russkaia starina*, vol. 15 (1): 9–38; vol. 15 (2): 237–265; vol. 15 (3): 471–499; vol. 16 (5): 1–32; vol. 16 (6): 207–238; vol. 16 (7): 399–440.

Geertz, Clifford. 1980. *Negara: The Theatre State in Nineteenth-Century Bali*. Princeton: Princeton University Press.

Geertz, Clifford 2000. *Local Knowledge: Further Essays in Interpretative Anthropology*. Basic Books.

Georgi, I. G. 1996. *Opisanie rossiisko-imperatorskogo stolichnogo goroda Sankt-Peterburga i dostopamiatnostei v okrestnostiakh onogo, s planom*. St. Petersburg: Liga.

Glinka, S. N. 2004. *Zapiski*. Moscow: Zakharov.

Girtsel, I. K. 1789. *Sel'skoi Sokrat, ili opisanie ekonomicheskikh i nravstvennykh pravil zhizni filoso-fa-zemledel'tsa*. Moscow.

Gogol', N. V. 1978. *Sobranie sochinenii*. Vol. 7. Moscow: Khudozhestvennaia literatura.

Golovine, comtesse. 1910. *Souvenirs de la comtesse Golovine, née princesse Galitzine 1766–1821*. Paris: Librairie Plon.

Grimm, Friedrich Melchior. 1886. *Pis'ma Grimma k imperatritse Ekaterine II*. St. Petersburg.

Guberti, N. V. 1887. *Istoriko-literaturnye i bibliograficheskie materialy*. St. Petersburg.

Gukovskii, G. A. 1936. *Ocherki po istorii russkoi literatury XVIII veka: Dvorianskaia fronda v literature 1750-kh–1760-kh godov*. Leningrad: Gos. izdatel'stvo khudozhestvennoi literatury.

———. 2001. "Iz istorii russkoi ody XVIIII veka. Opyt istolkovaniia parodii." In G. A. Gukovskii, *Rannie raboty po istorii russkoi poezii XVIII veka*, edited by V. M. Zhivov, 229–250. Moscow: Iazyki russkoi kul'tury.

Harris, James. 1844. *Diaries and Correspondence of James Harris, First Earl of Malmesbury*. Vol. 1. London.

Hayden, Peter. 2005. *Russian Parks and Gardens*. London: Frances Lincoln.

Held, David, and Anthony McGrew. 2007. *Globalization/Anti-Globalization*. Cambridge: Polity.

Hughes, Lindsey. 1998. *Russia in the Age of Peter the Great*. New Haven: Yale University Press.

Ian'kova, E. P. 1989. *Rasskazy babushki: Iz vospominanii piati pokolenii zapisannye i sobrannye ee vnu-kom D. Blagovo*. Leningrad: Nauka.

Ibneeva, G. V. 2009. *Imperskaia politika Ekateriny II v zerkale ventsenosnykh puteshestvii*. Moscow: Pamiatniki istoricheskoi mysli.

Iosad, Alexander. 2016. "Curiosity, Utility, Pleasure: Official Discourses of Natural Philosophy and Their Alternatives in Russia in the Run-up to 1762." In Schönle et al., 2016b, *The Europeanized Elite in Russia, 1762–1825*, 46–65.

Ivanova, L. V., ed. 2001. *Dvorianskaia i kupecheskaia sel'skaia usad'ba v Rossii XVI–XX vv*. Moscow: URSS.

Johnson, James H. 1995. *Listening in Paris: A Cultural History*. Berkeley: University of California Press.

Jones, Gareth W. 1984. *Nikolay Novikov: Enlightener of Russia*. Cambridge: Cambridge University Press

Jones, Robert E. 1973. *The Emancipation of the Russian Nobility*. Princeton: Princeton University Press.

———. 1984. *Provincial Development in Russia: Catherine II and Jakob Sievers*. New Brunswick: Rutgers University Press.

Kahan, Arcadius. 1966. "The Cost of 'Westernization' in Russia: The Gentry and the Economy in the Eighteenth Century." *Slavic Review* 25, no. 1 (March): 40–66.

Kahn, Andrew. 2002–2003. "'Blazhenstvo ne v luchakh porfira': Histoire et fonction de la tranquilité (*spokoistvie*) dans la pensée et la poésie russe du XVIIIe siècle, de Kantemir au sentimenta-lisme." *Revue des Etudes Slaves* 74 (4): 669–688.

Kamenskii, A. B. 2001. *Ot Petra I do Pavla I. Reformy v Rossii XVIII veka*. Moscow: RGGU.

Kant, Immanuel. 1922. *Gesammelte Schriften*. 2nd edition. Vol. 10. Berlin: W. de Gruyter.

Kappeler, Andreas. 2001. *The Russian Empire: A Multi-Ethnic History*. Translated by Alfred Clayton. Harlow, UK: Longman.

Karamzin, N. M. 1796. *Bednaia Liza*. Moscow.

———. 1802. *Istoricheskoe pokhval'noe slovo Ekaterine Vtoroi*. Moscow.

———.1964. *Izbrannye sochineniia v dvukh tomakh*. Vol. 2. Moscow-Leningrad: Khudozhestvennaia literatura.

———. 2003. *Letters of a Russian Traveller*. Translated by Andrew Kahn. Oxford: Voltaire Foundation.

Kauffmann, Angelica. 1924. "Memorandum of Paintings." In Victoria Manners and G. C. Williamson, *Angelica Kaufmann, R. A*, 139–174. London: John Lane, Bodley Head.

Keenan, Paul. 2013. *St. Petersburg and the Russian Court, 1703–1761*. Houndmills: Palgrave Macmillan.

Kir'iak, Timofei. 1867. "Potemkinskii prazdnik 1791 goda." *Russkii arkhiv* 5 (5–6): 673–694.

Kirichenko, O. V. 2002. *Dvorianskoe blagochestie: XVIII vek*. Moscow: Palomnik.

Khrapovitskii, A. V. 2008. *Dnevnik*. In Ekaterina II, *Iskusstvo upravliat'*, edited by A. Kamenskii. Moscow: Fond Sergeia Dubova.

———. 1874. *Dnevnik*. Edited by N. Barsukov. St. Petersburg.

Kliuchevskii, V. O. 1989. *Kurs russkoi istorii*. Vol. 5. Moscow: Mysl'.

Kobeko, D. F. 1884. "Ekaterina Vtoraia i Dalambert. Novootkrytaia perepiska Ekateriny s Dalambertom i drugimi litsami." *Istoricheskii vestnik* 15 (4): 107–142.

Kogan, E. S. 1960. *Ocherki istorii krepostnogo khoziaistva*. Moscow: Gos. istoricheksii muzei.

Kondakov, Iu. E. 2012. *Orden zolotogo i rozovogo kresta v Rossii: Teoreticheskii gradus solomonovykh nauk*. St. Petersburg: Asterion.

Korchmina, Elena. 2016. "The Practice of Personal Finance and the Problem of Debt among the Noble Elite in Eighteenth-Century Russia." In Schönle et al., 2016b, *The Europeanized Elite in Russia, 1762-1825*, 116–135.

Korchmina, Elena, and Andrei Zorin. 2018. "Karamzin and Money." *Cahiers du monde Russe* 59, no. 1 (Jan–March): 1-24.

Korovina, E. N. 2005. "Russkie usadebnye teatry (vtoraia polovina XVIII veka–pervaia chetvert' XIX veka." *Russkaia usad'ba* 11 (27): 49–60. Moscow: Zhiraf.

Kupriianov, Aleksandr. 2007. *Gorodskaia kul'tura russkoi provintsii. Konets XVIII–pervaia polovina XIX veka*. Moscow: Novyi khronograf.

Kuptsova, O. N. 2012. "Russkii usadebnyi teatr poslednei treti XVIII veka: Fenomen 'stolichnosti' v provintsial'noi kul'ture." In *Dvorianstvo, vlast' i obshchestvo v provintsial'noi Rossii XVIII veka*, edited by O. Glagoleva and I. Shirle, 578–597. Moscow: Novoe literaturnoe obozrenie.

Kurakin, A. B. 1815. *Souvenirs d'un voyage en Hollande et en Angleterre par le P. A. K. à sa sortie de l'Université de Leyde durant les années 1770, 1771 et 1772*. St. Petersburg.

Labzina, A. E. 2001. *Days of a Russian Noblewoman: The Memoirs of Anna Labzina, 1758-1821*. Translated and edited by Gary Marker and Rachel May. DeKalb: Northern Illinois University Press.

Lappo-Danilevskii, A. S. 1904. *I. I. Betskoi i ego sistema vospitaniia*. St. Petersburg: Tipografiia Imp. Akademii nauk.

Lappo-Danilevskii, K. Iu 1997. "O tainoi zhenit'be N. A. L'vova." *Novoe literaturnoe obozrenie* 23: 129–144.

Leckey, Colum. 2011. *Patrons of Enlightenment: The Free Economic Society in Eighteenth-Century Russia*. Newark: University of Delaware Press.

Lepekhin, Ivan. 1771. *Dnevnye zapiski puteshestviia doktora i akademii nauk ad"iunkta Ivana Lepekhina po raznym provintsiiam rossiiskogo gosudarstva, 1768 i 1769 godu*. St. Petersburg.

Levitt, Marcus C. 2011. *The Visual Dominant in Eighteenth-Century Russia*. DeKalb: Northern Illinois University Press.

Liubzhin, A. I. 2000. *Ocherki po istorii rossiiskogo obrazovaniia aleksandrovskoi epokhi*. Vol. 1310. Moscow: Izd. Moskovskogo kul'torologicheskogo litseia.

Lomonosov, M. V. 1957. *Polnoe sobranie sochinenii v 10 tomakh*. Moscow: AN SSSR.

Longinov, M. N. 1867. *Novikov i moskovskie martinisty*. Moscow.

Lopukhin, I. V. 1913. *Masonskie Trudy*. Moscow: Tovarishchestvo tipografii A. I. Mamontova.

———. 1990. *Zapiski senatora I. V. Lopukhina*. Moscow: Nauka.

———. 1997. *Masonskie Trudy. Dukhovnyi rytsar'. Nekotorye cherty o vnutrennei tserkvi*. Moscow: Aleteiia.

Lotman, Iu. M., and B. A. Uspenskii. 1984. "Pis'ma Karamzina i ikh mesto v razvitii russkoi kul'tury." In N. M. Karamzin, *Pis'ma russkogo puteshestvennika*, 525–606. Leningrad: Nauka.

Lotman, Iu. M. 1994. *Besedy o russkoi kul'ture. Byt i traditsii russkogo dvorianstva (XVIII–nachalo XIX veka)*. St. Petersburg: Iskusstvo-SPB.

———. 1997. "'Ezda v ostrov liubvi' Trediakovskogo i funktsiia perevodnoi ku'ltury v russkoi kul'ture pervoi poloviny XVIII veka." In Iu. M. Lotman, *O russkoi literature: Stat'ii i issledovaniia*, 168–175. St. Petersburg: Iskusstvo-SPB.

Loudon, J. C. 1835. *An Encyclopedia of Gardening*. Vol. 1. London.

Lubianovskii, F. P. 1872. *Vospominaniia*. Moscow.

Maikov, P. M. 1896. "Perepiska Ekateriny II s A. P. Levshinoi." *Russkii vestnik* 247, no. 11 (November): 310–359.

———. 1904. *Ivan Ivanovich Betskoi. Opyt ego biografii.* St. Petersburg: Tipografiia tov. Obshchestvennaia pol'za.

Maksimovich, L. M. 1789. *Novyi i polnyi geograficheskii slovar' Rossiiskogo gosudarstva.* Vol 6. Moscow.

Marasinova, E. N. 1999. *Psikhologiia elity rossiiskogo dvorianstva poslednei treti XVIII veka: po materialam perepiski.* Moscow: ROSSPEN.

———. 2008. *Vlast' i lichnost'. (Ocherki russkoi istorii XVIII veka).* Moscow: Nauka.

Masson, Nicole. 2002. *La poésie fugitive au XVIIIe siècle.* Paris. Honoré Champion.

Marker, Gary. 1985. *Publishing, Printing and the Origins of Intellectual Life in Russia, 1700–1800.* Princeton: Princeton University Press.

———. 2000. "The Enlightenment of Anna Labzina: Gender, Faith, and Public Life in Catherinian and Alexandrian Russia." *Slavic Review* 59, no. 2 (Summer): 701–739.

Martin, Alexander M. 2013. *Enlightened Metropolis. Constructing Imperial Moscow, 1762–1855.* Oxford: Oxford University Press.

Maza, Sarah. 1997. "The 'Bourgeois' Family Revisited: Sentimentalism and Social Class in Prerevolutionary French Culture." In *Intimate Encounters: Love and Domesticity in Eighteenth-Century France,* edited by Richard Rand, 39–47. Hanover: Dartmouth College and Princeton University Press.

Mézin, Anne, and Vladislav Rjéoutski, eds. 2011. *Les Français en Russie au siècle des Lumières.* 2 vols. Ferney-Voltaire: Centre international d'étude du XVIIIème siècle.

Mironov, B. N. 1990. *Russkii gorod v 1740—1860-e gody: demograficheskoe, sotsial'noe i ekonomicheskoe razvitie.* Leningrad: Nauka.

Mironov, Boris. 2012. *The Standard of Living and Revolutions in Russia, 1700–1917.* Edited by Gregory L. Freeze. New York: Routledge.

Montesquieu, 1973. *De l'Esprit des lois.* 2 vols. Paris: Garnier.

Mordvinov, N. S. 1902. Arkhiv grafov Mordvinovykh. Vol. 5. St. Petersburg.

Munro, George E. 1997. "Food in Catherinian St. Petersburg." In *Food in Russian History and Culture,* edited by Musya Glants and Joyce Toomre, 31–48. Bloomington: Indiana University Press.

———. 2008. *The Most Intentional City: St. Petersburg in the Reign of Catherine the Great.* Madison: Fairleigh Dickinson University Press.

Murav'ev, M. N. 1957. *Stikhotvoreniia.* Leningrad: Sovetskii pisatel'.

Nemirovskii, I. V. 2004. Dva "voobrazhaemykh" razgovora Pushkina. In *Lotmanovsii sbornik,* vol. 3. Moscow: OGI.

Nesin, V., and G. Sautkina. 1996. *Pavlovsk Imperatorskii i Velikokniazheskii 1777–1917.* St. Petersburg: Neva.

Newlin, Thomas. 2001. *The Voice in the Garden: Andrei Bolotov and the Anxieties of Russian Pastoral, 1738–1833.* Evanston: Northwestern University Press.

Nicolas Mikhailovitch. 1905. Le comte Paul Stroganov. 3 vols. Paris: Imprimerie nationale.

Nicolas Mikhaïlowitch. 1909. *L'Impératrice Elizabeth, épouse d'Alexandre 1er.* Vol 1. St. Petersburg: Manufacture des papiers de l'Etat.

Nisbet, Robert. 1980. *History of the Idea of Progress.* London: Heinemann.

Nora, Pierre. 1996. *Realms of Memory: Rethinking the French Past.* Vol. 1. New York: Columbia University Press.

O'Hagan, Timothy. 2007. "Jean-Jacques Rousseau (1712–1778)." In *Fifty Major Thinkers on Education: From Confucius to Dewey,* edited by Joy Palmer et al., 55–59. London: Routledge.

Ovchinnikov, G. D. 1992. *Literaturnaia deiatel'nost' F. V. Rostopchina.* PhD Dissertation. Russian Academy of Sciences Institute of Russian Literature. St. Petersburg.

Pallas, Peter Simon. 1788. *Voyages de M. P. S. Pallas en différentes provinces de l'empire de Russie, et dans l'Asie septentrionale.* 5 vols. Paris.

Papastergiadis, Nikos. 1997. "Tracing Hybridity in Theory." In *Debating Cultural Hybridity: Multi-Cultural Identities and the Politics of Anti-Racism*, edited by Pnina Werbner and Tariq Modood, 257–281. London: Zed Books.

Papmehl, K. A. 1983. *Metropolitan Platon of Moscow (Petr Levshin, 1737–1812): The Enlightened Prelate, Scholar and Educator*. Newtonville, MA: Oriental Research Partners.

Piéjus, Anne. 2000 *Le théâtre des demoiselles: Tragédie et musique à Saint-Cyr à la fin du grand siècle*. Paris: Société française de musicologie.

Pogosian, Elena 2010. "K predystorii 'Torzhestvuiuschei Minervy': I. I. Betskoi i M. M. Kheraskov v krugu organizatorov maskarada." In *Permiakovskii sbornik*, edited by Nataliia Mazur, 111–127. Moscow: Novoe izdatel'stvo.

Ponomarev, S. I. 1868. *Vysokopreosviashchennyi Filaret, metropolit Moskovskii i Kolomenskii. Materialy dlia ocherka ego zhizni i uchenoi deiatelnosti*. Kiev.

Porfir'eva, A. L., ed. 1998–1999. *Muzykal'nyi Peterburg. Entsiklopedicheskii slovar'*. Vol. 2–3. St. Petersburg: Kompozitor.

Poroshin, S. A. 2015. *Zapiski sluzhashchie k istorii velikogo kniazia Pavla Petrovicha*. Moscow: Kuchkovo pole.

Pumpianskii, L. V. 1937. "Trediakovskii i nemetskaia shkola razuma." In *Zapadnyi sbornik*, 157–186. Moscow: ANSSSR.

Pushkin, A. S. 1962–1965. *Polnoe sobranie sochinenii v desiati tomakh*. Moscow: Nauka.

Radishchev, A. N. 1958. *A Journey from St. Petersburg to Moscow*. Cambridge, MA: Harvard University Press.

Raeff, Marc. 1957. *Michael Speransky: Statesman of Imperial Russia, 1772–1839*. The Hague: M. Nijhoff.

———. 1966. *Russian Intellectual History: An Anthology*. New York: Harcourt, Brace, and World.

———. 1983. "The Russian Nobility in the Eighteenth and Nineteenth Centuries: Trends and Comparisons." In *The Nobility in Russia and Eastern Europe*, edited by Ivo Banac and Paul Bushkovitch, 99–121. New Haven: Yale Concilium on International and Area Studies.

———. 1984. *Understanding Imperial Russia. State and Society in the Old Regime*. New York: Columbia University Press.

Rasskazova, L. V. 2014. "'Umenie zhit' v derevne': penzenskie usad'by i vladel'tsy posle Manifesta o dvorianskoi vol'nosti." *Russkaia usad'ba* 19 (35): 162–172. St. Petersburg: Kolo.

Reddaway, W. F., ed. 1971 [1931]. *Documents of Catherine the Great*. New York: Russel and Russell.

Reyfman, Irina. 1999. *Ritualized Violence Russian Style: The Duel in Russian Culture and Literature*. Stanford: Stanford University Press.

Rjéoutski, Vladislav. 2013. "Le français et d'autre langues dans l'éducation en Russie au XVIIIe siècle." *Vivliofika: E-Journal of Eighteenth-Century Russian Studies* 1: 20–47.

———. 2016. Quand le français gouvernait la Russie. L'éducation de la noblesse russe, deuxième moitié du XVIIIe siècle—première moitié du XIXe siècle. Paris: L'Harmattan.

Rogov, K. Iu. 2006. "Tri epokhi russkogo barokko." In *Tynianovskii sbornik*, edited by M. O. Chudakova, 12:9–101. Moscow: Vodolei.

Roldugina, Irina. 2016. "Otkrytie seksual'nosti. Transgressiia sotsial'noi stikhii v seredine XVIII v. v Peterburge: po materialam Kalinkinskoi komissii (1750–1759)." *Ab imperio* 2 (August): 29–69.

Roosevelt, Priscilla. 1995. *Life on the Russian Country Estate: A Social and Cultural History*. New Haven: Yale University Press.

Rostopchin, Fedor. 1806. *Plug i sokha, pisannoe stepnym dvorianinom*. Moscow.

Rostopchin, F. V. 1849. "Puteshestvie v Prussiiu." *Moskvitianin* 1 (January): 69–92; 10 (May): 77–90; 13 (July): 3–14; 15 (August): 121–139.

Rousseau, Jean-Jacques. 1971. *The Political Writings*. Edited by C. E. Vaughan. Vol 1. New York: Wiley.

Rzhevskaia, G. I. 1871. "Zapiski Glafiry Ivanovny Rzhevskoi." *Russkii Arkhiv* 9 (1): 1–29.

Samarin, A. Iu. 2000. *Chitatel' v Rossii vo vtoroi polovine XVIII veka*. Moscow: Izdatel'stvo MGUP.

Schwartz, I. G. 2008. *Lektsii*. Donetsk: Weber.

Schönle, Andreas. 2000. *Authenticity and Fiction in the Russian Literary Journey*. Cambridge, MA: Harvard University Press.

———. 2007. *The Ruler in the Garden: Politics and Landscape Design in Imperial Russia*. Oxford: Peter Lang.

———. 2013. "Julies Garten in der 'Nouvelle Héloïse': Rousseau und die Ideologie der 'Verbesserung' in Russland um 1800." *Die Gartenkunst* 25 (1): 113–122.

———. 2016a. "Self-fashioning, Estate Design, and Agricultural Improvement: I. I. Bariatinskii's Enlightened Reforms of Country Living." In *The Europeanized Elite in Russia, 1762–1825: Public Role and Subjective Self*, edited by Andreas Schönle et al., 136–154. DeKalb: Northern Illinois University Press.

———. 2016b. "The Instability of Time and Plurality of Selves at Court and in Society." In Schönle et al., 2016b, *The Europeanized Elite in Russia, 1762–1825*, 281–299.

Schönle, Andreas, and Andrei Zorin. 2016 "Introduction." In Schönle et al., 2016b, *The Europeanized Elite in Russia, 1762–1825*, 1–25.

Ségur, Louis Philippe, comte de. 1859. *Mémoirs, souvenirs et anecdotes*. 2 vols. Paris.

Semevskii, V. I. 1888. *Krest'ianskii vopros v Rossii v XVIII i pervoi polovine XIX veka*. St. Petersburg.

Shamrai, D. D. 1940. "Tsenzurnyi nadzor nad tipografiei Sukhoputnogo shliakhetskogo kadetskogo korpusa." *XVIII vek* 2: 293–329.

Shepelev, Leonid. 2004. *Tituly, mundiry i ordena Rossiiskoi Imperii*. Moscow: ZAO Tsentrpoligraf.

Shishkov, A. S. 1824. *Sobranie sochinenii i perevodov*. Vol. 2. St. Petersburg.

Shkvarikov, V. A. 1939. *Planirovka gorodov Rossii XVIII i nachala XIX veka*. Moscow: Izdatel'stvo Vsesoiuznoi akademii arkhitektury.

Slezkine, Yuri. 1994. "Naturalists Versus Nations: Eighteenth-Century Russian Scholars Confront Ethnic Diversity." *Representations* 47 (Summer): 170–195.

Smith, Douglas. 1999. *Working the Rough Stone: Freemasonry and Society in Eighteenth-Century Russia*. DeKalb: Northern Illinois University Press.

———. 2008. *The Pearl: A True Tale of Forbidden Love in Catherine the Great's Russia*. New Haven: Yale University Press.

Smith-Peter, Susan. 2008. *The Russian Provincial Newspaper and Its Public*. Pittsburgh: Center for Russian and East European Studies, University of Pittsburgh.

———. 2015. "Making Empty Provinces: Eighteenth-Century Enlightenment Regionalism in Russian Provincial Journals." *REGION: Regional Studies of Russia, Eastern Europe, and Central Asia* 4 (1): 7–29.

Smolich, I. K. 1994–1997. *Istoriia russkoi tserkvi*. 8 vols. Moscow: Izd-vo Spaso-Preobrazhenskogo Valaamskogo monastyria.

Soloviev, S. M. 1895. *Istoriia Rossii s drevneishikh vremen*. Vol. 27. St. Petersburg.

Speranskii, M. M. 1907. "Ob usovershenstvovanii obshchego narodnogo vospitaniia." *Russkaia starina* 132, no. 12 (December): 730–735.

Stites, Richard. 2005. *Serfdom, Society, and the Arts in Imperial Russia: The Pleasure and the Power*. New Haven: Yale University Press.

Staehlin, Jacob. 2001. "Obshchii plan vospitaniia i uveseleniia molodogo kavalera ot 12–13 do 14 let." In *Graf Nikolai Petrovich Sheremetev. Lichnost'. Deiatel'nost'. Sud'ba*, 217–231, edited by G. V. Vdovin. Moscow: Nash dom.

Sunderland, Willard. 2007. "Imperial Space: Territorial Thoughts and Practice in the Eighteenth Century." In *Russian Empire: Space, People, Power, 1700–1930*, edited by Jane Burbank and Mark von Hagen, 33–66. Bloomington: Indiana University Press.

Sushkov, N. V. 1858. *Moskovskii universitetskii blagorodnyi pansion*. Moscow.

Sverbeev, D. N. 1899. *Zapiski, 1799–1826*. Moscow.

Timkovskii, I. F. 1874. *Zapiski*. Moscow.

Tsimbaeva, E. N. 2008 *Russkii katolitsizm. Ideiia vseevropeiskogo edinstva v Rossii XIX*. Moscow: KLI.

Tomlinson, John. 1999. *Globalization and Culture*. Cambridge: Polity.

Topograficheskoe opisanie Khar'kovskogo namestnichestva s istoricheskim preduvedomleniem o byvshikh v sei strane s drevnikh vremen peremenakh, vziatym k ob"iasneniiu deianii i khronologii. 1788. Moscow.

Trudy—Trudy Vol'nogo ekonomicheskogo obshchestva 1 (1766); 5 (1767); 16 (1770).

Velizhev, Mikhail. 2016a. "The Moscow English Club and the Public Sphere in Early Nineteenth-Century Russia." In Schönle et al., 2016b, *The Europeanized Elite in Russia, 1762-1825,* 220-237.

———. 2016b. "The Political Language of the Europeanized Military Elite in the Early Nineteenth Century: The Unpublished Diary and Letters of Vasilii Viazemskii." In Schönle et al., 2016b, *The Europeanized Elite in Russia, 1762-1825,* 176-196.

Vernadskii, G. V. 1999. *Russkoe masonstvo v tsarstvovanie Ekateriny II.* 2nd ed. St. Petersburg: Izd-vo im. N.I. Novikova.

Veselova, A. Iu. 1999. "Iz naslediia A. T. Bolotova: stat'ia 'O pol'ze, proiskhodiashchei ot chteniia knig.'" *XVIII vek* 21: 358-367.

Vil'chkovskii, S. N. 1992 [1911]. *Tsarskoe Selo.* St. Petersburg: Titul.

Vinskii, G. S. 1914. *Moe vremia, zapiski.* St. Petersburg: Ogni.

Vishlenkova, E. A. 2002. *"Zabotias' o dushakh poddannykh": religioznaia politika v Rossii pervoi chetverti XIX veka.* Saratov: Izd. Saratovskogo universiteta.

Volkov, N. E. 2013. *Dvor russkikh imperatorov v ego proshlom i nastoiashchem.* Moscow: Kuchkovo pole.

Vsevolodskii-Gerngross, V. N. 1913 *Istoriia teatral'nago obrazovaniia v Rossii.* St. Petersburg: Direktsiia imp. Teatrov.

Vsiakaia. 1769. *Vsiakaia vsiachina.* St. Petersburg.

Wilmot, Catherine. 1934. *The Russian Journals of Martha and Catherine Wilmot.* London: Macmillan.

Wirtschafter, Elise Kimerling. 2008. *Russia's Age of Serfdom, 1649-1861.* Malden: Blackwell, 2008.

———. 2013. *Religion and Enlightenment in Catherinian Russia: The Teachings of Metropolitan Platon.* DeKalb: Northern Illinois University Press.

Wortman, Richard. 1995. *Scenarios of Power: Myth and Ceremony in Russian Monarchy.* Vol. 1. *From Peter the Great to the Death of Nicholas I.* Princeton: Princeton University Press.

Zaborov, P. R. 2011. *Voltaire dans la culture russe.* Ferney-Voltaire: Centre international d'étude du XVIIIe siècle.

Zhikharev, S. P. 1989. *Zapiski sovremennika. Dnevnik chinovnika. Vospominaniia starovo teatrala.* 2 vols. Leningrad: Iskusstvo.

Zhivov, V. M. 2002a. "Gosudarstvennyi mif v epokhu Prosveshcheniia i ego razrushenie v Rossii kontsa XVIII veka." In *Razyskaniia v oblasti istorii i predystorii russkoi kul'tury,* 439-460. Moscow: Iazyki slavianskoi kul'tury.

———. 2002b. "Pervye russkie literaturnye biografii kak sotsial'noe iavlenie: Trediakovskii, Lomonosov, Sumarokov." In *Razyskaniia v oblasti istorii i predystorii russkoi kul'tury,* 557-637. Moscow: Iazyki slavianskoi kul'tury.

———. 2008. "Chuvstvitel'nyi natsionalizm: Karamzin, Rostopchin, natsional'nyi suverenitet i poiski natsional'noi identichnosti." *Novoe literaturnoe obozrenie* 91 (3): 114-140.

———. 2009. *Language and Culture in Eighteenth-Century Russia.* Boston: Academic Studies Press.

———. 2010. "Handling Sin in Eighteenth-century Russia." In *Representing Private Lives of the Enlightenment,* edited by Andrew Kahn, 123-148. Oxford: Voltaire Foundation.

Zhukovskii, V. A. 1959. *Sobranie sochinenii,* 4 vols. Moscow-Leningrad: Khudozhestvennaia literatura.

Zisserman, A. L. 1888. *Fel'dmarshal Kniaz' Aleksandr Ivanovich Bariatinskii, 1815-1879.* Moscow.

Zitser, Ernest. 2005. "New Histories of the Late Muscovite and Early Imperial Russian Court." *Kritika* 6 (2): 375-392.

Zorin, Andrei. 2014. *By Fables Alone: Literature and State Ideology in Late Eighteenth–Early Nineteenth Century Russia.* Brighton, MA: Academic Studies Press.

———. 2016a. "Sentimental Piety and Orthodox Asceticism: The Case of Nun Serafima." In Schönle, et al., *The Europeanized Elite in Russia, 1762-1825,* 300-317.

———. 2016b. "The Emotional Culture of Moscow Rosicrucians: An Experiment in Alternative Europeanization." In Schönle, et al., *The Europeanized Elite in Russia, 1762–1825*, 201–219.

———. 2016c. *Poiavlenie geroia. Iz istorii russkoi emotsional'noi kul'tury kontsa XVIII–nachala XIX veka.* Moscow: NLO.

Index

Lightning Source UK Ltd.
Milton Keynes UK
UKHW012108030222
398167UK00001B/66